Greek Democracy and the Junta

Greek Democracy and the Junta

Regime Crisis and the Failed Transition of 1973

Ioannis Tzortzis

I.B. TAURIS
LONDON • NEW YORK • OXFORD • NEW DELHI • SYDNEY

I.B. TAURIS
Bloomsbury Publishing Plc
50 Bedford Square, London, WC1B 3DP, UK
1385 Broadway, New York, NY 10018, USA
29 Earlsfort Terrace, Dublin 2, Ireland

BLOOMSBURY, I.B. TAURIS and the I.B. Tauris logo
are trademarks of Bloomsbury Publishing Plc

First published in Great Britain 2020
Paperback edition first published 2021

Copyright © Ioannis Tzortzis, 2020

Ioannis Tzortzis has asserted his right under the Copyright,
Designs and Patents Act, 1988, to be identified as Author of this work.

For legal purposes the Acknowledgements on p. vii constitute
an extension of this copyright page.

Cover design by Adriana Brioso
Cover image: General Zoitakis, Stylianos Pattakos and
Colonel George Papadopoulos, Greece, 1967.
(© KEYSTONE-FRANCE/Gamma-Rapho/Getty Images)

All rights reserved. No part of this publication may be reproduced or
transmitted in any form or by any means, electronic or mechanical,
including photocopying, recording, or any information storage or retrieval
system, without prior permission in writing from the publishers.

Bloomsbury Publishing Plc does not have any control over, or responsibility for,
any third-party websites referred to or in this book. All internet addresses given
in this book were correct at the time of going to press. The author and publisher
regret any inconvenience caused if addresses have changed or sites have
ceased to exist, but can accept no responsibility for any such changes.

A catalogue record for this book is available from the British Library.

A catalogue record for this book is available from the Library of Congress.

ISBN: HB: 978-1-7883-1391-9
PB: 978-0-7556-3722-5
ePDF: 978-1-7883-1786-3
eBook: 978-1-7883-1787-0

Typeset by RefineCatch Limited, Bungay, Suffolk

To find out more about our authors and books visit
www.bloomsbury.com and sign up for our newsletters.

Contents

Acknowledgements		vi
Chronology of Events		viii
	Introduction: Why did the Junta not end in 1973?	1
1	From 'Difficult Democracy' to the 'Wrong Coup': Greece 1949–67	13
2	'Greece of Christian Greeks': The Dictatorship of 21 April 1967	31
3	The Early Liberalization, January–September 1973	55
4	The 'Unfinished Revolution' and the 'Castrated Parliament': The Elites and the 'Experiment'	77
5	*Fortuna* and the 'Experiment': Civil Society and the Polytechnic Events	115
6	The Americans Yet Again? The International Factor and the 'Experiment'	143
7	Concluding Thoughts: The 'Markezinis Experiment' between Oblivion and Myth	171
Notes		191
Bibliography		235
Index		249

Acknowledgements

The writing of any book is a spiritual and sometimes psychological challenge, let alone that of a book the subject of which is controversial and at the same time so little researched. It is also a very lonely and isolating process which, nevertheless, constitutes a test of self-questioning and also self-confidence. This book is not an exception to that rule, although it has the specificity that its basis was provided by a section of my doctoral thesis; it has been thoroughly re-researched, updated with many new publications that have come out since, enriched with foreign archival material and new interviews, corrected, revised and extended to its current length.

In the course of the original research that I conducted, I had the unique opportunity to meet and engage with several individuals of different political affiliations and positions at the time of the events described. Their responses to my questions were most productive in helping me reconstruct the historical framework of the dictatorship and of the 'Markezinis experiment', as well as try to guess why the protagonists of the time acted the way they did. Sadly almost all my interviewees have now passed away; I am grateful to all of them, regardless of their political ideas and attitudes on the events of 1973 and of my own views about those, as without their contributions this book would not have been possible. Many of them also opened up their personal archives for the sake of my research, for which I am even more indebted.

As for the recent research, it was greatly facilitated by the staff of the Foundation of the Friends of the People (*Idryma Filon toy Laou*) in Athens, who opened up the archive of Markezinis of the time of the dictatorship for me to consult, and to whom I owe a special debt.

I also wish to thank Tomasz Hoskins, editor of IB Tauris/Bloomsbury, first of all for his encouraging attitude during the time that the proposal was under review, as well as for his understanding and assistance during its writing.

Acknowledgements

To my beloved parents Athanasios and Chryssi I also owe a great many thanks for their continuous moral support during the research and the writing of the book, and especially for their trust in my capacity to deal effectively with such a controversial topic. Finally, the long and insightful discussions that I have had with my late uncle Evangelos Tzortzis on the subject have provided a stimulus for me to research and write on the issue of the dictatorship. His loss in the concluding days of the manuscript was a great blow for me, as he did not live to see the outcome of an effort to which he contributed so much. It is to his loving memory that I dedicate this book.

Chronology of Events

1949

August: End of the Greek civil war

1951

30 May: First post-war coup attempt by IDEA officers, following Papagos's resignation from the army in order to run in elections as leader of the party of ES (Greek Rally), fails due to reaction of Papagos himself.

1952

November: Papagos wins the elections and becomes PM.

1955

October: Death of Papagos; he is succeeded by Constantine Karamanlis.

1956

February: Karamanlis' newly founded party ERE (National Radical Union) wins the elections.

1958

May: ERE wins new elections; electoral collapse of the centre parties, left-wing EDA (United Democratic Left) becomes main opposition party.

1961

Summer: the various centre parties join forces under the leadership of George Papandreou and Sophocles Venizelos, forming the EK (Centre Union).

October: ERE wins the elections; EK refuses to recognize the result, denouncing the 'violence and fraud' used to extract a pro-ERE result, and starts the 'unrelenting struggle' against Karamanlis.

1963

June: Government crisis: following a disagreement with the Palace, Karamanlis resigns.

November: National elections and victory of the EK; Karamanlis leaves Greece; Kanellopoulos becomes new ERE leader.

1964

February: New elections; death of Venizelos; victory of the EK; Papandreou becomes PM.

1965

May: A left-wing officers' conspiracy (ASPIDA) is revealed, implicating Andreas Papandreou, son of PM; Papandreou denies the accusations.

July: Government crisis following a disagreement between Papandreou and the Palace on the issue of insubordination of the Minister of Defence to Papandreou; the latter resigns and a 'renegades' government' of EK defectors is formed but fails to win the parliament's vote of confidence.

September: Another 'renegades' cabinet' wins vote of confidence with the support of ERE.

1966

December: Collapse of the 'renegades' cabinet' following an agreement between Kanellopoulos and Papandreou on new electoral law and elections in the spring.

1967

March: After a disagreement with Papandreou on the elections' timetable, Kanellopoulos forms a government and calls elections for May.

21 April: The Colonels' coup.

13 December: After a failed counter-coup attempt, King Constantine leaves Greece. Papadopoulos becomes PM.

1968

September: The regime conducts a plebiscite on a new 'Constitution' which was never applied.

1970

August: The most serious inter-regime clash ends with the weakening of most faction leaders; Papadopoulos remains PM due to Ioannidis' support.

November: Formation of the *Symvouleutiki Epitropi* (Consultative Committee) as the first attempt to provide the regime with a proto-party.

1971

March: Papadopoulos assumes the Regency, at the peak of his power.

September: A second attempt to form a *Symvouleutiki Epitropi*.

1973

20–21 February: Athens students' demonstration ends in lock-up in the Law School building, which is evacuated the next day.

March: Further students' demonstrations lead to clashes with the police.

April: Creation of the *Ethnikon Politistikon Kinima* (Greek Cultural Movement – EPOK) in an attempt at forming another pro-regime party.

23 April: Two days after the sixth anniversary of the coup, Karamanlis issues a message urging the armed forces to restore democratic legality.

24 May: An anti-regime plot involving many Hellenic Navy officers is revealed and frustrated.

1 June: Papadopoulos announces the abolition of the monarchy, calling for a plebiscite on the form of polity in Greece and pledging a transition to democracy with elections in 1974.

28 July: Amidst allegations of fraud, the plebiscite produces a majority of 78 per cent for the Republic.

24 August: Papadopoulos is sworn in as 'President of Republic'. He is already holding talks with Markezinis on the formation of a new cabinet.

8 October: Markezinis is sworn in as the transition PM, leading the first all-civilian cabinet since April 1967.

October–November: Negotiations between Markezinis and opposition leaders on the timetable for elections end in deadlock.

4 November: Demonstrations and clashes with police following the memorial services on the sixth anniversary of the death of George Papandreou.

14–16 November: Students from various faculties occupy the Athens Polytechnic campus, demanding free and fair elections.

17 November: Escalation of demonstrations leads to major clashes with the police; the army intervenes to evacuate the Polytechnic campus, causing numerous casualties.

18 November: Papadopoulos declares martial law.

21 November: Markezinis visits the Ministry of Defence, pledging to carry on with the transition timetable for elections in February 1974.

25 November: Hardliners' coup, led by Ioannidis: end of the 'Markezinis experiment'.

1974

15 July: A coup instigated by Greek officers stationed in Cyprus topples President Makarios.

20 July: Turkey invades Cyprus; the Greek regime calls a general mobilization, which ends in chaos.

23–24 July: The dictatorship collapses; the army leaders, along with the politicians, confer and invite Karamanlis to return and form a transition cabinet. Democracy returns to Greece.

Introduction: Why did the Junta not end in 1973?

Every advantage in the past is judged in the light of the final issue.
Demosthenes, *Olynthiac* I: 11

[In democratisation studies] Greece literally defies classification.
Schmitter and Karl, 1991

One of the most poignant slogans that an observer of the large anti-bailout deal demonstrations in Athens in the early 2010s would notice was one claiming that 'the Junta did not end in 1973', identifying the governments which signed the 'memorandums of austerity' with the dictatorship of 1967 and insinuating a peculiar 'continuity' with that period of Greek history in the minds of the demonstrators. This discourse is indicative of the detrimental effect of the dictatorship on Greek political psychology and culture, which has not been overcome even given the more than 40 years that have lapsed since its end. Indeed, the dictatorship of the colonels has left its trace deep and vivant in the Greek psyche, perhaps more because of its demeaning and despicable collapse in July 1974 than because of its actual establishment in 1967. It has, for a good reason, become anathema in Greek collective memory, all the more given the ambiguous – to say the least – attitudes of a considerable part of both elites and people during its time in power.

One of the major, yet most unstudied, events of this seven-year rule is the regime's failed attempt to transform itself into some kind of civilianized form of power in 1973. It was arguably the most crucial year for Greece since 1967, a year full of events not witnessed for a long time, from mass and bloody demonstrations to outright military interventions. The core time of those events is the seven-week *reforma*[1] attempt – Greek style: this has been recorded as 'the Markezinis experiment', after the politician who assumed the impossible task of leading the liberalization attempt, along with the dictatorship's strong man, Papadopoulos. The attempt ended disdainfully amidst the bloody Polytechnic demonstrations and the regime's hardliners' coup, led by Brigadier Dimitrios Ioannidis, head of the much-loathed ESA (Greek Military Police). It has since slipped into oblivion and has been seen either as an inseparable part of the dictatorship, or at most as a clumsy attempt by Papadopoulos to evasively disguise his one-man rule of the previous years under a pseudo-democratic facade, which collapsed because of the peoples' reaction and/or the regime hardliners being alarmed by the Polytechnic events. The post-1974 institutionalized celebrations of the latter have very effectively demonized the 'Markezinis experiment' and merged it into the dictatorial timeline, thus presenting a linear and homogeneous account of the dictatorship from 1967 to 1974 and hiding its mutation during that time.

Yet, a closer look at those events challenges the conventional interpretations of the 'Markezinis experiment': the Greek political elites and civil society refused to support Markezinis only to get a 'worse dictatorship' in a few weeks and see the hardliners get back to the helm. The latter, as well as the military-as-institution, toppled the tandem Papadopoulos–Markezinis to protect their interests, perceived as threatened by the 'experiment', only to find themselves, a mere eight months later, humiliated by the imbroglio they created in Cyprus in July 1974. They now had to renounce their power and hand it back to the same political class they had toppled in 1967. The actual democratic transition arose from, and ultimately bequeathed to Greece, a severe external crisis transformed into a major foreign relations issue still unsolved 44 years on – the Cyprus issue. Was this series of events inevitable, and could a different development of the 'Markezinis experiment' have prevented it? Why did the self-transformation attempt occur in 1973 and not earlier? Was it stillborn because of the nature of the regime it supposedly tried to change? To what extent was it sincere or fake on the part of Papadopoulos? What were Markezinis' goals when accepting the transition premiership and was he indeed the puppet of Papadopoulos? Was there an alternative to the 'experiment' in 1973? Was the international factor helpful, or did it hinder (as Markezinis himself claimed years later) the transition attempt? All in all, why did 'the Junta not end in 1973'? Those are the questions this book will endeavour to address.

Disdain and oblivion: The 'Markezinis experiment' as a point of historical and political reference

Reviewing the existing literature on the 'Markezinis experiment' reveals an almost absolute dichotomy and diversity of opinions. For a start, there is no account focused on the 'Markezinis experiment' per se at all, exposing the dominant attitude among most of the scholars and journalists that have written on the dictatorship and who consider it identical to the regime and thus summarily refer to it as 'the junta'. On the other hand, among most of those that have paid attention to the 'experiment', there is a consensus that it was but a mere ruse on behalf of Papadopoulos to perpetuate his personal rule disguised under a democratic facade that would trick people and political elites into believing that the dictatorship was over and that democracy was to be restored, albeit in a piecemeal way. According to this view, Markezinis was the puppet of Papadopoulos who accepted the premiership in order to quench his ambition for power, even if it was a 'premiership granted'. The failure of the 'experiment' is explained, according to this analysis, by the reaction of civil society in the form of the Polytechnic students' uprising that exposed the facade of the attempt, due to its bloody suppression, as well as of the overambitious hardliners of Ioannidis who refused to concede to Papadopoulos' prerogative for absolute control under the ruse of regime change. In this analysis, the success or failure of the experiment makes little difference: the one-man rule of Papadopoulos simply continues in a different form.

Yet, this opinion overlooks some facts that change that simplistic account of the 'experiment'. To start with, it came after the first signs of awakening of civil society (the student unrest of early 1973), as well as of the first organized attempt after the 'royal coup' of December 1967 to dynamically challenge the regime in the spring of that year. Those were proofs of a comeback by the 'frozen' Greek society after six years of inertia and passivity, the effects of which on the regime have gone unaccounted. Also, the last days of the summer of 1973 saw the complete lifting of martial law, as well as the release – for the first time in many years – of all political prisoners. This tendency was also reflected in the Markezinis cabinet, the first all-civilian one after six years: even the Minister of Defence was not ex-military, something unusual even by pre-1967 Greek standards. Also, the stance of Papadopoulos early in the summer of 1973 was more hard line than after the formation of the Markezinis cabinet in the autumn, thus showing some signs of a willingness to grant further concessions to the opposition. Furthermore, it has been overlooked that the reaction of the junior hard-line officers was caused not only by their objections to the overpowerful Papadopoulos, but also by the fact that they were watching the 'revolution' giving way to the same political class it had overthrown six years before. Apart from the above, the military as an institution for the first time since 1967 seemed to have a say of their own in politics, a trend that would become obvious during the actual transition to democracy one year later. Last, the political opposition's rejection of the 'experiment' was not as unanimous as many have thought; some of its members were anything but negative to the possibility of success by Markezinis.

On the other hand, the positive accounts of the experiment almost unanimously assume a narrative apologetic not only to Markezinis, but also to the dictator himself. They take at face value Papadopoulos' statements of goodwill to end the dictatorship and contrive a gradual and piecemeal yet genuine and sincere transition to democracy, that was undermined by the hardliners of Ioannidis and/or by members of the 'old political class'. Another current of the same apologetic analysis assumes an absolute conspiracy theory, blaming the failure of the 'experiment' on the adverse American factor that had 'written off' Papadopoulos and Markezinis due to their supposed independent stance during the Yom Kippur War, which coincided with the formation of the Markezinis cabinet. Presumably the two refused to allow the use of Greek air space and naval facilities to the US Navy and Air Force, thus angering the State Department and the Pentagon and prompting an American-inspired overthrow, the long hand of which was Ioannidis and his followers in the army. Interestingly, this is also the theory adopted by Markezinis himself to explain his downfall. For the part that blames the demise of the 'experiment' on the politicians, the above apologists of Papadopoulos/Markezinis, for their part, underrate the suspicion that Papadopoulos' initiative understandably raised among the political opposition, as well as the fact that some of the 'old political elites' were not as opposed to the 'experiment' as might be assumed. On the other hand, those who blame the failure on the American factor overlook the fact that the same stance on offering bases and facilities was assumed by almost all European governments, yet rejection of the US request did not result in any of those governments being overthrown by US intervention. This conspiracy-ridden oversimplification is at the core of almost all pro-regime accounts of the 'experiment', thus further blurring analysis of the factors that contributed to its demise.

In contrast, this book will focus on the regime's nature and its problematic, if not impossible, self-transformation process, as it was further accentuated by the lack of elite and societal support, in order to explain the failure of the 'experiment'. It will reject ideologically-ridden, evaluative-laden and conspiracy-burdened accounts, and will trace the origins, development and demise of the 'Markezinis experiment' in terms of what it really was: a Greek case of a failed *reforma pactada*, a regime self-transformation and liberalization attempt that collapsed because of the exclusively monolithic military nature of the dictatorship that imposed itself on Greece in April 1967. Also, this study will stress that it was a regime plagued by acute internal divisions and continuous struggles among the factions that imposed it. The book will furthermore recount the regime's failure or negligence to secure support either from social forces which might have offered it some base for a self-transformation into something like a political movement, or from any political elites or groups which might have served as a political party, as well as the lack of a stable ideological platform that could provide it with a manifesto or agenda for a potential transformation into a political organization. This isolation inevitably produced suspicion about the dictator's real intentions when he engineered the transition in 1973, and understandably caused an initial negative reaction by political opposition elites and civil society. Nevertheless, it will be pointed out that even this initially clumsy and restricted transition did open a window of opportunity for some more substantial move towards liberalization in the autumn of 1973, which was, however, put to sudden death by the omnipresent and omnipotent regime hardline leader Ioannidis – the only figure that Papadopoulos had failed to neutralize, check or retire during his days as the strong man of the regime. The failure of the 'experiment' marked the final countdown of the dictatorship, as it never recovered from its hopeless isolation accentuated by the hardliners' rule, who turned to a nationalist venture in Cyprus to make up for the impasse they were in, resulting in Turkish intervention in the island and their final demise in July 1974.

The 'Markezinis experiment' in historical and comparative perspective

In order to account for the circumstances and reasons for the failure of the 'Markezinis experiment', one needs first to understand what it actually was about and what kept it from hatching into a proper democratic transition, and led to its inglorious end after a mere seven weeks. For this to be done, the failed transition will be set in the framework used in the democratization literature to analyse similar transitions by regime transformation that took place during the so-called 'third wave of democratization'.

Introduction: Why did the Junta not end in 1973? 7

First, though, a short historical account shows that the 'Markezinis experiment', notwithstanding its peculiarity, was not a unique case in Greek political history. For example, a coup in 1909 saw a group of military officers, disillusioned by the nepotism, inefficiency and corruption in Greek politics, and willing to make up for the dishonest and humiliating defeat in the short Greek–Turkish conflict of 1897 as well as promote the irredentist cause of Greek territorial expansion, topple the government with a *pronunciamento* but without assuming power. Instead, recognizing the complexities of military rule, they effectively resisted the temptation to take direct control of the state and instead imposed a constitutional amendment, which restructured the armed forces, as well as a series of institutional and political reforms aimed at modernizing the Greek party system, electoral law and public administration, and contrived the calling of Eleftherios Venizelos into the Greek political scene, by forcing new elections.[2]

A similar case occurred in 1924. The Venizelist officers, following the Greek army's dishonest defeat and subsequent withdrawal from Asia Minor, resulting in the uprooting of Greek populations from that area, rose in revolt in September 1922 against the anti-Venizelist royalist government, which they toppled in a few days. Assuming full control of the state this time, they brought to trial (and sentenced to death) some members of the previous cabinets presumed responsible for the military and humanitarian disaster suffered by the Greeks, abolished the monarchy, established a republic (for the first time in a century), suppressed a counter-coup attempt by monarchist officers, and started catering for the urgent needs of the more than one million Greek refugees from Asia Minor. Almost eighteen months after their coup, in the spring of 1924, they transferred power over to the newly elected National Assembly which, in turn, produced a government. Thus, for the first time ever, the Greek military willingly withdrew from power, having nevertheless left their trace in the institutional and political structure that was to remain for the next twelve years and set a precedent the repetition of which was to be attempted but not achieved half a century later.

This was anything but the end of military intervention in politics, though: the interwar period in Greece was one riddled with coups which tormented the young and weak democracy until 1936, when the dictatorship of ex-general Ioannis Metaxas put an end to the political turmoil and imposed a rigid police state. After the Axis occupation of Greece in 1941, what was left of the Greek army was reorganized in Egypt under the aegis of Great Britain, and participated in the Allied military effort. Still, ideological divisions among Greeks resulted in fierce confrontations and mutinies in the army and navy that had to be suppressed and led to purges of the army from left-wing and anti-royalist officers. The ensuing civil war years continued this trend, producing a fiercely anti-communist and corporatist-oriented officer corps by its end in 1949. It is this corps, parts of which conspired and brought about the dictatorship of 1967, which had to accept the regime's self-transformation in 1973 if Greece was to return to democracy in a peaceful way.

Thus the 'Markezinis experiment' was a case of democratic transition by regime self-transformation which has, in democratization studies, been known as *reforma pactada*, after the Spanish case of democratization which has since 1977 been the paradigmatic case of transition. Indeed, the similarities between the two cases are so substantial that, had the 'experiment' succeeded, one can assume that it would have been Greece rather than Spain that would have been studied as the exemplary *reforma* since it preceded the Spanish transition by four years. Such a regime-initiated transition is consensual, distinguished from other, non-consensual forms of transition such as collapse, revolution, coup or extrication, caused by a sudden loss of legitimacy that non-democratic regimes can suffer, forcing them to hand power over to civilians – the reason the dictatorship actually collapsed in 1974.[3] This consensus refers to both regime and opposition elites' willingness to initiate and accept the transition process, usually after negotiations on some basic and minimum convergence on the terms and conditions of the transition process. The features of this kind of transition, as is agreed in democratization literature, are based on the acceptance that 'it is both possible and desirable that political democracy be attained without mobilized violence and dramatic discontinuity ... [transition] groups within the dictatorial regime conclude that the costs of staying in power ... had reached a point where a graceful exit from power was desirable'.[4] Przeworski adds that 'faced with the alternative of an open, possibly violent, conflict – the outcomes of which may be highly beneficial but also quite risky – and of a democratic solution, which requires compromise but provides security, political forces involved in the regime transformation may opt for the democratic compromise'.[5]

However, the situation does not necessarily have to reach threatening levels for the dictatorial elite in power; rather, as Huntington claims, 'the established elites within an authoritarian regime ... see their interests served by the introduction of democratic institutions', and therefore they opt for reform.[6] In such cases, the regime elites pre-empt the opposition and 'unilaterally liberalise the political arena as a strategic move to prevent its removal and, more to the point, the installation of a democratic regime over which it has no control'.[7] O'Donnell and Schmitter conclude that regime softliners opt for democracy because 'some have gotten what they wanted ... and are prepared to withdraw to the enjoyment of private satisfactions' or 'wish to see the transition stop at a limited liberalization which protects their tenure in office' or even 'aspire to elected positions in the emergent regime'.[8] In view of that point, one can assume that the outgoing dictatorial elites would prefer to withdraw in good times since they are 'less isolated politically than during times of crisis, and are more likely to enjoy explicit or tacit support'.[9] It needs to be added that the decision for opening up to democratic transition does not necessarily imply a unanimous decision on behalf of the regime elites; rather, 'within the governing coalition some groups often came to favour democratisation, while others opposed it, and others supported limited reform or liberalisation'.[10]

An important thing to note is that in this conception, democracy need not necessarily be (re)introduced by democrats: 'we may allow for the possibility that circumstances may force, trick, lure or cajole non-democrats into democratic behaviour and that their beliefs may adjust in due course by some process of rationalisation or adaptation'.[11] Linz and Stepan conclude that 'democracy becomes "the only game in town" partly by belief and partly by elite calculation of the cost of compliance versus the cost of mobilisation for other governing alternatives'.[12] And Rustow argues that democracy might not have been the elites' original goal, but 'was sought as a means to some other end or it came as a fortuitous by-product of the struggle'.[13] However, the factor of 'miscalculation' can turn their expectations into a negative for them, especially when elections are held; 'even deeply manipulated elections may lead to surprising opposition victories. Even tightly controlled elections ... generate pressures for further reform.'[14]

The success of the transition will depend on the state structures and institutions of the dictatorship, and therefore the nature of the dictatorial regime is the first and most crucial factor in this process. Any study needs to focus on the elites that made the dictatorship, its potential success or failure to institutionalize itself, and the degree of coherence of the elites competing for power in transition, especially if their interests vis-à-vis the transition do not converge. The above questions were crucial for the outcome of the 'experiment', as they also concern the opposition elites. During this process, civil society can also achieve goals such as inclusive democracy and the rule of law. Thus the institutional arrangements that will characterize the new democratic regime will reflect, as Etzioni-Halevy says, 'the combined result of relations among elites and of relations between elites and the public'.[15]

Last, the weight of the international factor stressed by Markezinis and many of Papadopoulos' apologists needs some particular attention, as generally 'the international context is the forgotten dimension in the study of the democratic transition'[16] because 'domestic factors play a predominant role in the transition'.[17] The democratic transition, though, is 'a process in which political systems may well be especially vulnerable to international influences'[18] which are 'almost always present in a democratisation process'.[19] For a non-democratic state like Greece in 1973, it was in the interest of the elites to try to end their isolation by seeing the country rejoining the political and economic constellation

Introduction: Why did the Junta not end in 1973?

that was the EEC. As for the USA and NATO, they had always been the most prominent foreign influence in Greek politics in the post-war years.

The approach of this book will therefore be non-deterministic, taking structural preconditions as a context in which political action develops, rather than accurate predictors of outcomes; as Sorensen argues, 'there is no historical law that says that regimes must move from authoritarian to democratic'.[20] The unexpected and contingent dynamics of transition processes will receive close attention; often 'what starts as an effort by members of the old elite to rescue the status quo may take an unintended direction as other members of the elite, with more innovative dispositions, join in'.[21]

In terms of methodology the book makes use of primary material of two categories: archival research and interviews with personalities that lived in that time and occupied certain positions in the regime elite and opposition. The material available for research was limited: in general the state of the public archives in Greece is disappointing for the researcher, in so far as organization is concerned, not to mention that most documents are not available due to a 50-year disclosure rule. Apart from that, the procedural norms of accessing material held in the Greek Ministry of Foreign Affairs proved too tedious for the limited time that the author had at his disposal. In any case, the research tried to make up for the scarcity of public records by focusing on private archives (diaries, notes, letters, etc.) that were made available. British and US archives were of greater value, although the latter proved to be less rich than the author expected them to be, especially when compared with the comprehensive British Foreign Office sources. As for the interviews, their purpose was the collection of information that would help reconstruct the framework of the 'Markezinis experiment', explain the attitudes and decisions of the main actors and general society of the time and record the opinions of the interviewees on issues that have remained controversial, such as whether the regime indeed became dispensable or not and the reasons for the failure of the 'experiment'. Despite the fact that most of the main protagonists of the events covered in this book had died, the author was lucky enough to interview figures from across the political spectrum, from ex-dictatorship leaders Pattakos and Makarezos to ex-Communist leader Farakos, and from ex-PM Rallis to then member of *Rigas Ferraios* (the ex-Communist Party of Greece of the Interior) youth Mitsos. He was not so lucky with other personalities who refused to be interviewed, most of them basing their refusal on the superficial excuse that 'it is still early for such events to be accounted for in cool blood'. The fact that most of the interviewees have now sadly passed away is the best counter-proof to such an opinion.

Regarding the structure of the book, the first two chapters provide the historical framework of the 'Markezinis experiment', with Chapter 1 giving an account of the 'difficult democracy' that followed the civil war and the position of the military until the 1967 coup, while Chapter 2 outlines the developments in the dictatorial regime until 1973. Then the 'experiment' is placed in context, with Chapter 3 presenting the major events of the year that preceded the 'experiment', from the student demonstrations to the July plebiscite and Papadopoulos' assumption of the role of 'President'. Chapter 4 accounts for the reaction of the political and military elites to the 'experiment', giving the main reasons for its collapse. Then in Chapter 5 the reaction of civil society (in the face of the Polytechnic students' uprising) is explained. Finally, Chapter 6 explores the link between the 'experiment' and the international factor, namely the reaction of the EEC and of the US. Chapter 7 concludes the study by offering a brief comparison with the similar *reformas* of Spain and Turkey, as well as some thoughts on the legacy of the 'experiment', its (mis)interpretations and its falling into oblivion post-1974.

The author is happy to present this account of one of the most controversial incidents in modern Greek history, hoping that it will help throw light upon an event which still remains at best misinterpreted – if not neglected.

1

From 'Difficult Democracy' to the 'Wrong Coup': Greece 1949–67

There will be no elections . . . because there comes the time of the 'Unknown Colonel'.

Markezinis, speaking to the press in February 1967

All and no one.

Karamanlis' reply to the question 'Who was responsible for the 1967 coup?'

The developments that led to the 1967 coup were indirect consequences of the civil war, therefore the period from 1949 to 1967 calls for a detailed analysis of the political elites, social and institutional change and the military officers' corps. All prospects of the evolution of the Greek political system towards a proper liberal democratic settlement were blocked by a number of factors: the extreme polarization of Greek political life; the institutionalization of a rigid and partial legal framework against potential challengers of the post-civil war status quo; the emergence of the army as an independent centre of power, enjoying an organizational and institutional autonomy unthinkable for a Western democracy and prone to conspiracy and subversion; and the failed attempt at institutional modernization in the 1960s blocked. This opened the way to the April 1967 coup.

Politics and institutions from 1949 to 1961: The 'difficult democracy'

Although, for most of the civil war, Greece was ruled by a coalition government of the centre and the right, it was the latter that is considered to have been the winner in the struggle that ravaged the country from 1944 to 1949. Both political poles came out of the war fragmented; however, the right was quicker to unite its pieces in the new party of ES (Greek Rally) under Field Marshal Alexandros Papagos in 1951. The next year Papagos won the elections and stayed in office until his death in October 1955 when, in a controversial move, King Paul appointed Constantine Karamanlis as premier. Karamanlis formed a new party, the ERE (National Radical Union), which was to dominate the right until 1967. Karamanlis himself would stay in office until 1963, a length of service unmatched by any politician up to that point. The party of ERE was largely shaped by the dominant figure of its leader, had a quite vague ideological orientation and lacked both a stable structure and a clear programme, other than that of 'economic and social rehabilitation and progress'.[1]

It would take the groups of the centre another decade to achieve the same unity. The political space between ERE and the left comprised a number of parties plagued by the personal enmities and ambitions of their leaders and thus for many years they were incapable of forming a coalition that could effectively challenge ERE. The political vacuum between left and right would, in the 1950s and early 1960s, be occupied by various opportunistic and precarious coalitions that would sometimes include the left itself, ranging up to the fringes of the right and some of its dissidents. Although this particular setting offered ERE some easy victories, in the long run it proved a challenge to the stability of the political status quo. The prolonged incapability of the forces of the centre to find a common political platform worked to the advantage of the left-wing EDA in the elections of 1958, when it emerged for the first time as the major opposition party with 24.43 per cent of the votes. This was a success that proved hard to repeat, but for the moment, this left-wing party, fashioned in the image of the Communist Party of Greece (KKE), had become the major opposition party in the Greek parliament just nine years after the end of the civil war. The implications of this development were twofold: on one hand, it prompted the numerous political groupings which occupied the space between ERE and EDA to overcome their leaders' personal enmities and ambitions and join forces in one political coalition. This eventually resulted in the creation of the EK (Centre Union) in the summer of 1961, just before the next elections. It was a hastily formed coalition which was plagued by problems of coordination and regular conflict over the personal interests and ambitions of the faction chiefs, some of whom questioned the hegemony of the coalition leader, the 73-year-old George Papandreou. At the same time, the EK alarmed the 'deep state' and triggered a violent reaction against the left and its 'fellow travellers'.

On the left side of the political spectrum, the ideological and organizational domination of the KKE, though illegal since 1947, continued in the face of the EDA (United Democratic Left), a party formed by left-wing personalities and groups which at the same time maintained strong links with the KKE, the expatriated leadership of which had not renounced the possibility of a continuation of an armed struggle should circumstances allow. Moscow's tight control of the KKE, which faithfully followed the Soviet political and diplomatic agenda in the Cold War years, made consensus a chimerical expectation on the left as well. While the post-civil war institutions of supervised democracy influenced and hardened the stance of the left, its own basic decisions provoked a negative reaction by non-left political groups.[2]

In September 1946, after a contested referendum, the monarchy was restored in Greece.[3] Its return guaranteed to both internal and external allies the continuation of the country's pro-Western allegiance and anti-communist orientation. After the end of the civil war, backed by the American delegation in Greece and encouraged by the unwillingness of most political groups or leaders to resist its predominance, the monarchy tended to exceed its constitutional authority by seeking to control Greek political life – indeed, to such an extent that, for a number of years, there would be no major political development without the involvement of the Palace.[4] However, in the long run this posed a serious threat to the legitimacy of the monarchy: continuous, often overt, interference in politics cost the support of certain political forces, as well as fuelled anti-royal feeling among the population. None the less, the monarchy enjoyed a great deal of popularity during and after the end of the civil war, especially in the countryside, but by the early 1960s this support was beginning to wane.[5]

It was on an institutional and cultural level that the bitter legacy of the Greek civil war was felt most keenly, preventing the healing of the acute political divisions of the 1940s and perpetuating their consequences well into the 1960s. The post-civil war years saw a sharp contrast between constitutional theory and political practice. The state of emergency, introduced during the civil war, was extended long after the official end of that conflict in 1949 by means of institutional engineering and comprised a complex legal arsenal including a number of special laws and decrees targeting individuals 'conspiring or revolting or coming into contact with foreigners or participating in armed groups threatening the integrity of the state', or 'seeking to apply ideas having as [their] goal the subversion of the state or of the existing social system by violent means'.[6] The excuse for this programme was an announcement by the KKE in the autumn of 1949 that the armed struggle was not finished, simply temporarily suspended. The result was the intervention of the state in many facets of everyday life, from the issuing of passports to appointing civil servants, from manipulation of the electoral system to involvement in social and political activities, sometimes using the police and even the army; in extreme cases, the state of emergency practically nullified the constitutional guarantees of democratic institutions.[7] The executive was also able to claim some powers which were normally reserved for the legislature. So although Greece remained officially a democratic state, the guarantees of political, civil and individual rights recognized and protected under the 1952 constitution were in practice crippled by the application of this 'para-constitutional jurisprudence'.[8] This is why the democratic institutions in the country remained weak at this time, resulting in an 'exclusivist political system' which the French political scientist Maurice Genevoix called 'a difficult democracy'.[9] In the elections of October 1961, the army, police and security services together with the state bureaucracy coordinated their actions in order to reduce the electoral influence of the EDA and, to an extent, of the EK. The result, giving ERE 50.71 per cent of the votes, was promptly contested by the opposition parties on the grounds of 'electoral violence and fraud'.[10] The next two years were a time of bitter and unrelenting polarization which, coupled with the social repercussions of economic development, undermined any possibility of democratic consolidation in Greece.

In the early post-civil war years, Greece witnessed a steady but slow and unequally distributed growth and recovery from its post-war penuries, which turned it into 'a state-centred petty bourgeois society marked by the domination of the tertiary sector'.[11] The model of economic development that Greece followed was dependent on US aid, which took shape under the Truman Doctrine and the Marshall Plan. The aid was coordinated after 1947 by the AMAG (American Mission for Aid to Greece), whose goal was, as Veremis notes, the defeat of the left rather than the restoration of a democratic state and the economic development of the country.[12] There was also considerable foreign investment under privileged conditions, especially in the secondary sector. Apart from that, the state took control of some vital industrial activities, such as energy provision. In the first years after the civil war, Greece's economic policy was oriented towards 'boosting the supply and protection of the internal market, and import substitution'.[13] From the late 1950s, because of the shrinking of the agricultural sector and the key role of the state in the economy, particularly in industrialization, there was need for an enlarged civil service. Public administration thus became a promising field for relatively secure jobs and quite predictable career opportunities, much sought after by a people anxious to secure both their professional future and a social position. A new Greek middle class emerged, developing its own moral and cultural values.

This new middle class also reflected the rising number of those in self-employment, occupied mainly with petty commercial jobs and services which were rapidly expanding, creating more jobs and wealth. To all the above should be added the boom in (both private and public) construction and public works, a response to the urgent need to rebuild a country devastated by a decade of war and to restore and modernize its infrastructure. This was another source of job opportunities and, despite workers' low wages and lack of independent trade unionism to promote their collective interests, it helped raise the standard of living in Greece after the war. However, the rural exodus resulting from these changing employment patterns 'destroyed traditional political clientelist networks and caused inequalities and tensions leading to the rejection of traditional networks of patronage, and to the development of new political identities for large parts of the new urban groups'.[14] Last but not least, tourism, which began to emerge as an important factor in Greek economic development, added more invisible resources to many families, and promoted communication and understanding between Greeks and people from more developed (and more democratic) countries. By 1963, per capita annual income in Greece exceeded $400. As Haralambis puts it, 'the right wing did not achieve the economic miracle that it had claimed, however it had taken Greece out of poverty'.[15]

This rapidly changing economic environment had serious political implications as well. For a country undergoing major economic and social transformation, the limits and inefficiency of the existing legal and political framework became more exposed from the late 1950s. As Rueschemeyer, Stevens and Stevens have pointed out, economic growth and the social differentiation that it entails 'foster a population's interest and capability in political participation, and thus engender pressures for democratisation'.[16] According to Legg and Roberts, 'many people had already put the civil war behind them, and the mechanisms of the national security state had become an anachronism. In addition, despite the enormous strides in economic development, prosperity had not touched everyone'.[17] Large sections of the middle and working classes identified politically with the centre's call for change, while the ideological discourse of the ERE looked increasingly obsolete and was challenged (if not rejected) by many, most notably workers and students who began to form unions in order to promote democracy and the redistribution of wealth. The party of EK would capitalize on this discontent after 1961, with its 'unrelenting struggle', and finally bring down the ERE in 1963, but not before Karamanlis tried to take the initiative through institutional and political change.

Frustrated attempts at democratic consolidation, 1963–5

In the spring of 1963, Karamanlis brought to parliament a proposal for a constitutional amendment. It included provision for the creation of a Constitutional Court for the first time in Greek history, which was to decide on the legality of political parties. The proposal also set out to regulate the right to strike; restructure the civil service; limit the immunity of MPs; put some limits on the motion of censure in parliament; limit the competence and jurisdiction of courts in political crimes; and finally, it recognized some economic and social rights. According to Alivizatos, 'it worked in the logic of rationalisation of parliamentary functions, enhancing the executive for faster and more effective decision making.'[18] The amendment also sought to take away some of the powers of the 'deep state', as well as aiming for faster and more effective decision making.[19] The proposal, however, was rejected by the EK and EDA as one of authoritarian inspiration; it also met with the objections of many ERE MPs who were aligned with the Palace and opposed to the type of strong executive the amendment was aiming at. In relation to the mechanisms of the 'deep state', Karamanlis aimed to diminish the army's central role and also end the supervision of the Greek political system by the 'para-constitution'. The confrontation that ensued between Karamanlis and the Palace ultimately brought his time in office to an end, while the popularity of his main opponent, Papandreou's EK, was on the rise. Late that spring a political assassination, which revealed the latent power of the deep state, and a disagreement with the Palace over a royal visit to London, which served as a pretext, induced Karamanlis to resign. After losing the election of November 1963, he left for Paris. The road was now open for Papandreou, who won an absolute majority in parliament in the election of February 1964, ending 11 years of right-wing rule and raising hopes for a rebalancing of power in the direction of a more democratic political and institutional arrangement.

It would soon become clear, however, that the actual goal of EK was a change of government rather than a change of the power structure, as it was a 'heteroclite coalition of personalities whose political tendencies ranged from the left to the right wing [and] some of whom joined the centre because they could not find or were not given a place in the right wing'.[20] Once in power, the political divergence of its various factions proved insurmountable. There were major disagreements on a number of issues, from matters of economic policy to the relations with the army and the Palace, that plagued the short-lived EK administration and paralysed any attempts at modernization of the political and institutional structure of Greece. The factionalism in the party crystallized in the form of Papandreou's son Andreas on the one hand, leading what was called the 'centre-left' of the party, and the rising Constantine Mitsotakis on the other hand, leading the rest of the party factions.

Crisis and breakdown of democracy in Greece, 1965–7

The beginning of the end for the EK in office was the spring of 1965, when Andreas Papandreou was named as leader of a faction of officers conspiring to impose a dictatorship. The truthfulness of those allegations has since been the subject of more speculation than hard evidence,[21] however, they were enough to spark a fatal crisis in the EK. Although Papandreou firmly denied the accusations, the Minister of Defence,

Petros Garoufalias, started an investigation, ignoring the Prime Minister's advice to focus on the allegations of military participation in fraud in the elections of 1961. When in July Papandreou tried to replace Garoufalias with himself, he was met by a firm refusal from the King and subsequently resigned. The King responded by appointing successive governments made up of MPs who left the EK, refusing to follow Papandreou in his clash with the Palace, and supported by the ERE, and finally succeeded in obtaining a vote of confidence in parliament. Nevertheless, the country's constitutional order and political stability had taken a fatal blow. Large demonstrations were held in Athens and other big cities in the summer of 1965, denouncing the '*Apostates*' (Renegades) of the centre and calling for a restoration of constitutional order through new elections. Greece now faced its most severe crisis since 1949.[22]

What was left of the EK became a radicalized party under the covert leadership of Andreas Papandreou who, seconded by the EDA, assumed an extreme anti-monarchist stance, attacking the Palace, the right wing and the military, and calling for major institutional and political reforms; the ERE, for its part, was on the defensive and lacking significant public support. After almost 18 months, it withdrew its support from the 'Renegades' government and, with the blessing of the Palace, started a process of rapprochement with George Papandreou in the winter of 1966, with the goal of reducing tension and ultimately calling elections as soon as possible. Nevertheless, the radicals behind Andreas Papandreou in the EK and the right-wing hardliners in the ERE aimed fiery rhetoric and even threats at their opponents, polarizing the political situation even more. After long and arduous background negotiations, the King appointed Panayotis Kanellopoulos, Karamanlis' successor as leader of the ERE, as PM charged with the task of calling new elections on 28 May 1967. The measure of polarization was reflected in the desperate attempt of the ERE, the 'Renegades' and the small Progressive Party of Spyros Markezinis to join forces and invite Karamanlis to return to Greece and lead their coalition, in the hope of defeating the radicalized EK of Papandreou.[23] The refusal of Karamanlis induced the King to ask George Papandreou and Kanellopoulos to form a coalition government if the polls did not produce a clear majority. Most scholars agree, however, that had the elections taken place, there would have been a majority for the EK – that is, for Andreas Papandreou, now controlling most of the party with his radical MPs.[24] As the support for the EK's left wing was increasing, and regardless of whether after its electoral victory the EK would introduce more substantial reforms or seek a compromise with the Palace, that victory would de facto produce a more radical political settlement than that of February 1964: it would mean 'the start of a process of abolition of the unequal balance between army/Monarchy on one hand and parliament/government on the other hand'.[25] In view of the pending elections, the Palace and some politicians from the right wing began to consider plans to declare a state of emergency in case of 'major disruptions' on the way to the polls, thus implicating the army once again in a desperate attempt to block the EK.[26] It was intended to be a limited intervention, led by the higher military echelons under the direction of the King, should an opportunity arise for such a move. The surprise coup in the early hours of 21 April frustrated those plans and revealed the importance of the military in Greek politics, a factor that needs to be weighed in this context.

The armed forces and the path to the 'wrong coup'

The army factions' intervention of April 1967 can be explained by examining three elements of the military organization: professionalism, ideology and social status. The combination of these three factors worked heavily against the democratic institutions in Greece from the end of the civil war until the coup.

Professionalism

The urgent need for more officers created by the civil war resulted in the swelling of the officer corps to unprecedented numbers. Furthermore, 'as in other developing countries, the army was a career open to talents, adapted to young countryside men with no other social or economic qualifications',[27] thus guaranteeing a climb up the social ladder. However, junior officers were not as well catered for in terms of good opportunities for career advancement,[28] which led to congestion in the middle ranks after the civil war. General Panourgias noted in a report of June 1967 to Karamanlis that while there were over 2,000 captains in the army, the number of promotions was between 100 and 150 per year. This meant that it would take about 20 years for this backlog to be cleared.[29] This problem was exacerbated from the 1950s onwards 'by political and royal favouritism which distributed promotions not according to merit but by proof of loyalty'.[30] The army was thus not immune to clientelism and, as Zacharopoulos has noted, 'deliberate endeavours were made by political leaders to develop clientage networks within the military'.[31] This situation was not only damaging to the military officers' career opportunities, but also affected their loyalty to the political regime they were supposed to preserve not only from external but also from 'internal' threats, as they viewed them. From their point of view, having 'saved the nation from the throes of communism', army officers refused to accept their unconditional return to the barracks, believing that their prominent role in Greek politics during the civil conflict should be perpetuated.

Ideology

As Alivizatos points out, the Greek post-civil war army 'unilaterally hyper-politicised, having too little respect for parliamentary institutions and democratic legality, deeply influenced by a particularly wide conception of "communist danger" ... was prone to understanding its task as being beyond, if not above, the constitution'.[32] Indeed, the purge of almost all left-wing and republican affiliated officers in the civil war years had turned the Greek military into 'a homogeneous, die-hard, right-wing organization no longer reflecting the contradictions of the political society'.[33] Moreover, this ideology of unyielding nationalism and anti-communism would soon develop a lack of respect for parliamentary democracy altogether. Influenced by the aforementioned favouritism and clientelism, military officers' radicalization would reach dangerous levels, especially after the elections of 1958, when some officers 'became concerned (a) that communism was still a major threat in Greece, and (b) that politicians were either unwilling or incapable of doing anything to meet the renewed communist challenge'.[34] This radicalization turned many officers not only against politicians of all parties, but also against the Palace for tolerating this favouritism, especially after the higher ranking officers had reached their desired posts. What was new and extraordinary about these officer factions was that they did not identify themselves, the army and the *patria*, which they believed they represented, with any other institutional pillar of the Greek polity. It was this image of themselves that inclined them towards intervention in politics.[35] As Moskos has pointed out in his classic analysis of traditional armies, the 'duty, honour and country' principles are values in the minds of the military.[36] It is in this period that a particular group within the army began to regard the Nasserite dictatorship in Egypt as a blueprint for a military 'developmental dictatorship' Greek-style, one which would bring about the radical changes that Greek politics and society needed and which the political elites and the Palace were incapable of or unwilling to make.[37] As long as the military held such 'interventionist and messianic views',[38] they posed a substantial threat to democracy.

Social status and prestige

Last but not least, the high social prestige that Greek officers had enjoyed – due to the above-mentioned easing of tensions and social mobility in an ever liberalizing social and cultural context, as well as due to their own persistence in viewing themselves as an elite beyond society – was beginning to erode by the 1960s. The political tensions that emerged after the election of 1961 did little to appease their feeling of social isolation and estrangement, nor did their identification with obsolete and oppressive extreme right-wing politics in the eyes of many civilians. In the final years before the dictatorship, this social disdain had reached unacceptable levels for the military who experienced a social resentment of sometimes unprecedented intensity.[39] The combination of this development with the other two factors mentioned above produced the revival of an old malaise in the Greek army – factionalism.

Factionalism, conspiracies and the path to military intervention

The Greek armed forces were never immune from factionalism and conspiracies from the time of the National Schism of the 1910s; however, what differentiates the Greek army after the civil war is the new form that factionalism took after 1941, when the remnants of the army escaped in Egypt. The various secret officers' organizations eventually came together as one group, which remained uncontested in the Greek army until the late 1950s: IDEA (Sacred Link of Greek Officers). The new fraternity aimed at serving the professional interests of its members, as well remaining off-limits to republican and non-right wing officers. The ensuing civil war provided IDEA with a golden opportunity to pursue those interests under the banner of the anti-communist struggle.[40] In May 1951 some of the members of IDEA staged a coup in order to impose the man they saw as their natural leader, Field Marshall Papagos, as premier.[41] The attempt failed only after Papagos himself, who had already retired from the army, refused to endorse it. It did, however, achieve its goals in a different way one year later: Papagos became Prime Minister in November 1952, which for most of the IDEA members meant appointments to high-ranking positions in the army pyramid with the consent of the Palace, which thus believed it had the loyalty of the armed forces guaranteed. Therefore, IDEA was practically dissolved. However, this did not mean the end of factionalism; on the contrary, numerous factions still existed in the army, formed by officers of lower rank than the original IDEA members. The most important of the post-IDEA factions appeared in 1958. It was called EENA (Union of Greek Young Officers), its leading figure the future dictator, Major Papadopoulos. These groups comprised officers who had fought and won the civil war on the battlefield rather than in staff positions, and were characterized by extreme anti-communism but also by a sense of victimhood, having lost out in the division of the spoils by their superiors. Within these groups, then, a certain anti-elitism appeared, turning gradually against the Palace in resentment at its opulence and also against well-placed superior officers and politicians, considered corrupt and 'soft' in the fight against communism, especially after the 1958 elections. This was the turning-point in terms of the loss of civilian control of the army and the countdown to the conspiracies that led to the 1967 coup.[42] As long as the higher ranking military believed they could check such plotting, the army seemed to be controllable. However, this was an illusion: factionalism was steadily turning the middle and lower ranking officers against all obstacles that, in their eyes, stood in the way of their professional advance and social prestige, as well as against the modernization of Greece (as they saw it) and the toleration of communism's revival. For most of these officers, the entire political system needed to be dismantled, so that Greece could move in a direction which they approved, from the monarchy to their superiors. Nevertheless, they still showed some loyalty to the post-civil war pillars of the Palace and the ERE; there is evidence that they took an active part in the manipulation of 1961 election.[43] However, after 1963, when the ERE lost the election, they started contemplating more radical solutions.

Some authors contend that this is a proof of their right-wing affiliation. This is true only to a certain extent. Most of the factions felt more secure under the ERE, yet it also became a target for their anti-parliamentary fervour.[44] As for the Palace, it made the mistake of underestimating the danger to the Crown from the anti-constitutional and ever-growing 'semi-autonomous parallel military power' (in the words of Meynaud), as well as assuming that these factions had the same loyalty to the monarchy as their institutional superiors.⁴⁵ As if all this was not enough, the EK provided another source of turmoil when in power on the sensitive issue of factionalism, as the ASPIDA whistle was blown in the spring of 1965, and it is no coincidence that the most serious crisis of the post-civil war period focused on the army and its control. Papandreou responded to the revelations about his son's involvement in the ASPIDA group by ordering an enquiry about the army's involvement in manipulation of the 1961 election. The decision of the EK government to proceed with an investigation into the role of ASPIDA while the Defence Minister, Garoufalias, had refused to authorize a general enquiry into the 1961 election ultimately proved to be the spark for the crisis of July 1965. As the crisis unfolded, and following the collapse of the 'Renegades' government which had provided an illusion of 'stability' in the country, the failure of both EK and ERE leaders to resolve their differences and the calling of elections in the spring of 1967 placed the army in a dilemma: it either had to accept a new EK victory, in which case it 'would lose its leading position with inevitable internal consequences for those holding posts within it; or else, the army had to prevent this by the overall abolition of parliamentary rule'.⁴⁶

The 'wrong coup' of 21 April 1967

In the 21 months between the crisis of July 1965 and the April 1967 coup, and amidst growing fears for the future of democracy, two parallel military conspiracies were unfolding. The first one, which most people focused on at the time, was that by the military hierarchy, conspiring under the auspices of the King and with the tacit knowledge of some leaders of the ERE; and the second, far more threatening and better organized, was that of the lower and middle ranking officers who eventually beat their superiors in the race to overthrow Greek democracy.

The Palace and a part of the ERE, having realized that the most probable outcome of the election would be a victory for the radicalized EK under the leadership of Andreas Papandreou, now contemplated a 'limited' intervention if necessary, which might involve 'the suspension of some fundamental articles of the constitution under a civilian government and in full agreement with the leadership of the army'.[47] The problem for this group, however, was the lack of a specific plan of action as well as agreement on what precisely was to be done and when it would take place. The political wing of the group, the ERE of Kanellopoulos, was wavering between half-hearted support for intervention before the election or risking the election going ahead and then judging the situation. The King himself and the generals were undecided as to how far the intervention would have to go, considering both a full-fledged dictatorship and a constitutionally-limited state of siege in the case of an emergency.[48] The Palace and its associated politicians, however, took royal control of the army for granted, which was their big mistake,[49] as the middle ranking officers were quietly but efficiently preparing their own coup in the background.

The groups that organized the April coup had months earlier acquired access to the necessary information that would allow them to move military units in Athens and the big cities without arousing the suspicions of their peers or superiors. Keeping a close eye on political developments, as well as on the Generals' moves and plans, they took advantage of the fact that their superiors had them transferred to sensitive units and posts in view of their own plans for an eventual royal intervention.[50] Obviously, theirs was to be a radically different intervention from that of the King and the Generals, one that, in the words of Theodorakopoulos, 'called for a complete reversal of the status quo'.[51] The Generals and the King were contemplating a coup for either the end of April, or a few days before election day.[52] Having first-hand, insider information about that possibility, as well as access to contingency military plans for a declaration of a state of siege, the 16 faction leaders decided to take advantage of the indecisiveness of the Generals who now hesitated in response to the Palace's mood.

They skilfully applied their meticulously devised plan of action on the morning of 21 April, presenting a *fait accompli* to the surprised Generals, the right wing and the Palace[53] and submitting Greece to military rule for the first time in more than a generation.

Conclusion. Was the dictatorship of the Colonels inevitable?

The social and political transformation that Greece had undergone in the 1950s and early 1960s and the failed efforts of the established political order to conclude the incomplete democratization of the country's political structure had ground to a halt in the spring of 1967, presenting the monarchy, the right and the military with some difficult choices. As Keeley says, 'the intervention planned among the higher echelons of the Army would be executed in the name of the King and its motive would be the will to save the Monarchy from the attacks of its opponents, mainly of Andreas Papandreou'.[54] The latter, in turn, leading the centre-left and the EDA were pushing their left agendas of 'maximalist and inexorable demands',[55] thus putting to the test the military and right-wing hardliners' faith in elections as a means of sorting out the chaos they saw coming; in their view, the centre-left's tactics challenged the King's supremacy in politics, and he was contemplating whatever might be necessary to avoid having to accept the people's verdict in the election. The Palace and the ERE, for their part, correctly saw in the left and centre-left's agenda a readiness to turn the King into a purely symbolic head of state, stripped of any substantial power that the monarchy now had in the Greek political system.[56] In this way, and without realizing it, they were opening up the possibility of military intervention not by the military hierarchy, but by the junior officers, the ones who really controlled the army. It is impressive, as Kanellopoulos himself would admit years later, that 'the only danger not discussed was the one that actually emerged on the 21st of April'.[57]

There were numerous indications of an irreversible crisis in Greece in the spring of 1967. The monarchy appeared obsolete and decadent – out of touch with the demands of the time. The government, the civil service and the political parties seemed to be stuck in the past, with politics functioning by means of patronage and corruption, political issues personalized, and debates failing to conform to democratic structures and inspire an attitude of toleration, thus igniting fanaticism and intolerance. Political actors pursued strictly personal agendas, failing to work together when faced by a threat to democracy. Finally, there existed an army officer corps which viewed itself as the ultimate arbiter of political and national issues and was eager to intervene when its perceived predominance was questioned. One can agree with Voulgaris that the failure of the Greek political system and its actors in 1967 to break out of the impasse created by the persistence of highly divisive post-civil war politics and structures opened the door for the colonels to use the military might they commanded for their own ends.[58]

2

'Greece of Christian Greeks': The Dictatorship of 21 April 1967

The fundamental weakness of [the] colonels' regime was its failure to consolidate, to institutionalize, and to legitimate itself.

Diamantouros 1986: 145

The military oligarchy is not a complete regime. It has neither a comprehensive programme nor a perspective into the future . . . it has no provision for succession.

Legg 1969: 241

The dictatorship of the colonels has been viewed by many as a compact and united authoritarian regime that enjoyed an internal consensus among its factions on the way the country was to be ruled. It was far from that, however, as a study of its leaders' goals and ambitions reveals a different picture: inter-regime clashes between faction leaders, subversion and conspiracy, a climate of uneasiness not only about sharing the spoils of their victory, but also – and perhaps most importantly – on the kind of plan they had in mind for their – and the country's – future. The ambition of most of the 21 April plotters was limited to guaranteeing for themselves power and privileges for their lifetime, but others felt there should be an attempt to remake Greek society, although their ideas about how this was to be achieved were nebulous. For the few who, like Papadopoulos, had a clearer blueprint of the structures they wanted to see installed, it proved to be a complex venture that finally led to the impasse of 1973 and the attempt to resolve it by means of the 'Markezinis experiment'.

The nature of the dictatorial regime and the aims of its leaders

The dictatorship of 21 April was imposed by a number of heteroclite factions of mid-ranking officers (ranging from captains to colonels) who took advantage of their knowledge of state contingency plans for the management of an internal insurrection (the 'Prometheus Plan') as well as of the hesitation and dithering of the monarchy and of their superior officers on the issue of whether they should intervene before the election date. Although these factions were united in the goal of usurping power by force, they were anything but in agreement on what to do with it once their coup had prevailed. Because of their social roots and ideological disposition, as well as their corporate perceptions, the nature of the dictatorial regime has remained a subject of controversy, reflective more for the contempt in which it was held than any dispassionate analysis. Some regarded it as fascist or totalitarian, while others saw in it a typical bureaucratic-authoritarian case in the pattern of the Latin American dictatorships of that time.[1] One further school of thought, following the pattern of Duverger, viewed the regime as a 'pseudo-fascist paternalist dictatorship'.[2] However, although one can trace elements of fascist ideology in it, it was not a fascist regime, due to the absence of organized corporatist institutions in the country and a lack of close links between the regime and the people, such as a movement or political party.[3] Veremis, influenced by the typologies offered by Clapham and Philip, speaks of a 'veto regime', which none the less 'lacked the degree of military unity usually associated with this type ... [it was] a factional coup conducted against royalist senior officers as well as against democratic politicians ... [and] degenerated in many respects to the level of a factional regime'.[4]

There were no fewer than 14 factions that came together to make the 'Revolution', comprising some 167 officers.[5] Believing the position of the army within the power structure of Greece to be in peril from the likely power shift that would result from the upcoming elections in the spring of 1967, they acted both to protect the military and to preserve their own corporate interests within the structure of the army, as well as share the spoils of their coup once they had secured power. One should also be conscious of the influence of the Metaxas dictatorship years as well as of the civil war on most of those involved in this venture.[6] On the social level, the humble origins of most of the plotters[7] had produced a fierce anti-elitism which, for many, had been transformed into a nebulous social radicalism. Combined with a hard-line nationalist stance, this induced some officers to see the army as a tool of modernization and social progress in a Nasserite paradigm.[8] The regime was thus anything but homogeneous, comprising divergent groups holding (at times) contradictory goals. This point, as well as the inter-regime dynamics and power plays, has often gone unnoticed and needs to be given attention, since it might explain why the regime evolved in the way it did up to the crisis that produced the 1973 *reforma*.

Apart from the obvious common goal of preventing the elections, the development that would jeopardize the dominant position of the army in the country, the 21 April plotters were more divided than united on the issue of what to do once they had seized power. As Woodhouse notes, they 'had no agreed long-term policy except to maintain ... power. They were responding to events and opportunities [rather] than creating the new social order which they professed to envisage.'[9] However, Papadopoulos should be exempted from this general observation, as he was 'the only one really politically thinking man among the insurgents'[10] and the one who had a vision of the path the regime should take in order to guarantee for the army and the officer corps a long-lasting institutionalized predominance in Greek politics and society. Papadopoulos had in mind a reformation of the country's institutional and social structure, so that it would more easily accommodate the army as the dominant institution, with himself as its leader. Such a transformation should, in Papadopoulos' mind, integrate some elements of the 'old political class' while simultaneously creating a new generation of loyal statesmen. It should also accelerate the economic growth of Greece, and reverse the shift of some Greeks to the left by pursuing their 'reeducation', so as to make them endorse the goals of the 'Revolution'. Eventually there would be elections held at a chosen time with the appropriate parties and politicians – and, most importantly, with the desired results.[11] Papadopoulos had no timetable for how long the regime should last. The other members of the triumvirate, Pattakos and Makarezos, had similar, though not identical, views regarding the aims and duration of the regime, and the holding of elections.[12]

If such were the aims of the leaders, other factions did not have the same objectives. For the majority of the more radical and extremist groups (the future 'hardliners') the 'Revolution' was about giving them access to higher posts in the army, as well as to influential and much coveted positions in the state administration for as long as possible. In addition, they rejected any idea of restoring even a supervised democracy as a matter of principle; what they had in mind, in Pedaliu's words, was basically a regime 'designed to eradicate opposition and create armed forces that owed everything to the regime and had a stake in its continuation'.[13] The most representative of those officers were Ioannis Ladas, George Aslanidis and, most notably, Dimitrios Ioannidis. This divergence is at the core of developments in the Greek junta between 1967 and 1973.[14]

Developments and faction struggles within the regime, 1967–72

The first period of the dictatorship was characterized by an underground power game between the colonels and the Palace supported by the royalist generals. The Prime Minister appointed at the King's insistence on 21 April was senior public prosecutor Constantine Kollias. Also, other justices and diplomats took up governmental posts, as did the most notable plotters: Papadopoulos, Pattakos and Makarezos. Obviously the real power was in the hands of the officers who occupied the more important ministries and other key posts (the Ministries of Defence, Public Order, Interior, etc.).[15] The mutual suspicion and distrust between the insurgents and the Palace did not last long, however, as the new rulers set out to secure firm control of the armed forces. They started appointing many pro-regime officers to key posts in the army while at the same time retiring others who were known for their devotion to the throne.[16] After the first surprise, King Constantine started organizing his counter-plot against the colonels, in which he was joined by the rest of the high-ranking officers who were presumably preparing to move in May 1967. During the autumn of that year there were continuous rumours that a counter-coup was brewing, as indeed the Palace and the monarchist officers were in a rush to frustrate the plans of the colonels and their collaborators to establish total control of the army. However, the very fact that such an action was openly discussed proved that the pro-Palace plotters were never going to seriously threaten the colonels' control of the army: their preparation was too conspicuous and their organization too clumsy to succeed. At the same time, the insurgents were subtly pushing the King to act by circulating rumours that purges were being prepared against army officers loyal to the Palace.[17] The royal coup was planned to take place in the autumn, but was postponed by a crisis between Greece and Turkey in Cyprus in September, and the diplomatic negotiations that followed. Finally, on 13 December the Palace and the generals moved against the colonels. Their action, however, failed and was neutralized in a matter of a few hours. The King and his generals made the mistake of assuming that the use of Constantine's name would legitimize the counter-coup and be enough to convince the military to shift their allegiance from the colonels to the Palace. This was a total miscalculation: the colonels and their allies in the army were fully informed about the intentions and the timetable of the King and the higher officers and were simply waiting for their opponents to make their move. When they did, the colonels were able to check the counter-coup as it just started to unfold: the royalist officers and their collaborators were arrested without putting up any serious resistance. The counter-coup fell apart within 24 hours and the royal family and Prime Minister Kollias fled to Rome, where they would remain until the dictatorship ended in 1974. The colonels appointed General Georgios Zoitakis, a man totally obedient to them, as Regent, and Papadopoulos assumed the premiership. The royal attempt to change the regime was thus over, and with it the monarchy as a seat of power in Greece.[18] Control of the country was now firmly in the hands of the colonels, whom Woodhouse described as 'an unstable alliance of diverse and ambitious rivals'.[19]

According to one of the plotters, speaking years after the dictatorship had collapsed, 'The causes of Papadopoulos' downfall and the failure of the Revolution were created from the morning of the 22nd of April ... instead of looking forward, [the insurgents] just had in mind how to undermine each other's position'.[20] Indeed, as Grigoriadis points out, 'the history of the dictatorship after 1968 is one of continuous backstage initiatives of the opponents of the leader [Papadopoulos] and of unabated clashes with him which ended up in internal crises that profoundly shook the regime'.[21] The first clash occurred as early as the opening weeks of the regime, when, as already noted, most of the faction leaders were vying for posts in the government. At Papadopoulos' suggestion, any officer who wanted to assume a government position would first have to retire from the army. This led to the most prominent faction leaders' retirement, 13 in total leaving the service. Of course this also meant that the retired plotters would lose their power and influence over the army, where Papadopoulos aimed to preserve control by keeping his supporters in key positions. However, the *eminence grise* of the regime, Colonel Ioannidis, did not retire but chose to stay in his newly-assumed post of head of the much-loathed Greek Military Police (ESA) that was to be the regime's principal tool of repression.[22] Ioannidis would be the only major figure of the regime never to occupy a governmental post, remaining totally committed to controlling the army. Based on a wide network of trustees that he created for himself, starting from the School of Military Cadets (the *Evelpides*) and eventually including many junior as well as senior officers in most of the key military units, Ioannidis' omnipresent ESA grew so large that it incorporated a staggering 16 per cent of the Greek ground forces' personnel.[23] It was used both for policing the armed forces and checking the people's reactions against the regime, its ranks including some of the most infamous torturers of the dictatorship, a role that on occasion Ioannidis himself took on. He presented himself to his followers as the embodyiment of the 'conscience of the Revolution', the man who was always eager to encourage the hopes and listen to the concerns of military officers, making common cause in the effort to consolidate the military control of Greece.

Internally, the regime was structured around the so-called 'Revolutionary Committee' comprising the leaders of all the major regime factions. It was supposed to be a collective organ where all the major junta members would have a say on the course of the revolution. However, Papadopoulos gradually managed to amass all important powers in his hands, bypassing the official control system. None the less, this was not achieved without fierce resistance from other faction leaders.[24] Papadopoulos took charge of the ministries of Foreign Affairs and Defence and finally, in 1972, after one more internal settling of accounts, the Regency. Yet the image that Greeks – and others – had of a one-man regime was not a true picture of the dictatorship, as it hid the power struggles taking place behind the scenes. Meynaud was right to claim that 'despite being apparently the dominant personality of the regime, Papadopoulos did not cease to depend on decisions of the collective organ of the "revolution"'.[25] For the hard-line factions, the most pressing issues were the question of the King's return, which they had vetoed, and, more importantly, the 'civilianisation of the Revolution', which they vehemently opposed. For the purists among them, there was an ethical issue too: Papadopoulos' transformation from *primus inter pares* to *primus solus* seemed to make a mockery of the 'social principles of the Revolution', enjoying as he did a lavish lifestyle and showing favour to the plutocrats.[26]

This situation brought to a head a major internal crisis in the late summer of 1970, the most defining one of all the regime had been through so far and the one that proved the power of Ioannidis. Following rumours that Papadopoulos was planning to announce the lifting of martial law, which they considered to be a sign that he was preparing for a transition to civilian rule, most faction leaders backed a *pronunciamento* against him. During a stormy session of the Revolutionary Committee in late August, ex-colonels Ladas and Aslanidis, supported by other faction leaders, demanded that the Revolutionary Committee become the key decision-making organization in all matters of national interest and that all plans for elections be abandoned. Papadopoulos pretended to offer his resignation, which was accepted, and agree to their proposal of a new Prime Minister, allegedly Makarezos. With Papadopoulos seemingly having lost the game, and to the astonishment of everyone, 'Ioannidis brought the argument to an abrupt end by declaring himself on Papadopoulos' side because that was the general wish of the Army'.[27] The plot thus collapsed and Papadopoulos reasserted himself as the uncontested leader of the regime; the real winner, however, was Ioannidis, who established himself in Papadopoulos' eyes as his saviour and most trusted supporter. What Papadopoulos did not seem to realize at the time was that this was a mere ruse by Ioannidis, who was steadily advancing himself as the real overlord of the army while pretending to gauge the officers' disposition, presumably for the benefit of Papadopoulos. Ioannidis was the exemplary conspirator – a skill he would deploy against Papadopoulos when the time was right.[28]

After this incident, and feeling a new sense of security with the support from the head of ESA, Papadopoulos believed he could now proceed to transform the dictatorship in the way he wanted to. He weakened the positions of Pattakos and Makarezos, naming them Vice-Presidents of the government without specific portfolios. He also removed all the major faction leaders from the government, appointing them as District Governors in remote areas of Greece. As he said to a pro-regime editor, his plan was to neutralize the opposing faction leaders by retiring them, as well as some 200–300 hard-line officers, before proceeding to 'normalization' which would include the return of the King.[29] This was both too ambitious and too vague a plan, as it did not take into account the critical question of how the officers would react to these plans. Indeed, Papadopoulos' vision was detached from reality, since he was still under the illusion that he knew how the officers were disposed towards him.[30] In fact, he felt secure enough to appoint himself as Regent in 1972. Finally, in the summer of that year, Papadopoulos started speaking to his inner circle of the need to put an end to the Revolution: his associate Georgios Karter recalls a meeting in July 1972 when Papadopoulos told him that 'the Revolution is out of fuel. A second Revolution is now necessary, a political and short term one that will restore normality in the country.'[31] But yet again, Papadopoulos was vague as to how, when and with whom this would take place, as well as on the time scale. For the knowledgeable, this vagueness related to Papadopoulos' (and the regime's) inherent problem: the lack of a concrete plan to return the country to some form of normality, a problem accentuated by the stance of the 'old politicians' towards the regime, as well as the regime's own failure to create the basis of a new political movement.

The regime and the political elites, 1967–72

From the start, the regime leader was faced with the dilemma of ruling either by simple force and violence or by applying a controlled 'liberalization' in which the power holders would have the right to direct how politics was conducted. Unless the King and (after his departure) the politicians cooperated with the regime, the result might be oppressive rule. However, such were relations between the regime and the ex-politicians that the prospects were not hopeful. Efforts at rapprochement were stymied either because politicians feared being stigmatized as collaborators with an unpopular dictatorship or because regime hardliners were fundamentally opposed to any form of civilian rule. Indeed Markezinis was one of the very few members of the pre-1967 political class with whom the regime had any contact.

The name on everyone's lips as the man who might break this impasse was Karamanlis. He maintained a long public silence during the dictatorship, occasionally broken by interviews and statements urging the regime to hand over power peacefully. This was his attitude in the early days of the dictatorship, as indicated in his reply to a letter he received from the regime's first Prime Minister, Kollias, in June 1967. Karamanlis considered the imposition of the dictatorship to have been 'a reaction against the situation in Greece which all Greeks agree ... was miserable, even if they disagree on who was responsible for it ... it is a pity that this reaction did not come from the political world so that the military initiative [would have been] unnecessary'. Karamanlis then went on to outline the conditions necessary for a return to political normality:

> [The mission of the regime should be] the sanitisation of public life and the rapid restoration of Democracy on a more secure basis ... It is only in this sense that the army supported the regime, the public opinion accepted it and those who could have reacted tolerated it ... I am unaware of the intentions of the Revolutionary Government. I hope that it is aware of its mission and has the capacity to bring it about ... [I]n case it cannot do so, it should leave the initiative to the Head of the State, offering him its support.[32]

In his first interview with *Le Monde*, in late November 1967, Karamanlis again called for the colonels to give up power and for a peaceful and orderly restoration of democracy. Developments a month later ensured that this would not happen. Karamanlis was next heard from in late September 1969, when he accused the regime of weakening the armed forces and undermining the economy, which it kept in international isolation. He suggested that if the colonels would not give up power voluntarily, then the army officers should intervene. As a result of his intermittent pronouncements, Karamanlis had 'created an unbridgeable rift between the ERE followers and the junta, which lost the possibility of even an indirect legitimisation which would allow the regime to evolve along the pattern of Salazar's Portugal'.[33]

By then Papadopoulos had realized that he needed to provide some proof of his intention to return to some kind of 'political normality'. The drafting of a constitution in 1968 gave him an opportunity to do this. The text was prepared under the auspices of a committee of pro-regime jurists and, while it recognized some basic civil liberties such as freedom of the press and of political parties, it suspended indefinitely the guarantee of individual rights as well as regulations covering parliamentary and local elections. Furthermore the new constitution granted the Regent the authority to exercise both executive and legislative power without any time constraint. The constitution also recognized the military as the ultimate source of political authority and guarantor of national integrity and social order, with the Head of the Armed Forces empowered to act autonomously of the government.[34] The constitution in effect enshrined the military as praetorians of the polity and its future development. The draft was approved by a plebiscite in September 1968, though it had not been subject to any serious public debate and certainly no opposition or even criticism was permitted. Still, its very existence allowed Papadopoulos to consolidate his own position, 'basing his authority increasingly on the constitution and at the same time trying to ease the army out of the government. He presented the regime not as a dictatorship but as a "parenthesis" that was necessary to put thing[s] straight.'[35] In producing a constitution, Papadopoulos hoped to win over some ex-politicians to his cause.

He did in fact find some ERE ex-MPs willing to negotiate on those terms. The party was split into two groups, the largest of them following Kanellopoulos' vehement refusal to cooperate with the regime and denouncing it at every opportunity. Another group, however, small but not negligible, was open to the idea of a compromise with the colonels on the basis of accepting the legitimacy of the regime by endorsing the constitution and recognizing Papadopoulos as its leader. This group found a representative in ex-Foreign Minister Evangelos Averoff, whose efforts to build the infamous 'bridges' between the regime and a part of the old political class started in 1969 and dragged on until 1971, while he was keeping Karamanlis informed of his initiatives. In this effort, Averoff was guided by the conviction that after the failure of the royal coup of December 1967 there was very little possibility of a dynamic way to bring the regime down, and that only a political process could perhaps convince the colonels to hand over power.[36] Averoff's conditions were that the constitution should be implemented and free and fair elections be called by a transition government. In a letter to Ioannidis in the summer of 1973, he explained the rationale for his 'bridge-building' initiative:

> [I]n the spring of 1971 I had planned a bridge [between politicians and the regime] because I thought that the longer the Revolution lasted, the more difficult the transition from the Revolution to a democracy would be ... we missed many opportunities but it is never too late ... if you [the colonels] fail, the only solution will be that of a harsh dictatorship which, along with your end in power and your condemnation by history will also bring long-term and dreadful damage to Greece.[37]

Averoff was soon to be disillusioned: as he wrote to Karamanlis in 1971, 'the colonels, no matter what they said ... never intended to restore democracy'.[38] These efforts inevitably met with a negative reaction from anti-regime politicians like Kanellopoulos, who declared in a press statement in the summer of 1970 that 'some politicians, thankfully very few, speak of realism. But their "realism" is utopian. Concession to an authoritarian regime is not a step closer to democracy. It simply strengthens the authoritarian regime.'[39]

Nevertheless, in private most politicians were not as negative about the prospects of a negotiated regime transition as their outspoken declarations seemed to imply. Greek-born US University Professor Theodore Couloumbis made numerous trips to Greece and Europe between 1971 and 1973, in which he recorded his talks with many representatives from all sides of the political spectrum. His observations suggest that most of them appreciated the impasse that the country had reached and did not object to some kind of compromise that would allow the regime to end martial law and call free and fair elections under a transition government under Karamanlis or another figure.[40] For example, Kanellopoulos informed Couloumbis in August 1971 that politicians were ready to contest elections as soon as they had the chance, and eight months later Karamanlis told him that his minimum terms for returning to Greece were that Papadopoulos apply the 1968 constitution, call elections and retire, or charge a transition government (approved by as wide a representation of the political spectrum as possible) with organizing those elections. Later that month, Konstantinos Mitsotakis in Paris came close to agreeing that his own terms for returning to Greece were the lifting of martial law and an amnesty for around 80 per cent of political prisoners. And again, Kanellopoulos detailed the options for return to democracy: 'a) An eight-month government with increased authority is formed b) Papadopoulos calls elections and then retires c) He runs in elections with his own party but they are called by a transitional government. He added that he preferred options b) or c) to nothing at all, despite his conviction that the 1967 plotters should be put on trial.' Ex-EDA leader Ilias Iliou also confirmed to Couloumbis that his party could support a Karamanlis solution in order to get Greece out of the impasse it faced.

In a similar vein, the Dutch ambassador to Athens, Karl Barkman, was told by EK leader George Mavros in the summer of 1971 that 'he not only thinks it possible Papadopoulos will allow elections to be held in the near future, but tells me that his party [the Centre Union] and Panayotis Kanellopoulos [the ERE] would in principle be prepared to participate'.[41] An important factor in pushing some politicians towards negotiations with Papadopoulos was the conviction that the longer the dictatorship lasted, the more likely it was that the colonels would be there to stay.

Ultimately, some ex-ERE and EK deputies agreed to meet and discuss with Papadopoulos the prospects of their participation in his cabinet. Although these deputies 'were not of the front rank, they professed themselves optimistic about the outcome'.[42] Indeed, in discussions between 1969 and 1972 Papadopoulos met some 22 former MPs – 15 from the ERE and five from the EK – though their leaders denounced the meetings. In a cabinet reshuffle in the summer of 1972 one former ERE MP became Deputy Minister to the Prime

Minister and an EK MP became Deputy Minister of the National Economy. This, however, was as far as the collaboration between minor political figures and the regime could go.[43]

The attitude of Karamanlis, Kanellopoulos and Mavros did not deter Papadopoulos from seeking politicians who were prepared to collaborate with the regime. In February 1968 he first met and discussed that option with Markezinis, encouraged by the latter's abstention from anti-regime statements up to that point. A leading figure of Greek Rally in the 1950s, successful Minister of Economic Coordination in the Papagos government,[44] Markezinis had left the party after a disagreement with Papagos in 1954 to form his own Progressive Party, which never attracted more than 3 per cent of the popular vote when it ran independently.[45] Although he had been an outsider in the Greek political world ever since, Markezinis had both insightful political views and an ability to perceive future trends in Greek politics, as his perceptive comment on 'the unknown colonel' who would stop the elections of 1967 proves. After a second meeting, Markezinis showed Papadopoulos a draft article in which he explained that the goal of the revolution should be to proceed to civilianization. However, hardliners managed first to delay and then prevent publication of Markezinis' article. In the meantime, Papadopoulos realized that Markezinis' intention was to create a new political party with the aid of the regime, something that made him have second thoughts about working with Markezinis. Nevertheless, they had another meeting in late 1969, although nothing of substance resulted from it. Apart from his own doubts, Papadopoulos was constrained by the hostile reaction from within the regime to cooperation with Markezinis, the Prime Minister telling his intimates, 'I am being subverted by my fellow *Evelpides* cadets!'[46] The meetings with Markezinis continued half-heartedly and intermittently up to 1973, but Papadopoulos had already lost faith in the Markezinis and, as he confessed to Karter, did not trust him to form a government since he was convinced that Markezinis was motivated solely by self-interest.[47]

None the less, Papadopoulos and other regime leaders made strenuous efforts to convince Greek politicians and the wider world that they were sincere about restoring some form of democracy. In August 1969, Panayotis Pipinellis, Papadopoulos' Foreign Minister, presented the Council of Europe and some foreign governments with a document describing the next steps on the regime's path to establishing civilian rule. The 'Pipinellis Memorandum', as it was subsequently known, stipulated that by September 1970 martial law would be ended throughout the country; that by mid-December, 14 fundamental-institutional laws would be introduced as promised in the 1968 constitution; and finally, that by the end of 1971 there would be a return of full parliamentary democracy in Greece with the holding of free elections.[48] Makarezos was actively involved in the drafting of the memorandum, which reflected his view that the colonels 'should leave office by the end of 1971 *at the latest*' (his emphasis).[49] However, the Pipinellis Memorandum was a dead letter, due to the ongoing inter-regime clashes and the death of Pipinellis a year later, which put an end to this attempt at timetabling a transition to civilian rule.

As for the relations between the opposition elites and groups, they remained fragmented and cold for a long time; despite the fact that many of them had been arrested and had shared the same prisons and/or places of exile, the pre-dictatorship divisions in the opposition were not easy to overcome in a climate of doubt and of disagreement over how to deal with the regime and over the prospects of a future transition to democracy. As many politicians were imprisoned, exiled or placed under police surveillance, communication and coordination was difficult. Besides, there were rifts in all the major political groups. Even the EK did not escape a major fracture: already troubled by the 1965 schism, its more centrist wing began to align with Georgios Mavros, coming close to the ERE wing of Kanellopoulos in opposition to the regime, while the more radical or centre-left faction followed Andreas Papandreou. After leaving Greece in January 1968, the latter chose to form his own group, the Panhellenic Liberation Movement (PAK), and make his own stand against the regime: 'he set about assiduously undermining other anti-junta groups. His favoured tactic was to enter alliances but then work to discredit his supposed colleagues so that anti-junta opposition became synonymous with him personally'.[50] The hegemonic tendencies of the KKE and Papandreou's PAK 'reflected the pre-1967 fears of the Left that it might get totally absorbed by the Centre ... as well as a divergence over what forms the resistance against the dictatorship should take, the PAK speaking even of armed resistance, which the KKE considered potentially damaging'.[51] On the left, too, the division of the KKE into two parties following the 1968 Soviet invasion of Czechoslovakia set the two KKEs against each other: 'instead of speaking to their followers on what was to be done against the junta, [the KKEs] were trying to convince them on the [merits] of their own views'.[52] Furthermore, both KKEs became absorbed by an internal debate about the causes of the dictatorship, which simply revealed how 'they were distanced from country's problems ... they could not realise the deep social changes happening so they went on with their revolutionary rhetoric with excerpts from Marx and Lenin's work which might be theoretically interesting but had no convincing response for the Greek issues'.[53]

For the first time, the credibility and passivity of the left was now questioned, with Farakos admitting that 'in contrast to what had happened in the German and Italian occupation years, when the left became the trusting place of the hopes of so many Greeks, during the dictatorship its success was limited ... and this cannot be attributed only to the breakup of the KKE'.[54] Efforts to coordinate the opposition forces and form some sort of a united front against the dictatorship foundered on various areas of disagreement, and for the first five years, despite a shared experience of regime oppression, the groups involved failed to move beyond discussions so that by the end of 1972 no tangible results had been achieved. As Karakatsanis noted, 'various factions opposing the colonels' regime engaged in private talks about ways to rid Greece of the colonels. A formal compromise or agreement was never reached, however'.[55] The British ambassador noted in April 1972 that 'the democratic opposition of the "old" politicians is ineffective ... A return to the pre-1967 political regime should be considered improbable. If there is a change, this will most probably come from a new military coup that will lead to a more authoritarian regime than the current one.'[56]

The regime and civil society

'Papadopoulos and his colleagues had a vision, however misty, of the sort of Greece they were trying to create, but they never managed to convey this vision to the people, or to inspire them in any way.'[57] This admission by one of the most pro-regime authors somewhat understates the failure of the dictatorship to gain legitimization and win the hearts of the Greek people. This failure reflected the fact that the regime 'represented an effort by the Greek military's more reactionary elements to remake the nation's society in their own image and establish a political framework that would ensure the armed forces' primacy'.[58] On the other hand, it must be acknowledged that for a long time the Greek people did not actively resist the dictatorship: there was no acceptance of the colonels, but there was passivity. Their attitude gradually shifted from a 'shrugging indifference' to one of 'increasingly widespread impatience and resentment'.[59] It was this clear lack of resistance which led a regime official to boast to Polytechnic Dean Konofagos in the early years of the dictatorship that 'if all Greeks spat on us we would drown in their saliva; but they do not do it'.[60] There are a number of explanations for this, in addition to the most obvious one – the lightning strike by the colonels which caught everyone by surprise and which included the arrest of almost all the politicians, trade unionists, party and youth members and leaders and student representatives who might have organized some reaction against the new regime. The initial fear which inevitably accompanied the dictatorship paralysed the will of the would-be opponents of the colonels. In the words of Manesis, fearful of the omnipresent police, 'citizens were turned into "private beings" dealing with their everyday life as they usually would'.[61] Furthermore, as Notaras has pointed out, in the early days some were inclined (or wanted) to believe that 'the foreign factor will kick the colonels out the same way it got them in' or that the dictatorship would be a temporary phenomenon due to its inability to establish a popular basis, views that merely served as excuses for inertia.[62] There were also deeper causes of this passivity. Yannopoulos correctly notes that 'the failure of the leaderships of the left and the centre to grasp the realities of the Greek situation in those days, and their incompetence in forestalling the trend towards dictatorship, has led to an apparent feeling of mistrust toward the old political leaderships and parties by the party cadres, the political activists and especially the young.'[63] This aversion contributed to the lack of an organized reaction, which would normally have been undertaken by the political parties.

Gradually the situation began to change: after the first shock and surprise, certain individuals (mainly retired officers, released trade unionists, intellectuals and some party cadres who had managed to avoid arrest) began to organize secret nuclei of subversion and contemplate a more dynamic opposition to the colonels. During the dictatorship years more than 30 such organizations were created. The best known were the 'Free Greeks', set up by retired military officers in 1968; the Patriotic Front (PAM), created by the famous composer Mikis Theodorakis and fellow EDA/KKE members; the Democratic Defence, which comprised many academics, most notably future Prime Minister Costas Simitis; and the already-noted Panhellenic Liberation Movement (PAK) of Andreas Papandreou, which was formed abroad but had a small operational branch in Greece. Most of these organizations shared a common fate – exposure and dissolution by the very effective regime security, their members either arrested and imprisoned or exiled, or smuggled out of Greece. It is also an important point to note that, as Notaras, himself a member of a resistance group, put it 30 years later, what characterized these groups was their fragmentation, the small number of participants, their very short duration – most carrying out only one or two actions before being dissolved – and the fact that their activities were aimed primarily at showing that dissent existed in Greece rather than at toppling the dictatorship.[64] Although, according to one study, the resistance groups placed more than

170 bombs in Athens alone between 1967 and 1974, this had little impact on the dictatorship.⁶⁵ The most serious incident was an attempt on Papadopoulos' life in August 1968 by Alexandros Panagoulis, a member of an underground group, but the dictator survived. As for mass reaction against the dictatorship, two major events can be considered as proof of an anti-dictatorial spirit among the majority of the Greeks. The first was the demonstration by tens of thousands of Athenians in early November 1968, after the funeral of ex-Prime Minister George Papandreou. These scenes were repeated in September 1971 at the funeral of the prominent Greek poet and 1963 Nobel Prize-winner George Seferis. Both events may have registered the opposition to the dictatorship by an oppressed people but at the same time did not seriously undermine the stability of the regime.

Finally, a major reason for the fragmentation of the opposition – as with the ex-political parties – was the mistrust that existed between most of the groups. And again, the name of Andreas Papandreou appears in many studies as a key factor impeding the coordination of action among anti-regime resistance groups. In the words of Murtagh, 'Papandreou destroyed the possibility of a unified opposition, seeking instead to secure his personal position at the expense of other resistance groups which he saw as a threat to his political future. Thus, by the early 1970s, the resistance had lost much its momentum.'⁶⁶ A National Resistance Council was eventually created abroad, comprising the most important opposition groups, but with the exception of PAK, since Papandreou once again chose to abstain from joint action, with the excuse that the programme adopted by the National Resistance Council did not provide for the organization of a referendum on the future of the monarchy.⁶⁷ All in all, as Murtagh points out, 'the resistance had kept [Papadopoulos] isolated internationally but it could not topple him'.⁶⁸

One further factor in keeping resistance to the dictatorship at low levels in its early years concerned the economy under the colonels and its effects on society. The regime did not change the basic features of the economic policies of its predecessors; however, it did focus on rapid economic growth through a rise in consumption. The colonels embraced 'orthodox' economic philosophy regarding the role of the free market, with the state assigned the role of creating the social and economic infrastructure. Emphasis was also placed on industrialization and during the dictatorship the secondary sector surpassed the primary one for the first time in the country's history. This was not achieved without a degree of import substitution; however, as growth depended on exports and the competitiveness of the Greek industry was comparatively low, the colonels resorted to foreign loans in order to further fuel consumption. This situation was aggravated by the regime's decision to write off farmers' debts, raise pensions and reduce the interest on student loans. The colonels also sponsored public works, mainly in construction, as well as workers' housing programmes.[69] Although this gained them some popularity, particularly in the countryside, it also significantly raised the deficit of Greece, which in turn led to a rise in taxation and to a further increase in foreign loans and thus in the national debt. It is true that for the first years of the dictatorship the economy was booming and thus, in the words of Legg and Roberts, 'the continued economic growth reduced the incentive to actively oppose the new leaders'.[70] This situation of passivity misled some – mostly regime apologists – to believe that, in the words of Theodorakopoulos, 'if Papadopoulos had stood for election in 1970, he would probably have won by a landslide, especially after three years of uninterrupted political peace, economic progress and social harmony'.[71] However, to regime opponents like Yannopoulos, writing in 1972, 'the Greece of today resembles a nation of sleepwalkers'.[72]

But this euphoria did not last long. The colonels proved too short-sighted in restructuring the Greek economy, public administration and institutions to face the challenging demands of a proper modernization. Their limited plans for social security and welfare never materialized either.[73] Therefore, the Greek economy was unprepared for what was to follow in the later part of the dictatorship: by the end of 1972 the economy was already showing signs of stagnation, the regime having missed the chance to adjust its policies while the economic climate was still good. Besides that, the rule of the colonels had degenerated into a system of nepotism and favouritism, privileging those who had connections in the civil service and the army, and of sleaze and corruption that started turning even the most hard-line officers into fierce critics of Papadopoulos' toleration of these developments.[74] A letter from Averoff to Papadopoulos in April 1969 dramatically portrays the decadence of the regime and its acceptance of precisely what it was supposed to have been committed to eradicating – corruption and stagnation:

> The spiritual unity of nationally-minded Greeks has been shattered ... most of those who participated in large [pro-regime] rallies often recount in private the bullying they went through so as to make those rallies appear huge ... Young people have an evident tendency to cooperate with the left ... The civil service is underrated to an unknown point ... purges have fuelled irresponsibility and flattery ... there are persisting rumours of big scandals, favouritism, and nepotism ... [the regime] cannot find expedient collaborators. On the economy, seven businessmen out of ten will tell you that they are undergoing a crisis ... as economists say, the policies of spending money have raised the cost of production, the competitiveness of Greek exports is reduced, and a policy of overbrowning money undermines the currency.[75]

The regime tried to win the hearts and minds of the Greek people by using state propaganda. Radio and television were employed to this end, while in schools, universities and the civil service celebrations and festivities praising the 'Revolution' were the order of the day. The inauguration of public works was advertised as a proof of the 'affection of the National Government [for] the Greeks'. The regime used nationalist and traditionalist slogans to try to inspire people with a sense of identification with the grandeur of ancient Greece and Byzantium, similar to the approach of the Metaxas regime a generation earlier. Regime-staged public celebrations often ended with kitsch imitations of 'the glorious historic adventures of the Greek nation'. This nationalist discourse also had traces of anti-Westernism: many speeches and articles by pro-regime intellectuals, journalists and officials belittled 'western rationality and atheism' in contrast to the praise heaped on

Greek Orthodox piety. Not surprisingly, the colonels excelled at anti-communism, claiming that they had prevented a communist takeover planned for May 1967, although practically no evidence was produced to substantiate this assertion.[76]

There is one final point to be considered regarding the people's attitudes to the regime: as Haralambis has noted, the clientelist relationship between the dictatorship as the distributor of privileges and the citizens as receivers of those privileges reinforced political toleration of the regime, since 'with the price of the loss of one's individual and collective autonomy, one could enjoy ... the privileges of the state's distributive functions'.[77] The lack of collective action was very noticeable in Greece for most of the dictatorship years. As the political scientist Mancur Olson has observed, individuals in large unorganized groups (such as the Greek people under the dictatorship) 'have no tendency voluntarily to act to further their common interests' because a rational individual 'will not be willing to make any sacrifices to achieve the objectives he shares with others'.[78] This describes perfectly the behaviour of the Greek people for most of the dictatorship period, with a combination of factors – such as fear and memories of the civil war, rising standards of living until 1972, the unreliability of the pre-1967 political formations and the failure of anti-regime groups to articulate convincing alternative narratives that could lead to a transition to democracy – resulting in passive acceptance of, though not consent to, the dictatorship.

This situation prompted Papadopoulos, in November 1970, to form a group that might be considered the nucleus of a possible future pro-regime party. It was called the *Symvouleutiki Epitropi* ('Consultative Committee') and was supposed to comprise scientists, professionals, jurists and other technocrats. This appointed body would serve as a 'proto-parliament' that would advise the government on the applicability of laws and decrees and later on assume some of the functions of the executive, with its members chosen partly by academic and professional organizations and partly by the localities. However, the Consultative Committee lacked widespread appeal and failed to attract the type of people who might serve as a link between the regime and ordinary citizens, let alone satisfy the demand for a proper representative government body. Although there was an attempt to revive it one year later, it was ingloriously dropped in 1972.[79] The most convincing explanation for this failure is offered by the regime apologist Theodorakopoulos, who conceded that the Colonels' exaggerated fear of any progressive ideas, plus their feeling that 'the revolution was their own property, a kind of irrevocable privilege, had systematically obstructed participation by the politically minded, educated and active individuals who believed in the revolution'.[80] Even if some were seriously considering jumping on the regime bandwagon, by 1972 it was too late, as the tide had started to turn and the dictatorship was steadily beginning to lose its grip on Greek society. EDA leader Ilias Iliou spoke to Couloumbis in April 1972 and drew a strikingly different image to the one of the early days of the regime, speaking of 'a mounting expression of public discontent ... the press is getting more critical [of the colonels] day by day ... and the police are more relaxed, fearing a change and possible reprisals', though he saw no serious threat of a change except for a possible intervention by the armed forces, warning that 'the new regime they will impose will be more puritan and tyrannical'.[81]

By the end of 1972 the situation in Greece presented a paradox: although on the outside the regime looked as if it was there to stay,[82] it had lost its main asset – the capacity to inspire fear among the people.[83] Achilleas Mitsos, having recently returned from the USA where he did his PhD in late 1972, recalls that:

> By that time the people had started not fearing the junta. One night I went to eat in a small restaurant with a group of friends. After a few glasses of wine, as we were in high spirits we started singing a song of Theodorakis ... to my surprise, we were joined by people on other tables and, in a few minutes' time, more than half the people in the restaurant were singing. I could not imagine that this would be possible based on how I remembered the situation before going to the USA.[84]

Moreover, the regime had failed to create anything new in terms of the country's institutional structure or to present the Greek people with a credible mechanism for its transformation into anything other than what it was – an authoritarian regime. In its ranks, conspiracies and factionalism were brewing – as always – and there was no serious channel or link of support to the 'old politicians'. Despite their best efforts, the colonels had not avoided 'a continuous institutional deadlock, which was precisely the legal expression of their political isolation'.[85] Finally, the economic slowdown was already being felt by the end of that year, and perhaps more importantly, the first cracks in the oppressive system were becoming evident, such as the permission of representative elections in universities for the first time under the dictatorship, thereby giving students an opportunity to mobilize against the colonels. It was from this area of civil society that the most spectacular surprises were to emerge in the first part of 1973 – the year of the *Metapolitefsi* that failed.

3

The Early Liberalization, January–September 1973

In a dictatorship, the fear of loss of power turns into a passion stronger than the desire to get it in the first place.

Karamanlis' message, 23 April 1973

The year 1973 was arguably the most eventful one of the dictatorship; 'a baffling and frustrating year', in the words of the British ambassador in Athens. What happened – and perhaps more importantly, what did not happen – changed everything in the country and set the pace for the actual transition of 1974. This is because the regime had reached an impasse: 'a point at which the regime has clearly boxed itself into a corner, in which it can neither create new political institutions itself, nor do deals with existing political groupings'.[1] It was the point at which Papadopoulos was prompted to start the process of *reforma* in the summer, which he believed was compatible with his prerogative. Nevertheless, he would face unexpected developments that would put him in a dilemma as to whether to make further concessions, which might oblige him to retire earlier than he had intended, or revert to authoritarianism, which would also carry unacceptable costs. As Whitehead has noted, democratic transitions are 'processes of change which do not necessarily end in predetermined outcomes of equilibria or consolidation, and which may not proceed in predictable and necessary sequences'.[2] The transition from authoritarian rule of 1973 thus evolved in two phases, the first of which was the period when Papadopoulos attempted to establish a 'democracy' on his own terms.

The student demonstrations and their aftermath

'From early 1973 the effects of our failure to deliver on our fundamental pledges started becoming visible' admitted Makarezos; indeed, by that time 'the regime was at an impasse: the effort to restore Greek society to health had stalled with the economic difficulties at the time in a way that was obvious to all, and yet the regime had no viable plans for the future'.[3] It was now that Papadopoulos became anxious to accelerate the process of restoring some form of parliamentary rule. Zournatzis recalls him saying that 'we must definitely hand power over to civilians during this year!'[4] He was aware of the constraints that the economic downturn[5] placed on the timing of his efforts to stage a controlled transition. He also knew that he had to address the reaction of the hardliners if the transition was to stand any chance of success.[6] In addition, he still sought potential collaborators among the opposition and had to take into account the international pressure to democratize as well restore Greece's position in relation to the EEC.[7] However, problems cropped up earlier than he had anticipated in the whole process – and from a most unexpected quarter – with the beginning of student protests in February.

During their time in power, the colonels, despite being conscious of the need to keep the anti-regime reaction in the universities under control, had none the less underestimated the dynamics of the student movement. The methods employed to achieve and maintain that control – the appointment of a governmental commissar 'to supervise the application of laws' in the universities; the staffing of the universities with lecturers and staff who were regime loyalists; the dissolution of all student organizations and severe reduction of student participation in university affairs; the suspension of male students' military exemption because of a lack of 'nationally-minded behaviour' – simply created a 'suppressed reserve of passive resistance'.[8] Indeed, a report by two pro-regime professors acknowledged that 'the Revolution has not thus far offered any ideological or political possibilities within which a student movement might develop'.[9] In November 1972 the colonels allowed elections to university student councils for the first time, though they did their best to rig the process in order to produce pro-regime councils. Things did not turn out quite as they had planned, however, with many students denouncing the whole process and demanding free and fair elections. The police intervened against improvised demonstrations on a number of campuses in Athens and other cities. This crude attempt at manipulation by the regime further radicalized many students, so that most faculties had become hot spots of anti-regime activity by the beginning of 1973.

In early February the regime announced its intention to introduce a decree suspending students' exemption from the army in cases of disciplinary action or of non-participation in lectures and exams. Some students were indeed forcibly drafted. The reaction was swift: demonstrations were organized in Athens demanding revocation of the decree, a more liberal administration in the faculties and more participatory rights for students. The protests culminated in the occupation of the Law School building on 21 February, and only after prolonged negotiations with the police was the building peacefully evacuated on the night of the 22nd. In contrast and at the same time, elsewhere in Athens there were clashes between demonstrators and police. More violence followed in March, when police attacked and broke up peaceful student gatherings in the centre of Athens.[10] In a speech delivered to an academic conference in March, Papadopoulos blamed the turmoil on the campuses on 'an organized minority'.[11] The extent of student opposition to the regime was even evident among its own followers, as noted in the report by the two professors quoted above.[12] But what was particularly significant about these demonstrations was the presence of workers alongside the students, something the regime had not encountered before and a sign that the civil society in general was becoming restless.[13] 'Peace and order' was restored, but the impact of the demonstrations was considerable, as academics, intellectuals and politicians like Mavros and Kanellopoulos openly expressed their support for the students. On the other hand, the conclusion that the military diehards drew from these events was that even minimal concessions were potentially destabilizing as they only fuelled the demand for further concessions by the regime, concessions which in their eyes would be a sign of weakness to their enemies. Another factor to take into consideration was a report by a regime-appointed commissar of the Polytechnic School in late spring which predicted that the students would make a dramatic comeback in the university elections scheduled for 1974.[14]

Papadopoulos appeared unconcerned by developments on the campuses, or at least did not want to let them distract him from his plans for a controlled civilianization. This was evident in his speech in March when he warned that 'if turmoil occurs in issues concerning the public order and security of this country during the critical time of 1973 and 1974 ... not only myself, not only the Revolution, but the Greek people too will collapse'.[15] The reason he needed 'public order and security' was shown in early April, with the creation of the 'National Cultural Movement' (*Ethnikon Politistikon Kinima* – EPOK). In a certain sense this was a continuation of his effort (which had started with the 'Consultative Committee' in 1970) to create a political movement that would serve as a pro-regime party when elections were eventually called. As its constitutive text stipulated, 'the movement's pro-reform nature and programme ... must create the impression that something new is taking shape ... [that] does not leave out members of the old political parties ... [I]t is important that EPOK be populated by, on [the] one hand, personalities from [a] range of the political spectrum [except the left], and on the other hand by partners of the current political power [holders].'[16] Papadopoulos' aim seems to have been to include as many young and previously non-party-affiliated people as possible in the venture, in order that his planned civilianization process appear fresh and give the impression of a new start. However, a US government report at the time stressed that '[the] manner in which EPOK [is] being developed suggests [that the] PM [is] aiming for a "tame" and captive parliament'.[17] Despite all the palaver, EPOK proved to be a very short-lived phenomenon. Not only did it fail to attract public interest and participation, it also faced a hostile reaction from politicians as well as other regime leaders, who saw in EPOK an attempt by Papadopoulos to create a personal party to help him monopolize power indefinitely.[18] As early as May, Markezinis learned in private conversations that 'the interest of Papadopoulos in EPOK has withered away'.[19] EPOK collapsed as ingloriously as had the Consultative Committee. Ultimately it was overshadowed by more important developments in the spring of 1973.

The failed naval conspiracy

On 23 April the daily *Vradyni* published a long statement by Karamanlis on the sixth anniversary of the coup, in which he stated:

> The restoration of democratic normality is not in the intensions of the government ... the people have already passed from the toleration of the early days to discontent and from discontent to general, open enmity ... the government has broken the unity of the armed forces. Pretending to be ruling in the name of the army, it is fatally harming its prestige, creating an unbridgeable gap between army and people ... with its extreme consumption policies and mindless borrowing it has exhausted the limits of the endurance of the economy ... but the greatest danger is the isolation and threat of a permanent cut off of Greece from Europe ... therefore, the national interest of Greece calls for the restoration of democratic normality ... [This government] cannot carry out any modernization of political life because it lacks the basic precondition for this – popular support ... it is said that the regime, in order to find a way out of the impasse it has created, is preparing an electoral coup. It seems that it believes it could overcome the reactions and extend its stay in power under a coat of supposed parliamentary rule. If this is true, it means that the government has lost its sense of reality and ... it does not realize that it cannot carry out fake elections without risking ... bloodshed ... and even if it wins, it will be a Pyrrhic victory because no one in Greece or abroad will recognize the result; thus the anomaly will continue ... [G]iven all the above the government needs to call the King and make way for an

experienced and strong government which, having emergency [powers] for some time and free from revanchist passions, will create the conditions that will allow the functioning of democracy in Greece and the timely and free decision of the sovereign people on their future.[20]

The statement reflected the disillusionment of the 'old political world' as it faced the prospect of the regime remaining in power. However, there were clear signs that the people's patience would not last forever, with an indirect appeal to the army not to permit the creation of a pseudo-democracy by the colonels and for the first time an open call for the creation of a transitional government to prepare for the restoration of democracy under the auspices of the King. For astute observers, these developments were a sign of things to come. Interestingly, two days before the statement of Karamanlis, Ioannnidis had also marked the sixth anniversary of the coup with a speech, in which he had said that the monarchy was a thing of the past for Greece, as 'it has paid to the nation all services it possibly could'.[21] None the less, forces for change were on the move, with a report from the British embassy only a few days after the Karamanlis statement suggesting that something was afoot in the army:

> ... the American Embassy have been considering [rumours] that the statement is linked to some move that the King may be about to make ... The hope is presumably that a pro-Karamanlis faction in the army would be willing to "impose" the proposed coup on the regime. But Papadopoulos would almost certainly hear of it before any move was made against him.[22]

Less than a month later, on 20 May, the pro-regime daily *Eleftheros Kosmos*'s editorial revealed the intentions of Papadopoulos to kick off a process of 'self-transformation' of the regime, as well as his thoughts on the issue of the King. 'There is a good chance', the editorial claimed, 'that the first step to the future political arrangements is the sorting of the form of polity, through [a] people's vote ... [A]s things stand now, there are indications that by the end of 1973 or in the first half of 1974 Greece will move toward a different form of rule.'²³ It is hardly a coincidence that just a few days later it was announced that the first anti-regime conspiracy since December 1967 had been neutralized.

Whatever support the regime enjoyed among the rank and file of the army, it was certainly far more extensive than that in the air force and the navy, which had both been largely inactive in the 21 April coup, but heavily involved in the failed royal counter-coup of December 1967. During the dictatorship years, purges of potential regime opponents were frequent, as were anti-regime plots.²⁴ A conspiracy involving the navy began to take shape in the spring of 1972. As well as officers in active service, a number of retired naval officers were also involved in the plot. The plan was to move a number of warships from various bases to the island of Poros, close to Athens, send an ultimatum to the colonels demanding their resignation and threaten a naval blockade of the Athens area if the colonels did not comply. If they met with success, the naval officers intended to appeal for the formation of a government of national unity, headed by Karamanlis, which would then call elections.²⁵ The plotters sought the political support of Averoff and ex-Defence Minister Garoufalias.²⁶ Averoff accepted, but said that a more influential figure than himself was needed to advance the cause, and so he approached Karamanlis. The latter, however, expressed doubts about the chances of success, commenting 'I cannot take responsibility for a movement over which I can have no control.' None the less, Averoff was left with the impression that if the mutiny occurred, Karamanlis 'would assist it with declarations ... aimed at achieving a compromise solution'.²⁷ Although it was claimed that the plot 'had no specific political or ideological background, as the officers who organized it had different political orientations',²⁸ it also had the backing of King Constantine, who was hoping for a second chance to restore his pro-democratic profile in the eyes of the people.²⁹

The attempt was doomed to fail, however, due to the confusion and disagreement in the ranks of the conspirators on how far they would go if their ultimatum was rejected, the lack of support from the army and the air force, and the tight control by the regime security services.³⁰

The ESA knew about the coup in advance, as a naval NCO involved in the plot had been under surveillance for months. He was arrested at the end of April and gave details about the preparations. On 23 May it was announced that a conspiracy by some naval officers had been uncovered and defeated. General Odysseas Anghelis, the supreme commander of the armed forces, personally supervised the suppression of the coup. Sixty-three serving or retired naval officers involved were arrested, as were Averoff and Garoufalias, whose cooperation with the conspirators was confirmed. The regime press downplayed the seriousness of the incident, saying it involved only a handful of plotters, but in an interview a few years later, Averoff asserted that the number of officers involved was much larger than admitted and that 'the dictatorship did not dare arrest all [the] officers implicated, hiding this weakness by granting [a] general amnesty to those arrested'.[31]

None the less, the affair was over in a few hours and regime control over the armed forces reasserted, with the exception of the destroyer *Velos*, participating in NATO exercises in the Adriatic Sea and currently anchored at the port of Fiumicino, Italy, where her crew asked for political asylum. This event aroused a great deal of interest abroad, understandably taken as an indication that at least parts of the armed forces no longer supported the dictatorship.[32] However, there were inter-regime political implications too: regime hardliners sought to blame the King as the chief mastermind behind the conspiracy, with ESA interrogators making 'continuous and obsessive efforts to extract from captive officers confessions and proof [of] the King's involvement in the plot'.[33] The failed coup therefore became part of the power game between regime factions. As Leontaritis claims, a few days after its suppression the hardliners, led by Ladas and Alsanidis, presented an ultimatum to Papadopoulos to abolish the monarchy.[34] Papadopoulos succumbed to their demand, but at the same time he struck back: simultaneously with the announcement of the abolition of the monarchy, he declared his decision to proceed with the 'civilianization of the Revolution' with himself as President of the Republic.

From *Dictadura* to *Dictablanda*: The new constitution and the plebiscite

The failure of the naval coup marks the turning point of 1973: although frustrated, its aftershock alarmed Papadopoulos, who sped up the transition process. He now realized that there was little prospect of progress with the politicians with whom he had been in contact up to this point, and decided to proceed with the version of transition that he believed best served his goal of keeping control of the country's politics. Just eight days after the defeat of the coup, on 1 June, Papadopoulos addressed the Greek people on radio and television, trumpeting his decision to democratize Greece, which was to become a republic. He also announced that a plebiscite would be held in the summer to approve the change and that an interim government would be charged with the task of calling general elections to be held no later than the end of 1974. Papadopoulos appointed himself 'President of the Republic' and informed his audience that the 1968 constitution would be amended, producing a 'constitutional refreshing' of the regime.[35] It was the classical case of the authoritarian leader who, according to Huntington, 'see their interests served by the introduction of democratic institutions [and] therefore ... opt for a reform that will provide sufficient guarantees for their security, impunity and corporate interests'.[36] It was in this way that Papadopoulos' version of transition began to move from a 'hard' to a 'soft' form of dictatorship. The first step towards a limited liberalization of the regime involved Papadopoulos seeking to 'unilaterally liberalize the political arena',[37] hoping this would work to his benefit. At the same time, he also aimed to neutralize the opposition of the King and show off his democratic credentials to the world. A British Foreign Office report observed that Papadopoulos

> ... (1) by precluding the return of King Constantine has eliminated [an] obstacle which [the] hardliners within [the] government are said to have put in [the] way of any forward movement towards parliamentary democracy; (2) has neutralised two main centres around which opposition elements are said to have been coupling

themselves (King and Karamanlis); and (3) has committed himself to a fixed timetable for elections which may ease international pressures on him provided he lives up to his expectations.[38]

Papadopoulos also aimed to neutralize Karamanlis because, as a US State Department report noted, 'he recognized Karamanlis' great ability, his popularity generally, and his relatively good standing with the army'. The same report observed that by seeking to implicate him in the naval plot, Papadopoulos 'has provided [a] basis to prevent Karamanlis' return to Greece and reentry into Greek politics, and even to deprive him of [his] Greek citizenship if this became desirable. [Papadopoulos] must believe that he has eliminated a most formidable potential rival.'[39]

According to the new constitution of 1973, the President would be elected for a seven-year term; have the responsibility for foreign and defence/security policy, appointing ministers to these posts, as well as the Chiefs of the Armed Forces, over which there would be no other civilian control. The constitution also inaugurated a Constitutional Court of 11 members, appointed by the President of the Republic, whose jurisdiction would cover the legality of political parties. A 'Council of the Nation' was introduced as a consultative body in times of emergency, during which the President had the power to declare a state of siege and martial law for 30 days without consulting the parliament; if the President sought to extend the state of siege (for a further 30 days), then he would need the consensus of the government. The new constitution granted the President a veto power over laws enacted by parliament, while the first two elections under the new constitution would be governed by an electoral law decided by the President. Only secondary matters were supposed to be decided by elected bodies, while decisions on important issues of national concern were removed from the legislature. Last but not least, the position of the army as guarantor of the national integrity, security and social order and as a shield against both 'external and internal enemies' remained unchanged from the previous constitution of 1968.[40]

It is obvious that the constitution was tailored to fit the desires of Papadopoulos, institutionalizing his absolute power and control, as well as the army's oversight of Greek politics for many years to come. According to Alivizatos, the presidential powers detailed in the constitution were comparable to those of Turkey or Chile.[41] This is confirmed by Barkman, who was told by some of Papadopoulos' intimates that he was 'in favor of a type of democracy more or less along Turkish lines, where he would retain a leadership position with the support of the Army. In the interim-stage before elections, he wants to take some former politicians [as] "bridge builders".'[42] In a report he sent to the Foreign Office, the British ambassador was sceptical that the new constitution meant real democratic change:

> By removing the King and announcing carefully calculated modifications to the 1968 Constitution, it would be possible to satisfy the demand for political evolution, while enabling the regime to remain arbiters of the situation ... it would be unrealistic to think that the steps announced by Papadopoulos toward political evolution will lead to the early establishment of truly democratic conditions and full political and civil liberties.[43]

All things considered, the total rejection of the new constitution by the international community came as no surprise. Kanellopoulos' verdict, in a statement of 12 June, reflected widespread opinion:

> The new form of polity is a rigid and open presidential dictatorship ... The presidential powers establish again, after the Second World War, a *Fuhrerprinzip* ... There will be a parody of a Parliament ... with shadow authorities which will be controlled by the leader of the presidential dictatorship ... [W]ith the new *coup d'état* of the supposed Presidential Republic, the people's rule is totally abolished.[44]

Furthermore, the declaration of the 'Republic' induced opposition leaders to get together for the first time in six years and coordinate their actions in response to the upcoming plebiscite. In the early summer of 1973 a 'Parliamentary Committee for the Restoration of Democratic Legality' was created, comprising 17 right-wing and centre politicians. They included Kanellopoulos, Mavros and Rallis, who had denounced the July plebiscite as not representative of the real will of the people. However, this committee was also hamstrung by a lack of coordination, with each political figure pursuing a more or less personal line of action.

How Papadopoulos ever hoped to rally support from the ranks of the opposition with this show of sultanism is puzzling. The answer seems to lie in his belief that his relaxation of policing and repressive measures (the carrot next to the stick of his rigid constitutional arrangements) would attract a positive response. The following steps were taken simultaneously with the declaration of the Republic and were aimed at convincing both civil society and the international community of his good intentions: a general amnesty was granted to all 'political criminals' (including the naval officers), with the last 300 political prisoners to be released by late summer; martial law was to be lifted throughout the country; and censorship was significantly reduced. As Shain and Linz put it, 'a critical factor ... is the belief of the opposition and the public at large in the incumbents' genuine intention; a view shaped greatly by the government's liberalization policies'.[45] It was this pattern that Papadopoulos was trying to apply, but the initial reactions of the public were not as positive as he had expected, indicating that he was still to convince politicians and society at large of his sincerity. In the words of Barkman, 'the general apathy with which the proclamation of the Republic had been received has slowly developed into a growing irritation and indignation among many segments of the population ... as a result of the way in which the further political developments [have been] announced and prepared'.[46] Yet, Papadopoulos seemed oblivious to these finer points, focused as he now was on securing formal approval of his 'democracy' in the plebiscite to be held on 29 July. This was 'the last chance of the regime to achieve the minimum consensus necessary to legitimize itself and hold onto power'.[47] The opposition denounced the whole process as a farce, Kanellopoulos summing up the attitude and arguments of most politicians:

> A genuine Referendum can only possibly be called under conditions of freedom. This presupposes the formation of a fair and impartial government. Any Referendum, in order to have some value, has the following preconditions: Abolition of the regime of terror; lifting

of martial law; rehabilitation of full freedom of [the] press, by reintroducing the pre-April 1967 legislation; [a] general amnesty for political crimes and release of all categories of – [both] civilian and military – political prisoners.[48]

As had been the case with the plebiscite of 1968, the state media was used extensively to influence the people and guarantee a positive vote, as were the police. However, in contrast to what had happened five years earlier, on this occasion the people were not prepared to be bullied into voting 'yes'. Despite what Kanellopoulos described as 'an unprecedented terror campaign ... against every individual citizen' and his warning that 'if the NO vote wins then tanks will be on the streets again and there will be a worse dictatorship',[49] by the summer of 1973 the political climate had changed so dramatically that people like Mitsos did not hesitate to voice their preference for a 'no' vote:

> We were continuously mocking the regime, even in the streets; we were hanging around publicly with big NO stickers like we would have done in any normal election time. This would have been inconceivable five years before ... and we were thinking that, though it sounded hard to believe, the regime was for the first time on the defensive ... and we needed to make the most of that situation in order to get more concessions out of them.[50]

On a different level, an article written by the anti-regime journalist Grigoris Psaroudakis in June 1973 in his journal *Christianiki*, carrying the title 'What democracy are you talking about Mr Papadopoulos?', is also representative of the political climate of those days. In the article, Psaroudakis claimed that the transition 'is a ruse of despair and will trick no one: instead of Democracy being brought back in practice, it is brought as an empty title!' In another article in July about the imminent plebiscite, he concluded that 'the slogan of all people must be a NO to the dictatorship in disguise ... Mr Papadopoulos' democracy is a mask of democracy, behind which lies the dictatorship ... [T]he people's answer to the dictatorial provocation must be a historic NO!'[51] The impact of these articles was considerable, yet their author was not arrested. Georgios Rallis had also grasped the change in the political climate, and urged Karamanlis to seize the moment and return to Greece to lead the 'no' campaign. As Rallis wrote to Karamanlis, 'if you do not return to Greece now I do not believe that anything is doable after the 20th of July; the current marvelous psychological climate will have withered away'.[52] Rallis claimed that the return of Karamanlis would cause a political earthquake in Greece, paralysing the regime and preventing it from rigging the plebiscite. However, other collaborators with Karamanlis were unsure about whether he should return, and finally he chose silence once again. Karamanlis would maintain this attitude towards political developments throughout the rest of 1973.

Nevertheless, there were some who would vote 'yes' in the plebiscite: apart from the economic elites, like the Greek Federation of Industrialists (SEB), who saw in the new arrangements a positive development for Greece's economy,[53] Markezinis for the first time publicly expressed his dissent from the rest of the 'old politicians', justifying his 'yes' vote in an interview with the United Press International agency by claiming that, although he disagreed with the plebiscite and with the many powers Papadopoulos had amassed as President, his vote would be positive because, in his words, 'a new continuity' was being introduced:

> Either we want it or not, a new process is underway ... nobody can tell what will happen; it will be a difficult process ... The civilianization will need realism, understanding of the problems facing us, and firm decision making. The international problems which directly concern Greece will also become more pressing ... thus any positively active stance has a potential positive contribution ... therefore, and with my mind on this, I will vote yes.[54]

Markezinis' point was quite simple though difficult for many to accept: given the balance of power in 1973, and the impasse Greece was in, the extremely limited 'democratization' that Papadopoulos was offering presented the opposition with something to discuss; it was a fresh start – no matter how fake that freshness seemed to many at the time. Markezinis was implying something that the other opposition politicians, notwithstanding their relentless anti-regime attitude, were missing: they could still not offer an alternative to Papadopoulos' proposals. And it was not only Markezinis who spotted this; on June 27, one month before the plebiscite, Barkman noted in his diary:

> The opposition is not making a positive political development much easier. They have – in typical Greek fashion – rejected everything that the regime has offered without themselves indicating a new direction. It would be political wisdom if the two major parties presented a positive programme, taking into account the actual situation, and a list with a number of new, younger candidates included and the older ones eliminated.[55]

However, the lack of alternatives did not mean that Papadopoulos had an easy victory on polling day. The plebiscite was approved by 78.4 per cent of voters and rejected by 21.6 per cent. Of those eligible to vote, almost 15 per cent chose not to. However, there were major differences between the results in Athens and the big cities on the one hand, and in the countryside on the other hand. While Athens voted 'yes' by 51.1 per cent and 'no' by 48.9 per cent, the Athens suburbs recorded votes of 59.6 per cent for 'yes' and 40.4 per cent for 'no'. As Barkman noted, 'most observers conclude that in Athens, with some exceptions, procedures were followed which reasonably reflect the real vote'.[56] A few weeks later, the British ambassador judged the result to be the product of coercion by the authorities and scepticism among the people as to whether a 'no' vote would make any real difference. He recounted how the regime

> ... monopolised advertising, radio and television; banned opposition meetings specifically requested in places where the government had already held its own; maintained martial law in Athens; harassed those campaigning for a 'no' vote even to the point of making arrests; arranged that the ballot papers should be of a different colour; and finally allowed the voting itself to be subjected to the degree of force and fraud that has already been exposed.[57]

Although Papadopoulos rushed to proclaim the result a positive vote for his programme, the truth is that, as Haralambis contends, 'the plebiscite, without being a vote in favor of Papadopoulos, was a vote against the King'.[58] Notwithstanding this, Papadopoulos had reached the optimum position for any authoritarian leader seeking a limited change, hoping 'to see the transition stop at a limited liberalization which protects their tenure in office' or perhaps aspiring 'to elected positions in the emergent regime'.[59] At the same time, though, the hardliners' reaction to the results was a factor to be taken into account, as the aforementioned British ambassador's report noted:

> The government ... were taken by surprise by the strength of the feeling against them; and the vigour of their reaction in the latter part of the electoral campaign is a measure of the disillusionment and the fright they were in ... [This] may strengthen the hand of those in the Government who oppose any move in the direction of liberalization and produce a tougher attitude.[60]

On 19 August 1973, Papadopoulos was sworn in as President of the Republic. His first act was to appoint his close supporter General Anghelis as Vice-President. New arrangements took place in the army too, where Papadopoulos was having an uneasy time. He created the office of 'Chief of the Armed Forces' to which he appointed General Dimitrios Zagoriannakos, another ally. Nevertheless, personal and factional enmities among high-ranking officers were not eased; furthermore, the most serious danger appears to have been the lower-ranking officers, the majority of whom were concerned about allegations of corruption in the military occupying governmental posts (and about 'the treason against the spirit of the 21st of April') in exchange for higher military or government posts and personal wealth. They were also concerned that the 'Revolution' was beginning to accommodate the same political class it had overthrown six years earlier.[61] This did not go unnoticed by higher officers such as General Grigorios Bonanos, then commander of the Third Army Corps stationed in northern Greece. He categorized the officer corps into three major groups, according to their attitudes: first, those who supported the regime, the most powerful among whom were affiliated to Ioannidis; second, the royalists opposing the regime, especially after the deposing of the

King; and third, the majority of officers, who were non-affiliated and would accept any political settlement without objection. Young and mid-ranking officers were regularly expressing their concerns to General Bonanos about the course of the 'Revolution': 'they were saying that the armed forces had started getting corrupted by the exertion of power, that [they] spotted signs of corruption and sleaze'. This situation led Bonanos to conclude that 'the course of the regime was not what it should be ... [it] had partly lost its orientation. And there was [an] urgent need of a corrective interference.'[62]

The figure who appeared to best understand the concerns of these officers was Ioannidis, who, even in the view of British diplomats, seemed 'to have counted for more than that of the hard line members of the Council of Ministers, with whom he has been loosely identified'.[63] There is evidence from various sources that Ioannidis decided to overthrow Papadopoulos almost as soon as the 'Republic' was proclaimed, because he accurately foresaw the advent of a regime tailored to Papadopoulos' needs and the restoration of the 'old politicians', which the revolution had pledged to prevent.[64] He began to meticulously assemble his plan of subversion, placing his trustees in the staff of the higher military officers as well as crack unit commanders that would be useful for his coup, charging them with collecting information about the disposition of their superiors.[65] To the casual observer, the army appeared to be under the secure control of Papadopoulos, but this was an illusion – the real power was slowly and quietly shifting to Ioannidis.[66] Papadopoulos had failed to guarantee the most important prerequisite for his *reforma*, which was about to start: the neutral – if not positive – position of the army.

Enter Markezinis

For the time being Papadopoulos had other concerns, the most important of which was the 'staged' transition to a controlled democracy. In the summer of 1973 he started negotiations with Markezinis on the formation of the transitional government. The fact that of all politicians it was Markezinis who agreed to negotiate with him speaks volumes about the opposition's lack of trust in Papadopoulos' intentions. As Makarezos conceded, 'our main effort concerning the modernization of Greece's political capital had failed. The EPOK proved a fiasco … therefore, given that failure and under the pressure of time, we were dragged to the a priori defective Markezinis solution … which was spectacularly trumpeting our failure to bring anything new to Greek politics.'[67]

Papadopoulos and Markezinis held six meetings between June and September, which were not without their problems. There were disagreements on various issues, such as the extensive presidential powers and the consequently limited executive authority, the issue of the electoral law, the presence of ex-military figures in a future cabinet, and foreign and economic policies in general. At the outset, a certain uneasiness was noted by Ioannis Passas, a businessman who was acting as mediator between the two men: the intentions of both Papadopoulos and Markezinis were to use the other to promote their own interests. Papadopoulos wanted to present the Markezinis government as proof of his goodwill and commitment to bring democracy to the country and also appease the anti-dictatorship pressures both internally and internationally. Markezinis wanted to become Prime Minister using the resources of the regime, something he could never have achieved otherwise. Passas blamed Markezinis for deferring and he advised Papadopoulos to drop the Markezinis solution and carry forward the liberalization plans with another political figure, even Karamanlis if possible. Despite this advice, Papadopoulos insisted on working with Markezinis, which Passas considered a fatal mistake. Markezinis faced difficulties in forming a cabinet because of the reluctance of many politicians to get involved. There were rumours that because of this negative reaction, some candidates who had initially agreed to serve under Markezinis now declined to do so, believing it was a lost cause. As Zournatzis recalls, Markezinis even asked Papadopoulos to 'lend' him some of the ministers of his last cabinet in order to fill some vacancies.[68]

Markezinis none the less seemed optimistic about the sincerity of Papadopoulos' intentions and remained driven by the prospect of attaining glory as the politician who returned Greece to normality.[69] He also believed he could make it to the elections if the army did not intervene.[70]

Another subject for discussions was amendment of the 1973 constitution towards a more liberal settlement. Markezinis pressed Papadopoulos to agree to the involvement of political forces and personalities like the KKE and Andreas Papandreou, as well a reduction in the role of the military in politics and in the competence of the constitutional court. These negotiations were inconclusive, although there was agreement that in relation to the elections, all political movements should be gradually allowed to participate. Markezinis also hoped to curtail the presidential powers, particularly those concerning matters of defence, internal security and public order. He said to Papadopoulos that 'regulating the President's competence is pointless if it goes against the will of the majority of the people'.[71] Of course, the constitution was but a mere text; real political life would prove its viability. The talks proved to be very time-consuming, despite Papadopoulos' desire for a swift conclusion. His apologists insist that an opportunity was missed: had the government been formed in August rather than October, and elections taken place in the autumn, there would have been a good chance to face down the opposition from students and hardliners.[72] Nevertheless, a snap election called so early would simply have confirmed the general suspicion of the opposition in Greece and the international community that the version of democracy about to be inaugurated was a fake one. Despite the reservations of Passas, Papadopoulos was prepared to allow Markezinis space for the formation of his cabinet without particular concerns about losing time. Whether he was confident that things would work out as he planned, or simply gambling that he could accomplish his plan, unaware of (or even underestimating) the changes in the country which he would soon have to face, is a difficult guess. Markezinis, on the other hand, had a specific roadmap for the elections in mind, which he adhered to pedantically, though at times he seemed unprepared for the difficult task that lay ahead. Eventually, in September it was announced that the talks had reached a fruitful conclusion and that Markezinis would be the new Prime Minister. A number of questions remained open, however, such as the issue of the Constitutional Court, the President's powers and the timing of the elections (vaguely set for early 1974), but these were to be resolved at a later date.

The first phase of the Greek *reforma* was thus concluded. On the surface it still seemed that Papadopoulos was the master of the transition game and that he had the wind in his sails, having somehow reinvented himself as the repentant conspirator who was now putting democracy back on track, even though it was on his own terms and even if it was to be a *democradura*: a limited and problematic democracy where 'the existence of institutions beyond government and parliamentary control (such as, most notably, the army and the Head of State) hinder the smooth functioning of the democratic constitution'.[73] In the words of Woodhouse, Papadopoulos 'recognized that the purpose of revolution must be to produce something new. He could only vaguely imagine what it was to be, but he was confident that he alone among his colleagues would eventually succeed in bringing it to fruition. Whether he really contemplated ever renouncing power of his own volition can never be known'.[74] Nevertheless, he was walking on thin ice: the plebiscite lesson was that the majority of politicians did not accept his personal rule, and Markezinis was too minor a figure to attract to his *reforma* the proper recognition and support it desperately needed. And then there was the hidden factor of the attitude of civil society, something that, coupled with the weak popular appeal of Markezinis, could eventually create problems for him. As a British Embassy report to the Foreign Office stressed, '[Papadopoulos] is unlikely to find a civilian government, particularly one led by Markezinis, entirely docile ... [S]trikes, coupled with student unrest could put the president into a nasty corner'.[75]

But the most dangerous issue for Papadopoulos was the stance of regime insiders: 'he no longer had the support even of his closest colleagues. Makarezos and Pattakos had resigned in the last days of September when they saw which road Papadopoulos was taking.'[76] More ominously, military hardliners were planning a dramatic reaction, with Markezinis oblivious to how far they were prepared to go.[77] Eventually, on the eve of the first civilian government in Greece for almost six and a half years, Papadopoulos was confronted by a difficult problem, for he 'had not only failed to go far enough for the Greek democrats ... [but] had also gone too far for his critics in the junta and the Army'.[78]

4

The 'Unfinished Revolution' and the 'Castrated Parliament': The Elites and the 'Experiment'

I did not have any illusions: in the elections I would get 15%. I hoped, however, that finally the old parties would participate and we could come to terms on forming a government.

Markezinis, in Konofagos 1982: 113

Regardless of the attitude and motives of Mr Markezinis himself, it would be impossible for democracy to be born out of tyranny.

Kanellopoulos, in Grigoriadis 1975c: 39

We shall have a dictatorship, send all our opponents to exile on the islands and stay in power for thirty years!

Ioannidis to Pattakos, December 1973

The reasons for the failure of the *reforma* of 1973 are to be found in the refusal of the hardliners, headed by Ioannidis, as well as of the Greek mid-ranking officers, to concede the change of power that the 'Markezinis experiment' promised. The fact that it was tailored to the needs of Papadopoulos added to these groups' disdain for the whole venture, though this was not the main reason for their negative reaction: in 1973 for the Greek officer corps, professionalism was, as Danopoulos has put it, 'a stimulant to intervention rather than de-intervention and democratisation'.[1] Dominated by their self-image as defenders of the *patria* and the values associated with it, the hardliners could not but radically oppose the idea of the 'Revolution' handing back power to the same political class from whom it had taken power six years earlier and which, in their eyes, was identified with inefficiency, corruption and sleaze, faults associated with Papadopoulos himself. They followed the evasive 'untouchable' Ioannidis who seemed to guarantee a restoration of the values of 21 April. On the other hand, the apologists for Papadopoulos still blame the 'old politicians' almost as much as the military diehards for wrecking the 'experiment', accusing them of having acted selfishly and neglecting the national interest, which should have led them to support Papadopoulos and Markezinis and progress towards elections as a prelude to settling all other matters once more 'normal' times had been restored. Yet, this opinion downplays the positive reception of the experiment by some, including a number of left-wing figures. These conflicting interpretations of events lead to a seemingly contradictory conclusion: that it was Markezinis' fault that his 'experiment' lost momentum among the politicians, not because it was stillborn, but rather because of the nature of the regime he set out to transform, which proved an impossible task. It will be the aim of this chapter to show how and why this result occurred.

'Why is the Revolution finished?' The 'experiment' and the military

The main obstacle to the 'experiment' was the army hardliners; as in similar cases, a democratic transition will be precarious and most probably not viable if 'the incumbents cannot count on the loyalty of the armed forces'.[2] By the early autumn of 1973 'not only had the regime lost contact with its original ideals but it was also becoming increasingly divorced from its military constituency which was also its only political base'.[3] The brewing discontent with Papadopoulos and his followers in the army showed that the time was ripe for intervention by the diehards. In this situation, Ioannidis was the key figure. The control network which he had developed in the army was so extensive that 'everyone's impression ... [of] the great power of Ioannidis made most of the higher officers, as well as many younger ones, consider that it was their duty, if they came to Athens for any personal or service-related reason, to visit Ioannidis. They were thus expressing their faith and submission to him, trying at the same time to solve any problems they might have, begging for his interference.' This popularity of Ioannidis was in sharp contrast to the image of Papadopoulos, 'whose accumulation of so many offices and titles (President of Republic, Prime Minister, Minister of Defence) was harming the prestige of the regime and giving it an unacceptable image, which was not left unexploited by its opponents'.[4] Thus 'the Savonarola of the insurgents of the 21st of April', as Couloumbis described him,[5] was able to capitalize on the support of officers who were opposed to Papadopoulos, as well as of those who agreed 'to hand office to the politicians but felt that their collective interests were jeopardised if the Papadopoulos regime went on its isolated path'.[6] This undercurrent of dissatisfaction, aggravated by Papadopoulos' personal power and the sleaze in which many figures in the military-as-government were implicated, had one further source: the impression that the regime was giving way to exactly the same political class it had deposed six years earlier.

Moreover, many officers were concerned that the army might be used by the regime to back Markezinis' party in the planned elections.[7] Bonanos himself received a visit from Ioannidis in early September, during which the latter spoke of Papadopoulos with contempt, saying that the army was dangerously prone to corruption, nepotism and a lack of meritocracy, and that Papadopoulos' personal style of exercising power had alienated too many officers. It was at this point that Bonanos realized that something was brewing in the army against Papadopoulos, and that Ioannidis was working to a personal agenda. By the end of the month he was informed by a confidant of Ioannidis that a plan to overthrow Papadopoulos was taking shape.[8] All in all, the condition in the army in the autumn of 1973 did not bode well for a 'voluntary withdrawal' from power, a situation which occurs when 'the officer corps concludes that the army has accomplished its goals; realises that the political arena is more complex than previously thought and ... finally, fears that the worsening political, social and economic problems of the country may spur social upheaval and revolution.'[9]

The reaction of the hardliners in the government was bitter, though too weak to block Papadopoulos' way to his aimed-for supremacy. Their frustration at the perceived 'end of the 21st of April' was best summed up by ex-Colonel Ladas, who in a speech in October that was soon to become noted for a number of reasons, on the occasion of his handing over his portfolio to a new minister in the Markezinis cabinet, had posed the rhetorical questions, '[W]hy is the Revolution finished? How is it finished? Who brought it to an end?'[10] On the other hand, the reaction was also the result of personal bitterness at the loss of privileges linked to governmental posts. The most characteristic example here is Makarezos, the regime's number three, who had resigned from his post at the end of September, making clear that he did not agree with the type of *reforma* being implemented. At the time, rumour had it that he sought some high office, such as leadership of the Constitutional Court, and that Papadopoulos' refusal to grant him the position had led to Makarezos' resignation bearing a strong sense of grievance. Makarezos denied that this was the case, explaining his conduct in terms of his objections to the way the whole transition process had been organized.[11]

However, figures such as Ladas or Makarezos were not in a position to trouble Papadopoulos, as their actual power was practically negligible: once they were out of the army, they were stripped of any substantial support from the military networks and their remaining influence was limited to only a few officers. Moreover, they had lost all credibility among the junior hardliners, since they had enjoyed the spoils of power for six years. Thus a space was left free for Ioannidis, who, as the uncontested head of the diehards, began to meticulously unfold his two-part plan to overthrow Papadopoulos and Markezinis. First, as had been his ongoing practice, he ensured that trusted officers were strategically placed in all vital decision centres, from Papadopoulos' staff to high military command posts.[12] And second, he started playing a personal game of deceit against Papadopoulos. He would assure him that he was there to impose discipline on the junior officers, assure their obedience to Papadopoulos and guarantee their loyalty to the 'Revolution', using his personal prestige for these purposes. He also assured Papadopoulos that even if he allowed personal attacks against him, it was only to get accurate information about what the officers were thinking and to check their reaction to events.[13]

Despite Ioannidis' careful manoeuvring, Papadopoulos was not a person to be so easily fooled. To start with, he tried to reduce Ioannidis' influence in the army by appointing General Dimitrios Zagorianakos to the new post of Head of the Armed Forces.[14] He also hoped to remove Ioannidis from the army by luring him into the newly-created 'Military House of the President of the Republic' in early October. However, thanks to his network of informers, Ioannidis was already aware of this plan before it was officially broached with him by Papadopoulos and was therefore able to respond promptly, confirming that he was not willing to leave his current post.[15] Papadopoulos did not press the matter, instead trying to have Ioannidis transferred to command of a division in north-western Greece. Had Ioannidis been transferred there, his ability to continue conspiring against Papadopoulos would have all but disappeared. So he adamantly opposed this plan too and again confirmed to Papadopoulos that he had no intention of leaving his post as the ESA leader. Bonanos claims that he warned Papadopoulos, during the latter's tour in Thessaloniki for the 28 October National Day celebrations, that he needed to get rid of Ioannidis as 'he has rendered to the Revolution all services he could', hoping that Papadopoulos would get the coded message.[16]

What happened next remains a matter of much speculation. Some claim that Papadopoulos tried to retire Ioannidis, but the latter opposed this proposal and did not allow publication of the decree confirming his retirement. Another version of events suggests that the two men reached an agreement about Ioannidis' retirement, which would take place after the elections.[17] What is not disputed is that in the second half of October, Ioannidis requested one month's leave from the Chief of Staff, which he was granted, presumably to work on the details of his planned coup with his inner circle.[18] Ioannidis had regular meetings with this group in this time period and was even present during the Polytechnic uprising, in the suppression of which his ESA played a major role. The general consensus is that Papadopoulos remained confident that Ioannidis would not move against him, though some observers argue that he was not convinced that the danger Ioannidis posed to his plans was over, a judgement based on their interpretation of developments around the Polytechnic episode.

As for Markezinis, the short period that he was in office meant that his contact with the army was limited and he was in any case focused on preparing for the elections and negotiating with opposition politicians, matters which took priority over dealing with the officer corps. Only once was he heard complaining that he lacked any influence over the army, wishing he could have 60 per cent of the officers on his side. 'Politician as he was, Markezinis had not taken into account that support in military regimes is not based on percentage, as is the case in politics, but rather in the proper choice and placement of persons and military units that hold the army together.'[19] Nevertheless, institutionally Markezinis could not claim jurisdiction over the armed forces, for which the President – Papadopoulos – was responsible. So until the final days he totally lacked information about the predisposition of most of the officers and unit commanders towards his government.

The 'castrated parliament': The 'experiment' and the opposition elites

Unusually in cases of democratization, the phenomenon of the opposition leaders assuming what Huntington calls 'the standpatters' attitude towards the *reforma* is the second major cause of the failure of the 'experiment'. Whether motivated by distrust of Papadopoulos and Markezinis and concern about the possibility of a fake democracy under military supervision, or by personal ambition and calculation, most opposition politicians refused even to engage with Markezinis. However, across the political spectrum there were a few individuals who distanced themselves from this attitude, putting forward interesting arguments about the possibility of an alternative to the restoration of democracy, even if it was to be one not as inclusive as the opposition leaders and the people would have wished. Moreover, some opposition leaders were not as clearly against Markezinis before he took office as they seemed to be later in the process. Finally, as noted by some foreign observers, the argument against acceptance of the 'experiment' lacked an important element – the articulation of an alternative path to democracy, given the way things stood in Greece in 1973.

Markezinis started his short term as Prime Minister with a declaration of his government's aims, which he summed up with the phrase 'forgive, forget, and fair elections'. The first two features denoted the necessity, as in similar cases of a transition from authoritarian rule, of depolarization and convergence of the political elites of the regime and the opposition, blurring the lines of confrontation and restarting the political game on a new basis, different from the set-up in 1967. This would entail agreement on a platform of minimum conditions for the return to democracy, including the third element of Markezinis' slogan, free elections, with a commitment to respect their outcome without reprisal or recrimination by either side. This was the ideal scenario in terms of a negotiated democratic transition. Markezinis was conscious, however, that the presence of Papadopoulos was an obstacle to his plan and, as he said to Barkman, 'the President was clearly aware that his powers would of necessity be curtailed by an elected Parliament, and it was his impression that Papadopoulos would have retired from public life after some time'.[20] It would now be put to the test whether Markezinis' and Papadopoulos' plans for liberalization were 'sufficiently credible to provoke a change in the strategies of other actors'[21] – the opposition elites.

The right wing

On the right of the political spectrum, the key player, whose judgement on the 'experiment' would have a decisive influence on the rest of the

Greek political elites, was undoubtedly Karamanlis. His silence during the summer and autumn of 1973 was controversial and has been variously interpreted. Markezinis claimed that his government's objective was 'to secure a statement ... [from] Karamanlis, who was keeping his popularity and was the most probable next Prime Minister',[22] and that during one of his (Markezinis') trips to Paris, while still negotiating with Papadopoulos on the terms of the *reforma*, he had tried to meet with Karamanlis in order to obtain his approval on forming a transition government (though Markezinis' memoirs are ambiguous as to whether such a meeting did take place).[23] Arapakis claims that Markezinis' personal enmity towards Karamanlis was such that it 'did not allow him to seek a personal contact with him as soon as possible'.[24] Before deciding what he would do, though, Karamanlis sought information on the disposition of both the elites and the people, concerned that if he returned to Greece too soon, he might not be able to retain the interest of the people and would therefore reduce his chances of achieving much. Moreover, he was not prepared to become Prime Minister under Papadopoulos, as this would give the dictatorship an a posteriori legitimacy.[25] Many ex-politicians, especially from the ranks of the ERE and EK, faced a similar dilemma in the autumn of 1973: whether to refuse to participate in the elections and thereby miss out on subsequent developments, or become involved and thereby give legitimacy to the regime. This quandary is clearly portrayed in a letter sent in late August to Karamanlis from Constantine Tsatsos, ex-minister in the Karamanlis cabinets and later President of the Greek Republic. In that letter, Tsatsos expressed concern about what the rank and file of the ERE might do if Karamanlis did not endorse the 'experiment'. He was worried that the ERE might disappear as an electoral force if Kanellopoulos ran with second-rate candidates. Tsatsos speculated that some of them might be prepared to take their chances with a party led by Markezinis or Makarezos, as they would not want to be left out of a new parliament.[26] Woodhouse argues that Karamanlis' advice to the political parties was to 'prescribe specific conditions to the Colonels, which would amount to complete guarantees for free elections.

Then either the Junta would accept them, improbable as it seemed, in which case the deadlock would be ended; or it would refuse them, which would bring it into public disrepute and give a psychological boost to the parties.'[27] This accords with the opinion of Arapakis that if Karamanlis concluded that certain requirements, primarily a genuine commitment by the military to surrender power, were fulfilled, he could provide critical assistance to Markezinis in his effort to lead Greece to political normality. However, Makarezos, who claims to have been in touch with Karamanlis, receiving two letters from him after the Ioannidis coup, recalls that Karamanlis advised him not to trust Markezinis.[28]

Nevertheless, contradictory evidence also exists. According to his close associate and later minister in his cabinets, Ioannis Varvitsiotis, Karamanlis wanted the 'Markezinis experiment' to succeed,[29] but doubted that this would happen. As Mitsotakis said to Couloumbis, Karamanlis knew and approved of his return to Greece from Paris in early September; and Markezinis himself mentions that his minister Nikolaos Momferratos, who met with Karamanlis in Paris in early November, told him that the latter 'was not against the Markezinis solution' and that 'it was wrong that the politicians were competing with each other in rejecting it outright'.[30] Moreover, KKE reports rumoured that, in the early autumn of 1973, Kanellopoulos had privately accused Karamanlis 'of desertion and of compromise with the junta'.[31] A US Embassy report in late October cites information from a London-based correspondent of the daily *Makedonia* according to which Karamanlis was advising politicians 'to remain "flexible" until PM Markezinis provides "concrete evidence" of [his] plans to "return [the] country to normality." [The] politicians should set aside party considerations and personal ambition in order to achieve [a] basis for unity and agreement on [the] revision of [the] Constitution.'[32] Finally, Markezinis' son-in-law recalls a conversation with ex-Foreign Minister Christos Palamas who told him that Karamanlis had said 'it is a pity that the Markezinis opportunity was missed'.[33] However, this conversation took place in June 1974, a long time after the collapse of the 'experiment', hence Karamanlis was talking with the benefit of hindsight.

Overall it is uncertain what Karamanlis really thought about the Markezinis venture, as even his official biographers have to accept: 'the available historical data does not allow for an accurate recording of Karamanlis' views on that crucial dilemma [of participating or not in the elections prepared by Markezinis]'.[34] His tactical approach probably reflects a fact emphasized by his biographer, Tzermias, who claims that 'Karamanlis always thinks a lot before making every single move, and tries to make it so that there is always a way open for him to backtrack without major political cost.'[35] This point about Karamanlis' personality suggests that he was simply stalling for time by not assuming a clear-cut position. Considering the uncertainty about the attitude of both the army and the people to the Markezinis solution, Karamanlis chose to adopt a wait-and-see position, avoiding public pronouncements either for or against the 'experiment' and allowing other politicians to show their cards before he made any commitment. One was left to speculate what he would do if elections were called – and based on what guarantees of freedom and fairness – which meant that he could gauge with some precision whether or not a pseudo-democracy would come from the process. At the same time, Karamanlis knew that an increasing number of people in Greece, both within and outside of the regime, would begin to call for his return whether the 'experiment' succeeded, in which case clearing the path to new elections, or failed, when people might feel his return was even more urgent.[36] Stalling for as long as possible, Karamanlis confined himself to giving unofficial advice to others on how to handle the situation. The rapid collapse of the 'experiment' would prove the wisdom of this strategy.

Karamanlis' silence was in stark contrast to the approach of his ex-minister Georgios Rallis, who advocated a cautious though tentatively positive approach to the 'experiment'. In an article in the daily *Vradini*, Rallis perceived the Markezinis experiment as an opportunity for political 'normalization', which, under certain conditions, could be exploited and ultimately pay off:

> The task of senior and junior politicians [is] to get together in a united political group and seek to acquire a majority that will allow for a

radical constitutional amendment ... [T]he question is: is this united group allowed to run in the elections, while the antidemocratic regulations of the previous six years still apply? The answer is negative ... but abstention should be decided only after the regime has been blatantly proven reluctant to apply the regulations that make free and fair elections possible ... [N]on-participation in the elections is a mistake, since it will not shed any light [on] the real intentions of the regime either at home or abroad. If, on the contrary, on the way to the polls ... there is evidence of rigging [of the elections] then no one at home will dare be the apologist [of the regime], and those abroad who believe or pretend to believe in the 'civilianisation' will be obliged to accept that nothing has substantially changed. On the other hand, if abstention is decided prematurely, then certain opportunists will jump into the breach and the public opinion abroad, which is ignorant of the Greek situation, will fall into the trap. Should this happen ... the regime will have, once again due to our mistakes, achieved its purpose and it will be very difficult for the country to rid itself ... [of] the imposed pseudo-democracy, at least in the short run ... It is therefore imperative to come up with certain conditions, without which the terms 'free and fair' elections will be void of any content. If our demands are not granted, then it will be time for us to unite in abstention [from the elections].[37]

Some have claimed that it was in fact Karamanlis himself who had encouraged Rallis to publish the article. Certainly Rallis was the closest politician to Karamanlis, which gives this speculation a degree of credence.[38] However, after 1974 Rallis never confirmed that his article was influenced by Karamanlis, but rather asserted that it was an expression of his own personal and, as it turned out, well-founded doubts that there could be free and fair elections under Markezinis and Papadopoulos.[39] Coincidentally, the article was published on 13 November – the day before the start of the Polytechnic uprising.

Ex-minister Averoff, recently released from imprisonment for his association with the abortive naval plot, seems to have been more receptive to the 'experiment', which was consistent with his previous 'bridge-building' attempts. In October he spoke of the 'considerable effort' being made by the regime to restore democracy, which 'should not be condemned in advance'.⁴⁰ A few days later he told the British ambassador that

> ... he strongly supported Markezinis's attempt to build a bridge back to democracy ... The course Markezinis had chosen was the only possible middle way between the dangers of an extremist military take-over on the one hand and left-wing chaos on the other: and he was critical of the other 'old' politicians for hanging back ... However everything would depend on whether Markezinis made a genuine – and successful – attempt to call really free elections, and on whether Papadopoulos accepted the popular verdict.⁴¹

This was not the opinion of Varvitsiotis, who retained serious doubts that Papadopoulos intended to open the democratic game at all.⁴²

On the right, the most fervently adverse reaction to Markezinis came from Kanellopoulos, who from the very beginning refused even to discuss the prospects of participating in the elections planned. Kanellopoulos claimed that the *reforma* was a sham and that the regime had no intention of instituting genuine democratization. He said that 'regardless of the attitudes and motives of Mr Markezinis himself, it would be impossible for democracy to be born out of tyranny ... [A]ny settlement that would come out of the elections would necessarily prove right not the Greek people and those who fought against the dictatorship, but the crimes of the dictatorship itself.'⁴³ Kanellopoulos is said to have been inimical to Papadopoulos and Markezinis because of the bitter memories of the coup of 1967, which had toppled his government. In spite of the repeated pleas of Markezinis, Kanellopoulos remained resolutely opposed to him to the very end. Even Markezinis' assurances that Kanellopoulos had a very good chance of winning if he participated in the elections – which he again promised would be free and fair – were not enough to convince the latter to change his attitude. After one meeting with Markezinis, Kanellopoulos declared, 'I remain firm in my known position towards the situation that emerged after the 21st of April coup, a situation that, in spite of the motives of my negotiating partner [Markezinis], has not substantially changed.'[44] Markezinis noted caustically that for Kanellopoulos 'legality meant the return of the situation ... [as it existed on] the 20th of April 1967, that is, a Kanellopoulos cabinet that would proceed in calling elections'.[45]

The centre: The EK and the centre-left

In the former EK, things were not very different: most ex-leaders of the centre also opposed the 'experiment', though attitudes began to change quite noticeably as time passed. In late June, Mavros informed Barkman that the ERE and EK were considering drawing up 'a joint list of candidates and a programme under some other name' if elections were called, since the important thing was 'to get political life going again'. He added that 'only if demands were made upon the former politicians which they could not accept in honour and conscience (e.g. signing a declaration that the 'Revolution' had saved the nation), would they have to abstain from participating'.[46] One month later Mavros is said to have urged Markezinis at a public meeting to accept Papadopoulos' offer and immediately form a government. However, just a few months later, on 26 October, the same man summed up the opposition's rationale for rejecting the 'experiment', claiming that the planned elections had 'a single purpose: to legitimise the dictatorship, covering it ... [with] a castrated Parliament which will not have the power to debate, let alone decide, any of the nation's vital matters'.[47] What caused this dramatic change of heart in just three months? In defence of Mavros, one could argue that the Markezinis government failed to meet his expectations regarding a return to democracy. The reasons he offered Barkman for his change of attitude were that 'the powers that Papadopoulos had retained, [and] ... the "purge" of government officials and military officers which had taken place during the revolutionary period, had not been undone'. Barkman did not believe this explanation, suspecting that Mavros 'has changed his mind for fear of losing the left wing of his party (which he may well lose in any event) and [because] of the attraction that Markezinis may have for some of the right wing members of the Centre Union.'[48] Barkman also highlights the almost desperate attempts by Markezinis to convince Mavros and Kanellopoulos to participate in the elections, commenting that 'Markezinis had been ready to tell Kanellopoulos and Mavros that he himself would abstain if this would facilitate their participation.'[49] Ex-minister of the EK Constantine Mitsotakis remarked many years later that

> ... no matter how many openings Papadopoulos was to make, they could not possibly lead to democracy ... Papadopoulos had planned to establish in the country a kind of governance based on the Turkish pattern: a façade of parliamentary life, with the very powerful position of the regime moderator, the President of the 'Republic' and the armed forces behind him, ready to intervene when necessary. Any negotiation would credit the regime with an alibi. And I did not intend to give that.

As soon as it was announced that Markezinis would become Prime Minister, Mitsotakis decided to return to Greece from France, 'not in order to co-operate with him but in order to take action, using the openings of the regime for the advantage of the anti-dictatorial struggle. Because he believed that, under the new circumstances, the struggle could be more effective within Greece.'[50] He told Couloumbis that he did not trust Markezinis, 'who was always his opponent, but he believes that he deserves the benefit of doubt.'[51] The two 'renegade' Prime Ministers of 1965, George Novas and Stephanos Stephanopoulos, welcomed the 'experiment', although they had too small a political base to be credible contenders after 1965, as had Mitsotakis.[52]

Andreas Papandreou, on the other hand, would be Markezinis' most strident critic abroad. Interviewed by the daily *Apogevmatini* in early September, he said that 'everyone who participates in the elections and, generally speaking, in the political initiatives of the regime is a Quisling and will not be forgiven by the people.'[53] In October he reiterated this view in an interview with the daily *Makedonia*, where he stated that 'Participation ... [in] the elections is tantamount to collaboration, slavery and treason ... [It] means legalisation of the regime ... [I]t is naïve or conniving to advocate that we take advantage of the openings offered by the Junta.'⁵⁴ Papandreou continued to denounce the Markezinis government to the end.

The left wing: The KKE and EDA

The attitudes of the various constituents of the left to the Markezinis experiment have been, in contrast to what one might have expected, notably diverse. The KKE denounced the Markezinis government and rejected the 'experiment', calling it a farce. It should be noted that this was somewhat inconsistent with its own avowed policy during the dictatorship 'to exploit, even under the harshest conditions, any legal provisions that the people's movement may find'.⁵⁵ A possible explanation for this is the fact that in the summer of 1973 the party had detected 'a real danger that the political forces and a part of the people's movement [might] be tricked [by Papadopoulos and Markezinis] … and that the opportunistic view that "once we cannot do away with the junta, we need to rely on what we can now get and then aim at gradual later changes" might prevail'.⁵⁶ Nevertheless, according to a US State Department despatch, there was more to this attitude than met the eye. The telegram noted some 'indications' that '[the] Moscow-backed KKE (which has long sought recognition as legal party) is so desperate for recognition that it might be prepared to authorize participation in [the] elections in exchange for Markezinis' recognition (this position would seem to be supported by [the] Soviet Ambassador's remarks that participation in [the] elections should be as broad as possible)'.⁵⁷ Of course the fact that Markezinis never called the elections renders this analysis academic, yet it was an indication of the turn things might take even on the hard left if he had done so.

In contrast, the non-communist left seemed ready to accept the new political reality. The ex-leader of the EDA, Ilias Iliou, did not refuse to participate in the elections, arguing that the democratic forces could, if united against Markezinis and under certain guarantees of freedom and fairness, exploit the needs of the dictatorship for legitimacy, win more concessions and take advantage of possible developments in the future. He stated that 'it is a mistake that participation in the elections will legitimise the authoritarian regime'.[58] Leonidas Kyrkos, the leading figure in the 'KKE of the Interior', shared this view. He claimed that the *reforma* was a chance for the organized anti-regime forces and the people to assert their opposition to the dictatorship, making the most of the possibilities offered by the elections to highlight the shortcomings of the 'experiment':

> The people will be made to react against the dictatorship by the very process of the events, even against their will: when the elections were held, and the apparatus of the dictatorship set against the opposition forces, then the latter, backed by the mass public, would respond by escalating their reaction. [The democratic forces] had an opportunity to show everyone (international observers, journalists etc.) how violent and tyrannical the regime was ... and even in a Parliament where the junta would have the majority, there would be a powerful opposition, backed by a fiery people.

This escalation of the situation, Kyrkos concluded, depended on how violent the dictatorship's response to the opposition might be, possibly even igniting a civil war.[59] But Kyrkos's opinion was not shared by the majority of the members of the party's rank and file and was eventually rejected. However, the US State Department report quoted above also spoke of the 'contingency plans' of the party 'to form its own legitimate political party tentatively entitled "the Greek left". This party would be chartered by 100 "clean leftists", i.e. persons who have never been tried under Law 509 or for other political offences, in an effort to pass [the] scrutiny of [the] constitutional court and begin political activity.'[60] However, no other information exists to corroborate this analysis of a 'contingency plan', and again the matter was never put to the test.

Iliou and Kyrkos were not the only left-wing figures to assume a tentatively positive attitude to Markezinis. One more famous leader of the KKE of the Interior, Antonis Brillakis, who was in exile in Paris, met with Markezinis while the latter was there in September and told him that he was ready to return to Athens as soon as conditions would allow.[61] And Manolis Glezos, a respected communist member of the resistance and ex-MP of the EDA, told Barkman's Romanian colleague that 'it would be unrealistic for the opposition to abstain from participating in the elections'.[62] Furthermore, the composer Mikis Theodorakis said he was ready to return to Greece once Markezinis took over, 'even if his music was still banned by the regime'.[63] The Greek left, therefore, was just as divided on the issue of the 'experiment' as all other groups in the political spectrum, which augured well for Markezinis, had he been able to call the elections.

Among the civilian regime elites there was significant criticism of the way Papadopoulos was handling matters. For example, his former close associate Georgalas argued that Papadopoulos had to drop the idea of giving Markezinis the mandate. Georgalas sent Papadopoulos a letter urging him to give a chance to younger personalities to rule Greece or, should that not be possible, to call Karamanlis and offer him his full support in restoring parliamentary rule. But Papadopoulos was trying to avoid precisely what Georgalas was suggesting: the last thing he wanted in the transition process was to be overshadowed by Karamanlis, which was understandable given the big gap in the two men's popularity. Papadopoulos' rejection of this advice gave Georgalas the excuse to refuse to join Markezinis' cabinet. Papadopoulos was thus deprived of an able and trusted advisor. Georgalas claimed that he foresaw that Papadopoulos and Markezinis would fail.[64] Karter, another associate of Papadopoulos, gave the President almost the same advice as Georgalas: that 'he needed to find a new and charismatic personality to appoint as Prime Minister instead of Markezinis'.[65]

The economic elites welcomed the *reforma*, concerned as they were about the state of the economy and the international and internal political situation. They saw in the 'experiment' a possible way out of the impasse. The Greek Industrialists' Association gave its public backing to the plebiscite in July[66] and also welcomed the formation of Markezinis' government on the grounds that he was a man to trust in leading Greece to economic growth.[67] His previous record as Minister of Economic Coordination in the 1950s gave credence to this support. Nevertheless, the backing of the economic elites offered little comfort to Markezinis, as the really decisive factor in determining the success or failure of the 'experiment' was control of the army.

It is obvious that the 'first order understanding'[68] necessary for convergence of the regime and the opposition elites had not been accomplished by Markezinis. The explanation is twofold; on the one hand, the presence of Papadopoulos at the helm negated most of Markezinis' pledges of a genuine democratization; on the other hand, Markezinis put too much emphasis on the 'free elections' aspect of the 'experiment', to the point of raising suspicions that the transition would be limited to meeting what Linz and Stepan have called 'the electoralist fallacy', in which 'a necessary condition for democracy, free elections' becomes 'a sufficient condition of democracy'.[69] A British diplomatic report displayed insight on the political situation:

> It is difficult for us, conditioned as we are in Western European ideas, to understand the opposition's attitude ... In terms of Greek politics ... their position makes more sense ... [A]fter six years in opposition they are unwilling to cooperate in elections which may well result in something akin to the Spanish Cortes. They have no guarantee that this will lead to anything better and given the regime's record their distrust cannot be dismissed as unfounded.[70]

On the other hand, a democratic transition by regime transformation requires cooperation between the regime and the opposition, the outcome of which is to a large extent contingent upon the balance of power between the two sides. In the case of Greece in 1973, that balance was tilted heavily towards Papadopoulos' side. As professor of economics and fervent regime opponent John Pesmazoglou said to Barkman, many opposition politicians believed that 'a complete abstention could produce such pressures on Papadopoulos, that he might be forced to allow ... far-reaching changes in the regime [hoping that] the democratic forces would undoubtedly win the elections, in which case Papadopoulos' excessive powers would become irrelevant, even his staying on as President would then be quite unthinkable'.[71] On this point, the hopes of the opposition were misplaced, as they failed to take into account the rift within the regime ranks and the hardliners' stance.

The tactics of the elites and counter-elites in the course of the 'experiment'

As Couloumbis detected in October 1973, it seemed that the attempt by Papadopoulos and Markezinis to divide the opposition politicians was not as fruitless as many have since imagined. The next major step for the Papadopoulos–Markezinis partnership was, in Couloumbis's words, 'to legitimise its own government structure through participation in the elections'.[72] The first statements Markezinis made when he was sworn in as Prime Minister displayed 'a positive, decisive and pragmatic spirit', according to Barkman.[73] This also reflected the guarded welcome given to Markezinis' government by the foreign diplomats, something that encouraged him to work on giving a positive impression to the rest of the world. One important manifestation of this strategy was interviews with the foreign press, in which he emphasized his goodwill and sincerity. 'He claimed that he was fully maintaining his independence of opinion towards G. Papadopoulos and that in the new Parliament he would seek a radical amendment of the constitution, so that the powers of the President be curtailed.' In one interview he told *The Times*, 'if I do not agree with the President, I shall resign ... there is no other solution'. In another interview, with *Le Monde*, he even claimed to be an admirer of Lenin, adding 'if it was up to me, I would immediately legalise the Communist Party'. With reference to the opposition's reluctance to participate in the elections, he told *Der Spiegel* that he would 'organise [the] elections without martial law, with free radio, freedom of [the] press, free use of television, freedom of political rallies, party funding ... and [with] legal representatives as supervisors of the voting ... [W]hat excuse will the opposition [have to] abstain?' In the same vein, Markezinis declared on the day he took office that his government would 'secure for those who participate in the elections every chance to compete, communicate with the people and use state media'.[74] However, this steady stream of interviews – and particularly his reference to Lenin and to the legalization of the KKE – not surprisingly had the opposite effect on many officers to the one Markezinis desired.

When the concerns of these officers reached the ears of Papadopoulos, he advised Markezinis, as the latter recalled, 'to stop giving interviews for the time, not because he disagreed, as he told me, but in order not to cause him problems. I accepted reluctantly and cancelled about ten new interviews'.[75] In his desperate attempt to convince civil society at home and the international community of his good intentions, Markezinis overstepped the mark with the army, as he admitted in his private notes.[76] At the end of October, the opposition elites were divided on the question of participation in the elections, with the leaders of the ERE and EK refusing to discuss the situation with Markezinis, though as Barkman notes 'in other oppositional circles it is pointed out that this negative attitude makes no sense as long as there is no alternative'.[77] Markezinis was of course publicly committed to holding the elections and believed they could be critical in providing momentum for his *reforma*, hence his decision to give a televised press conference on 17 November in which he would reaffirm his decision to carry out free elections, in which the likes of Andreas Papandreou and other notable regime opponents would participate. As it turned out, he could not have chosen a less appropriate date for the conference.

Meanwhile, political activity intensified in what would turn out to be the last few weeks of the 'experiment', the aim of which was to make Papadopoulos and Markezinis retire or have them dismissed and replaced by Makarezos, which in turn would implicate Karamanlis. Makarezos had become an opponent of Markezinis, claiming that the latter 'was trying to make his own party with the support of the Revolution and ... [at] the expense of the other parties, while Papadopoulos wanted to rid Greece ... [of the] old political parties ... and [had] made the mistake of not sacking him [Markezinis] when he ... [realized] his ... [machination]'.[78] Makarezos started lobbying Papadopoulos to ditch Markezinis and retire in favour of Karamanlis, who would then seriously consider returning to Greece as President of Republic and appointing Makarezos as Prime Minister charged with calling the elections. Makarezos claims that he received two letters from Karamanlis expressing agreement with this plan. Unfortunately, the first letter arrived on the day of the Ioannidis coup and the second one in December, when all prospect of change had disappeared.[79] No further details exist about the letters or whether Karamanlis would have accepted the offer, the possibility also remaining that it was all a fantasy on the part of Makarezos. Markezinis certainly provides a different version of events, claiming that Makarezos visited him on 23 November and presented a plan in which Papadopoulos would resign and be replaced by General Anghelis, a development that 'would turn the elections [in]to a triumph for his [Markezinis'] party'.[80]

Other sources claim that Papadopoulos had seriously considered dismissing the Markezinis government, since it had failed to convince the major political party leaders of the propriety of the whole transition programme. The publisher of the pro-regime daily *Eleutheros Kosmos*, Savvas Konstantopoulos, argued that if the ERE and the EK 'recognised the new regime and cooperated with the President, Papadopoulos was prepared to proceed to new concessions (side-lining of Markezinis, elections organised by a transitional government, Constitutional amendment etc)', while Makarezos noted that 'Markezinis had disappointed Papadopoulos with his zigzagging and ambiguous handling of the civilianisation thus far'.[81] A further indication of the fluidity of the political situation was provided by an editorial in the daily *To Vima* at the end of October, which opined that 'the current cabinet is not the one to lead the country to elections'. Markezinis was supposed to have raised the matter of this editorial with Papadopoulos, who simply responded that it did not echo his views.[82] Nevertheless, there is no hard proof (but much speculation) that Papadopoulos was seriously considering removing Markezinis and seeking a different solution. Indeed, Markezinis had told Barkman on 23 October that Papadopoulos 'is aware that he cannot get very far with the support of the Army only, and that he needs someone for the political sector... [He] had apparently concluded that he had reached the extreme limit and was left with the choice of either effecting a change in a democratic sense or becoming the slave of the hard-liners'.[83] No one can be sure how Papadopoulos would have proceeded if he had abandoned the Markezinis solution.

Having made the commitment to the Markezinis experiment, he had no real option but to stick with it, for to have attempted a U-turn would have totally discredited him and made a puppet of the diehards. Papadopoulos 'was too ambitious to let himself backtrack like this, after all the ... [distance] he had gone since the early summer days'.[84]

Markezinis' troubles were not over, however, for he claims that there was another subversive attempt against him, arising in the context of the Polytechnic events in November. At the height of this episode, which he considered to have been orchestrated by 'those who wanted his overthrow' to bring him down, and after the declaration of martial law by Papadopoulos, he claimed that he refused to resign as PM because he wanted to see the civilianization process that he had started through to its conclusion.[85] Furthermore, when the unrest was over he met with Zagoriannakos, the head of the army, and Papadopoulos on 19 November to demand that martial law last no more than one month, since the constitution of 1973 had stipulated that martial law could only be extended beyond 30 days on the authority of the government, which Markezinis was resolutely opposed to. There was disagreement too over the date of the elections: Papadopoulos suggested 10 March while Markezinis argued for February. This was a matter over which Markezinis was prepared to resign, telling Papadopoulos, 'I am not made for ruling with martial law.' To his surprise, Papadopoulos offered him his resignation in turn, which Markezinis immediately turned down. The meeting was inconclusive, apart from the decision that Markezinis should visit the Ministry of Defence the next day to discuss the situation with the military leaders. Markezinis did not fail to notice that Papadopoulos looked 'evidently shaken' by the events of the preceding few days.[86]

The next day, 20 November, Markezinis made what was to be his last public appearance as Prime Minister. His visit to the Ministry of Defence was intended to obtain the support of the army on preparing the path to the February elections, claiming in his memoirs that 'had I not got the guarantee that the army would support me on way to free and fair elections, I would not leave the Ministry as Prime Minister'.[87] Speaking to the press, Markezinis 'strangely congratulated the Army on its "timely and bloodless intervention",[88] insisting that he was not an enemy of democracy, as proven by his desire for fair elections. Markezinis clearly still hoped that he could appease the military after the 'anarchist excesses' of the Polytechnic uprising. After the journalists and cameramen had left, Markezinis met the military leaders behind closed doors and obtained their backing for the elections. Later he would recall that 'amongst my interlocutors were those that would topple me a few days later', concluding that 'when those who were working on my overthrow saw me going to the Ministry of Defence ... determined not to resign, they also decided their next, final and fatal move'.[89]

Markezinis was anxious to get Papadopoulos to agree to the lifting of martial law by 17 December or, if this was difficult, to limit its extension to just a few days, since the constitution stipulated a 40-day election period and thus, if elections were to be held on 10 February, martial law had to be lifted in the New Year at the latest. His last meetings with Papadopoulos were inconclusive, as there was disagreement on the martial law issue, but at their final meeting, on 24 November, Markezinis made it clear to Papadopoulos and Anghelis that his continuation in office depended on their agreement to a press conference at which Markezinis would announce elections for February. Yet again, Papadopoulos offered to resign if that would facilitate Markezinis' plans. They eventually agreed to meet again, on Monday, 26 November, when the final decisions would be taken.[90] Markezinis was left with two strong impressions from these exchanges: first, that 'the President knew more than he said, but kept silent because he did not want to let me know too';[91] and second, that 'he seemed so absent-minded ... that I had the impression that something was going on, but I did not know what'.[92]

Chronicle of a coup foretold: Back to *dictadura*

One can only speculate what was in the mind of Papadopoulos in his last days in power. It is plausible, however, that he was focused on developments in the army and the rumours about Ioannidis planning a coup. Indeed, by the beginning of October, Ioannidis' faction had set a provisional date for their coup, according to Grigoriadis, of between 20 November and 10 December, and at the end of the month finalized a precise date of 25 November – which was duly fulfilled.[93]

The leader of the insurgents was in touch with a number of commanders of crack units stationed in the Athens suburbs and in the countryside. He had the tacit support of General Bonanos, leader of the Third Army Corps, stationed in northern Greece (although Bonanos later claimed to have had doubts about how 'useful to the nation' the coup would be).[94] Ioannidis also had General Phaedon Ghizikis, commander of the First Army, stationed in Thessaly, on his side. In Athens, Ioannidis' supporters controlled the important armoured corps training centre, as well as commando and paratroop units. Last but not least, the omnipresent and much feared ESA was involved in the coup.[95] The Polytechnic events unsettled the conspirators, with General Ghizikis, the day after the army had stormed the campus, proposing that the coup be postponed, since Papadopoulos' declaration of martial law might frustrate their plans. Ioannidis reassured Ghizikis that this was not a major disruption problem for them and that things would have cooled down by the 25th.[96]

All these preparations could not have escaped the notice of Papadopoulos, nor were the intentions of Ioannidis unknown: 'rumours of a forthcoming coup were on the streets; it was openly discussed even in the corridors of the Ministry of Defence for some time', recalls Makarezos. Various sources sent warnings about an imminent subversive action almost immediately after the Polytechnic events: Pattakos said he was forewarned on 19 and 20 November by the mayor of Athens, the British ambassador Hooper and even the US ambassador Tasca. He warned Markezinis and Papadopoulos in turn, though the latter attempted to calm him, saying that everything was under control. This led Pattakos to speculate that perhaps Papadopoulos was not unaware of what was happening, or even that he was actually involved in the coup.[97] The head of the State Intelligence Agency (KYP) also received reports about the suspicious movements of officers stationed in Ghizikis' HQ. However, as Zournatzis said, he did not communicate this to Papadopoulos, thus raising suspicion that he was also part of the conspiracy.[98]

Markezinis appears to have been much more worried about a possible coup than Papadopoulos. He says in his memoirs that he started receiving information about the hardliners' plans from a number of sources. A university professor with close links to London had told him in November that Ioannidis was preparing a coup, and, just days before the 25th, the British ambassador invited Markezinis and his wife to dinner and said quite openly, 'Are you sure that you will still be able to call the elections next week? I fear that you will not be in office by Sunday!'[99] The ambassadors of Germany, France, Holland and Italy also had information that something was afoot. Even Markezinis' son, then studying in the UK, called his father to warn him about the same rumours. Alarmed, Markezinis urgently asked to see Papadopoulos and share this information with him. To his astonishment, Papadopoulos assured him on 24 November that it was just rumours and invited him to a meeting with himself and Ioannidis, so that Markezinis could see for himself 'whether Ioannidis was capable of doing such a dishonourable thing. The meeting was to be held on Monday the 26th.'[100] That was about all Markezinis could ask Papadopoulos to do, since he had no authority over the armed forces. He retired to his flat to prepare the speech he would deliver to the Greek and foreign press the following week – in the press conference that would never be.

In the early hours of Sunday, 25 November, Markezinis was awakened by his personal police protection officer, who said he had been ordered back to his usual duty as the government had been deposed by a coup. Similar scenes took place in the homes of the Ministers of the Interior and of Defence, though they were not arrested. Papadopoulos, too, was awakened by a call from the head of the Greek police, who told him that mechanized infantry and armour were reportedly on their way to his villa. A while later, a lieutenant-colonel appeared and handed in a note from a 'Revolutionary Committee', which stated that at the 'demand of the Armed Forces, you have submitted your resignation; so have the Vice-President and the Markezinis government. You will follow further developments on the television. Your credit and that of your family will be respected.'[101] Papadopoulos was put under house arrest. Thus the 'Markezinis experiment' and Papadopoulos' six-year rule came to an inglorious end. At the same time, Greeks woke up to find themselves in a situation reminiscent of 21 April 1967. However, on this occasion everything happened much more smoothly and quietly than six years earlier. Practically no arrests were made and civilians were treated respectfully by the military. In one of the most tragic ironies of the seven-year dictatorship, the coup was initially welcomed by both the opposition elites and many people who did not understand who were really behind it and what their plans were.

The attitude of Papadopoulos has led to various theories on how he lost control of the plotters and what was really on his mind in the days leading up to 25 November. Bonanos was surprised that 'a regime that ruled for six years and had taken roots in the country could possibly collapse within one hour without the bleeding of a nose'.[102] Even a KKE report spoke of 'information available since the early autumn [of] 1973 on the clash between Papadopoulos [and] Ioannidis and on the possibility of a coup'.[103] Makarezos also stresses the 'inexplicable inaction of Papadopoulos' in view of the danger of his overthrow by Ioannidis and against all the available intelligence. Even years later, while in prison, Makarezos would repeatedly ask Papadopoulos about the Ioannidis coup but never receive an answer.[104] Pattakos believes that Papadopoulos fell victim to his power illusion and could not conceive that there might be someone smart enough to overthrow him, characterizing Papadopoulos' mindset as one in which 'my grandeur will not allow destiny to do me any harm'.[105] An alternative explanation is that Papadopoulos was exhausted by six years of inter-regime disputes and struggles and passively accepted his fate, even though he knew that a conspiracy was imminent. Makarezos gives some credit to this theory as he recalled a meeting with Papadopoulos after the Ioannidis coup, in which he said to Makarezos, 'I see my overthrow as a psychological liberation and I do not care about it.'[106] Some commentators argue that Papadopoulos had full knowledge of the Ioannidis coup and perhaps even acquiesced to it, so that he might 'be saved from the imminent internal rebellion of the junior hard-liner officers that regarded him as [a] "traitor of the ideals of the 21st of April"'.[107]

Any explanation of Papadopoulos' attitude during these last days has to take account of the uncertainty of such a complex situation as a transition from authoritarian rule, especially when opposing forces in control of military might are involved, as well as the flow of information or lack of it. Despite Ioannidis appearing to collect information about the officers' attitudes, thus presenting himself as Papadopoulos' supporter, the latter was not fooled by this charade.[108] His repeated attempts to retire Ioannidis from the army are proof of that. For all his psychological weariness after all these years of conspiracies, Papadopoulos was too ambitious and too agile to simply accept his fate at the hands of Ioannidis.[109] He did as much as he could to block Ioannidis' coup preparations, including mobilizing the army and introducing martial law after the suppression of the Polytechnic uprising. However, he was unaware of the extent of Ioannidis' network in the army and could not be certain when the latter would strike. He did not expect a coup to happen so soon after the Polytechnic episode and believed he was reinforcing his position with the declaration of martial law, which put all units on alert, regardless of whether or not their commanders were implicated in Ioannidis' coup. Despite this evidence, one of Papadopoulos' confederates, Georgios Karter, claims that although Papadopoulos was aware of Ioannidis' moves, he chose to withdraw peacefully rather than take part in a bloody confrontation. However, Papadopoulos did not give up for good: leaving Ioannidis to deal with the army and the people was a tactical move, to be followed in due course by a counterattack against Ioannidis. In the end, Papadopoulos was outrun by the chiefs of staff's initiative to call out the politicians in July 1974.[110] In November 1973 he was outmanoeuvred by Ioannidis' more highly-tuned conspiratorial skills.[111]

A short-lived *dictadura*: The aftermath

On 25 November, General Ghizikis was sworn in as President of the Republic.¹¹² Adamantios Androutsopoulos, a minor figure in the Papadopoulos cabinets but rumoured to have been a CIA agent, became Prime Minister.¹¹³ It is striking that the initial reaction of most former politicians and civil society to the new dictatorship was positive. In the words of Haralambis, 'the November coup initially appeared to be an act against the corrupt and tyrannical dictatorship of Papadopoulos... [and] an act of self-purg[ing by] ... the army [of] ... its pro-dictatorial element'.¹¹⁴ The new regime also bolstered its position by allowing rumours to circulate about the imminent return of Karamanlis or the establishment of a government by Kanellopoulos in the near future. It also took some popular steps, such as releasing some of those arrested in the Polytechnic demonstrations and some politicians from house arrest.¹¹⁵ This seemed to confirm that many opposition politicians were content to see the army intervene to topple Papadopoulos, which would be to their benefit. This was certainly the British ambassador's reading of the situation in mid-November:

> They [the opposition politicians] hope (on what grounds is not entirely clear) that the Army might support a move for the 'restoration of popular sovereignty' in which they would return to power without having spoiled their hands by collaboration with Papadopoulos. Many believe that the recall of Karamanlis as the head of a government of national unity would be the most effective way of achieving this ... They seem to have no policy beyond 'Papadopoulos out': and ... appear to have no alternative strategy in mind.¹¹⁶

The Greek elites and people had misinterpreted the reasons for the coup and not realized the true intentions of the new ruling group. The fact that a 'worse dictatorship' had been imposed did not take long to become evident. The feeling of frustration was most obvious in Kanellopoulos' statement on 3 December:

> I was glad to see that the Greek people immediately showed its will[ingness] to fraternise again with the armed forces which were,

only a few days ago, threatening them with their tanks and machine guns ... [L]ess than ten days later, everything has changed. I am saddened and worried; saddened, because I see that a great historical opportunity for Greece to get out of the impasse which it has been facing for seven years, has been missed. Worried, because I see that what has failed for so many years is being tried again.[117]

Indeed it was not long before the new regime showed its real face: martial law was not lifted; fewer detainees than expected were released from prison; and in early December the regime banned the publication of the pro-Karamanlis newspaper *Vradyni*. A general feeling of frustration prevailed when Androutsopoulos gave his inaugural speech, although no protest against the new junta was recorded.[118]

Evidence of the intentions of the new junta leader was given when he visited Pattakos in early December 1973. Ioannidis excused his coup on the grounds of Papadopoulos' failure to introduce a new political system and instead accommodating the same politicians that 21 April had overthrown. When asked for his opinion on the political situation in the country, Pattakos said that the time for dictatorships had passed, as the people had had enough of military rule, and advised Ioannidis to proceed with elections within the next six months. This is not what Ioannidis had expected to hear. 'He blushed, stood up, said angrily that "we are not playing. We shall have a dictatorship, send all our opponents to exile on the islands and stay in power for thirty years!" and left abruptly.'[119] Indeed, until the summer of 1974, Greece found itself under a 'worse dictatorship', in the words of Markezinis. Theodorakopoulos paints a graphic picture of what things were like: '[O]pponents of the regime trembled under a new reign of terror, with the military police cracking down on every ... liberal institution. Torture became an everyday occurrence; hundreds of people were arrested and thousands deported to Aegean islands.'[120] Indeed, deportation camps reopened early in 1974, hosting opponents of the regime, including some people that had previously served under Papadopoulos. Androutsopoulos boasted that 'the regime was powerful and, despite its internal frictions and personal enmities, retained power until the end because it was supported by the majority of the Armed forces. Therefore, no serious action ever threatened it.'[121] Despite its short duration and 'although the Ioannidis group included no more than forty officers, the army followed these new leaders wholeheartedly after Papadopoulos was overthrown ... [Ioannidis] continued to associate only with brother officers. He secured their promotions, cared for their families, seemed void of personal ambition and shunned all publicity.'[122] It was in this context that Averoff wrote to Ghizikis in early 1974, portraying the dismay of many Greek politicians, and of society in general, at what had happened and also their anxiety about what was to come, urging him to take the initiative in a direction which Averoff himself viewed as offering a solution:

> For about two days (November 25th and 26th) there prevailed everywhere a sense of general relief and joy, of lively optimism for the future, a feeling of devotion toward the Armed forces ... These feelings however were short lived. Hopes were disappointed. Of this everyone is now persuaded. Everyone is aware of an attempt to impose a long-lasting regime of government by the few; a regime created, supported and directed by the Armed Forces and only the Armed Forces ... [T]he prestige of the Armed Forces has never, during the country's independence, fallen so low ... We are sliding toward the left, toward a form of anarchism ... Let there be selected a person capable but above all one who inspires confidence ... Let the Premiership be assigned to him by the President of the Republic.[123]

Yet, in the first months of 1974 there were rumours that a new political solution was hatching, as there were second thoughts in the part of the army that supported Ioannidis but which was linked to the military-as-institution. On a visit to his former posting – with the Third Army Corps in Thessaloniki – in early 1974, Bonanos, now Supreme Commander of the Greek Ground Forces, delivered a speech to the officers claiming that there would soon be a civilianization of the regime on the President's initiative. Bonanos had informed Ghizikis and Ioannidis in advance about his speech, neither of whom was happy about his intentions and said that they hoped that he would not be precise about when this initiative would take place. Ioannidis told Bonanos 'we are not leaving any time soon; we will be here for many years to come'.[124] In an article published in the spring, Papandreou identified two factions within the regime: '[T]he first one is after a direct military government for an undefined time, with the cabinet as a smokescreen. The second one is looking for a deal with right and centre-right wing politicians, which would allow the armed forces a less evident role in the country's life.'[125] Nevertheless, Greece under Ioannidis was a 'frozen society', paralysed by tight regime control of all institutions, interest groups, opposition leaders and civil society.[126] Addressing the naval officers in February 1974, Ioannidis described the new dictatorship as

> ... a historical necessity which stopped the moral downturn of the 21st of April, as well as the untimely initiative of handing over power to politicians through a fake election in which the Armed Forces would be responsible for violence and fraud ... [T]he old politicians except Andreas [Papandreou] have aged and have lost touch with the people ... [T]he Armed Forces have the responsibility to carry on ruling the country and retain the ... [exclusive right to design] the process to restore democratic life without [the] participation of the old politicians. There is a danger that political control be handed to the left wing and a 'popular front' ... [T]he current government draws its power exclusively from the Armed Forces; if it does not ... [meet] up to their expectations it will be replaced.[127]

The total isolation of the military precluded any consensual transition to democracy, and it was only due to the junta's fiasco in Cyprus in July that the regime collapsed spectacularly within less than two days. As Markezinis noted, 'had the Cyprus disaster not happened, Ioannidis would not have handed power to the politicians, and his partners ... had no power to impose such a solution'.[128]

An account of the post-July 1974 developments would concern the history of the actual transition to democracy and is beyond the scope of this book. Nevertheless, it is useful to consider some factors that made the difference between the failed and the successful *Metapolitefsis* in Greece. It should be noted that the 1974 transition was the result of the regime removing itself from power, incapable of handling the situation created by its Cyprus adventure. The instigators of that change were the military as an institution, who undertook the initiative of recalling the politicians in order to take charge, since the situation both in terms of foreign and internal affairs was judged unmanageable by the military-backed Androutsopoulos government. They did not claim or seek any high office in the state hierarchy, as Papadopoulos had done, but rather retreated to the backstage, though not without hope of maintaining a certain degree of control over political developments, at least in the short term.[129] It is significant that this was the same military institution which, a few months earlier, had tolerated, if not tacitly supported, the Ioannidis coup; and it was the most fervent opponents of the 'experiment', Kanellopoulos and Mavros, who were initially asked to form a coalition government. So it was indeed 'back to 1967' for the leaders of ERE and EK, though not quite in the circumstances that they might have expected.

Nevertheless, this situation lasted only a few hours, as the second meeting of the military and political elites, that same evening, concluded that Greece needed a stronger and more prestigious personality to handle the transition, as well as the international implications of the Cyprus crisis. On this point they were right, as the popularity of Karamanlis with the army as well as the political elites and the people was unmatched by any possible rival. Here we can detect a second major difference with the Markezinis experiment: despite these episodes having a number of similarities, from an institutional and legal point of view, and most strikingly in terms of the mandate from a regime-appointed 'president of Republic', politically the difference is considerable, as nobody challenged Karamanlis' democratic credentials and intentions. Both opposition elites and the people welcomed his government (which comprised, in contrast to the Markezinis cabinet, politicians from a wide range of the political spectrum that could to a large extent be called representative of the people) and accepted his timetable for the first transition elections.[130] Moreover, Karamanlis abolished the 1973 constitution, replacing it with the constitution of

1952, which the colonels had abolished in 1967. In contrast to Markezinis, Karamanlis was in sole charge of the transition and offered no account of his actions to Ghizikis for the short time that the latter occupied the office of President. It is interesting that it took the Karamanlis government just under four months to call the elections, almost as long as it would have taken Markezinis if his timetable for the 10 February had been kept.

A final, and more clear cut, difference between the two transitions was in the handling of the military reaction. Karamanlis acted swiftly to remove most military units from Athens to the Turkish border because of the imminent threat of war, and when that threat receded, he retired all the regime-appointed leaders of the armed forces, replacing them mostly with officers with proven democratic commitment, some of whom had been persecuted by the dictatorship.[131] With total authority over the armed forces, he also recalled into active service many officers that the regime had forcibly pensioned off in the past six years, thereby guaranteeing the loyalty of military units' commanders. After a plot was revealed and suppressed in February 1975, he retired dozens more officers from the armed and police forces, purging these organizations of potential anti-democratic challengers.[132] It was not quite the 'forgive and forget' policy that Markezinis had advocated, but then Markezinis was constrained by having to operate under Papadopoulos. Karamanlis was not subject to such institutional control.

An opportunity missed or a ruse that failed?

The opposition's stance toward's the 'experiment' has been the focus of criticism by regime apologists, who perceive 'an opportunity missed' in the Markezinis venture. Their main argument is presented by Theodorakopoulos:

> A historic opportunity was lost, and catastrophic consequences were to follow from this irresponsible behaviour by the ex-politicians. If a climate of understanding had prevailed then, democracy would have

returned to Greece without a heavy price being paid, and probably with the same people who are now in the seats of power. Instead, democracy returned eight months later at the cost of thousands of dead and hundreds of thousands of homeless in Cyprus – developments which traumatized the Greek body politic for generations to come.[133]

In contrast, Farakos sums up the dominant analysis of the 'experiment' post-1974:

> It was chimerical to believe that under Papadopoulos and Markezinis Greece could become a democracy; there might have been some certain liberalization, but it would have fallen far short of the form of polity that the Greek people would have wanted ... [I]t was good that the 'Markezinis experiment' failed, because thus it facilitated the radical change of 1974.[134]

What both these opinions fail to note is the real reason for the collapse of the 'experiment': the existence of a strong pocket of regime hardliners who rejected any suggestion of handing over power to the politicians, and who had the means and the information they needed to stop the Greek *reforma* before it could acquire momentum. As long as this group held power, there was no hope of a self-transformation of the dictatorship of the colonels, unless Papadopoulos and Markezinis were agile and decisive enough to deliver a blow that would paralyse their reaction. As noted earlier, the only such move – the retirement of Ioannidis – was repeatedly frustrated, and Papadopoulos did not dare cut the Gordian knot of the hardliners' reaction. Instead, he chose to play the only game he had known for six years – deception. However, he was outwitted by the exemplary conspirator that was Ioannidis. A US State Department communication provided a trenchant analysis of his downfall:

> Papadopoulos fell because he was basically unable to put into concrete reality the coup of 1967. Even six years in power were insufficient to inspire him with a viable political, economic or social program, or with the requisite popular support ... In some respects Papadopoulos' weakness was his indecisiveness. He avoided confrontation at almost

any cost. Even when he knew that General Ioannidis posed a grave threat to his future he hesitated, and refused to take what seemed to be [the] inevitable steps to confront and eliminate Ioannidis from the Athens scene.[135]

It should also be remembered that Papadopoulos was facing the tacit opposition of another group: the military as an institution, who had become powerful enough to act autonomously and who believed they could dictate a limited transition on their own terms. They may have needed the hardliners' conspiratorial skills, but they refused to accept their predominance in the regime. The most characteristic figure in that group, the new Chief of Staff General Bonanos, tacitly accepted the Ioannidis coup but from the early days of the new regime showed his divergence from the latter, publicly speaking of a transition which would come shortly. Thinking they could dispense with Papadopoulos, this group engaged in a renewed underground competition with the hardliners over who was to take control of developments in Greece. The main area of contention was the new 'civilianization' plan, which on this occasion would be supervised by the military rather than Papadopoulos, leading to a renewed version of Papadopoulos' failed *democradura*, with the military acting as the praetorians. A full account of these developments would require a closer study of the actual transition of 1974, which is again beyond the scope of this book. Suffice to say that their ambition seemed to be coming true for a few hours in July 1974, when they overthrew Ioannidis and accepted a Kanellopoulos–Mavros cabinet. The return of Karamanlis, the new developments in Cyprus with Turkish operations in August, and their final retreat in the face of Karamanlis' firm decision to remove them from control in the army crushed their hopes irreversibly. In November 1973, nevertheless, they offered their tacit support to the diehards of Ioannidis. It was an alliance against which Papadopoulos stood no chance – albeit one as precarious and uneasy as all inter-regime alliances had been since 1967.

As for Markezinis, his limited control of the army (as well as his protracted preparation for the elections), which would have been his best source of information for the ruthless conspirators with whom he was dealing, had nullified from the beginning any slim chances he had of intervening in the inter-regime game. His high profile was a further disadvantage as far as the plotters were concerned. Bonanos believes that Markezinis' failure to call elections in early November was critical, as this would have taken the hardliners by surprise: '[H]ad the elections been called in the first five days of November, and had new developments got underway, then what took place afterwards [the Polytechnic events and the November coup] would not have happened.'[136] One might speculate that this was a necessary – though not sufficient – condition for the longer-term viability of the 'experiment'. Although there is no guarantee that this would have deterred the Ioannidis plotters, it would certainly have made the situation more complicated.

Conjecture about how a different outcome of the Greek *reforma* might have been achieved becomes more difficult when the opposition elites' refusal to negotiate is considered. While a number of opposition leaders were prepared to tentatively support the 'experiment', the majority did not, and in the case of the latter it appears to have been the presence of Papadopoulos at the helm that determined their attitude. As Barkman's record of the opinion of Pesmazoglou on 25 October notes, 'the attitude of the old political leaders ... is influenced less by rational considerations than by their psychological aversion from undertaking any political activities under Papadopoulos as President'.[137] This factor weighed heavily in their decisions, the British ambassador noting that, in terms of Greek politics,

> ... their position makes more sense than at first meets the Western eye. For obvious reasons, they reject the basic concept underlying the Markezinis venture – that if parliamentary government is to work in Greece, it must be controlled and guided. And while this is in itself perhaps a defensible proposition, they have rather more of a point when they continued that the control and guidance will come from one man whom they regard as having no authority deriving from popular sovereignty and whom they believe to be fundamentally opposed to genuine democracy and all that they themselves stand for.[138]

On this matter, however, the opposition erred in overruling the liberalization steps of the summer of 1973 as inadequate. In relation to participation, the optimum approach for the Greek counter-elites was that identified in Rallis's article.

The British ambassador agreed with his Dutch counterpart in a report to the Foreign Office as early as September, in which he stressed his impression that

> ... the rank and file of Greek politicians have still not learnt the lessons of the pre-1967 period ... They cannot be blamed for mistrust of the regime ... but the carping tone they take and the absence of any constructive criticism makes it appear to the outsider that they are not seriously interested in finding solutions to the country's political problems unless this is on their own terms.[139]

Barkman's thoughts were in line with Huntington's analysis, some two decades after the 'experiment', that 'opposition groups who wanted democracy should not have boycotted the elections authoritarian leaders did call'.[140] As elections never actually took place, though, the question has remained open (and never been answered) as to whether the democratic opposition could make some further gains on the way to the polls, since this would not depend on what Markezinis would *wish* to happen but rather on what Papadopoulos would *allow* to happen. It was precisely on this issue that Markezinis impressed the Dutch ambassador, in a meeting they had after the Ioannidis coup, in terms of what he appeared to have gained with Papadopoulos' agreement regarding the elections:

> In the polling-stations and even at [the] counting of the votes, observers would be allowed to be present, such as journalists and possibly international personalities whose democratic disposition could be in no doubt. Markezinis wanted to invite among others my Foreign Minister, Mr van der Stoel, to attend the last week of the elections. [Some] ... 31 Greeks who had been deprived [of] their nationality like Andreas Papandreou ... would regain Greek nationality and be allowed without any formalities, to return to their country and participate in its political activities.[141]

It can only be speculated whether the above steps would be indeed have been allowed by Papadopoulos, although his apologists like Passas maintain they would have, stressing the fault of the politicians for the collapse of the 'experiment':

> None of the political leaders had realised that Papadopoulos was sincerely aiming [at] ... civilianisation and would gradually, through free elections, achieve [the] full normalisation of political life, as it would be difficult and unwise on his behalf ... to proceed to full restoration of democratic politics, given that the more numerous and dynamic officers were hostile to civilianisation.[142]

One thing is certain: the 'experiment' of 1973 demanded more active and determined agents than Markezinis who, in Georgalas' words, 'was talking too much and doing too little'.[143] The 'experiment' also needed more realistic counter-elites, who should have left more space for negotiation in advance of the elections. In a certain sense, and although he once again writes apologetically, Theodorakopoulos makes an important point when he presents the paradox of a political initiative that was taken seriously only by the military hardliners: '[T]rying hard not to alarm the army by his concessions to the politicians, [Papadopoulos] found himself caught between the Scylla of the politicians headed by Kanellopoulos and Mavros, and the Charybdis of the hawks within the armed forces, who watched his balancing act with increasing disillusionment.'[144] This was the structural deficiency of the whole Markezinis venture: it was both 'too timid to convince the opposition, yet too far-[reaching] ... for the hard-liners and the military-as-institution [who refused] ... to extricate themselves from power'.[145] And there remains one major factor to be taken into consideration: the Polytechnic events of November 1973.

5

Fortuna and the 'Experiment': Civil Society and the Polytechnic Events

I took office without martial law and censorship, and had to face everyone's attacks as if they wanted to make up for their long silence during the time of the unpopular regime, the imposition of which was not my fault... and on the coming of which I had been sending early warnings. I nevertheless hoped that later, when the results would become tangible, my good intentions would be appreciated.

Markezinis, *Political Memoirs*: 222

Markezini buffoon.

Slogan of the Polytechnic demonstrations

The reaction of civil society to the Markezinis experiment is one of the least understood aspects of the failed *reforma* of 1973, the reason being its short existence and its overshadowing by the violent demonstrations of that November, first with the Papandreou memorial services and then, more importantly, with the Polytechnic uprising and its bloody suppression. The commonly accepted thesis is that the Polytechnic events 'signalled the irrevocable failure of the military dictatorship to achieve popular consent',[1] thus bringing the whole initiative to an impasse. The conventional wisdom that was subsequently developed presented the Polytechnic uprising as the reason for the downfall of Papadopoulos and Markezinis, an explanation that overlooks the deep rifts within the regime that had become completely unbridgeable by that point and the fact that the hardliners' conspiracy had been brewing long before November. On the other hand, a more conservative interpretation – if not exactly exonerating the regime – sees the events as simply an expression of some young students' discontent, which was exploited by certain politicians and offered a pretext for the hardliners to topple Papadopoulos and Markezinis, excusing their action by evoking memories of the 'chaos and anarchy' associated with the civil war, which required a restoration of 'law and order'. However, this episode still has some unanswered questions, such as the disposition of the people to the *reforma* in the early autumn and the reason for the escalation of the Polytechnic demonstrations to the point they got out of control. A more circumspect reading of these events stresses the contingency that is involved on both the students' and the regime's sides. As has been pointed out in the democratization literature, the factor of *fortuna* can change the course of a political process as subtle and sensitive as a democratic transition by regime transformation, which applies precisely in the case of the 'Markezinis experiment'.

Summer–early autumn 1973: 'Hard to believe, but they're retreating ...'

The swearing in of Papadopoulos as President in August 1973 was calculated to coincide with some steps towards liberalization, as he had promised early that summer. Indeed, on 20 August, martial law and the state of siege were lifted throughout the country and a general amnesty was granted to all political prisoners and exiles, leading to the release of the last 300 detainees. By early September, only about 15 political prisoners remained in custody, all sentenced under pre-1967 governments. Panagoulis, who five years earlier had tried to kill the dictator, also received a special pardon. At the same time, censorship was lifted. These developments, as Barkman noted in his diary, contributed to 'a public mood ... which is entirely new in Greece since the 1967 coup. The atmosphere has cleared considerably and expectations have arisen ... This has set the political tongues wagging and a lot of ink flowing, to such an extent that there is now almost complete freedom of the press.' He also claimed that 'Papadopoulos has improved his position with the public.'² It seemed that these progressive steps took opponents of the regime by surprise, with a KKE report acknowledging that '[the party] organisation did not rise ... to the occasion ... [I]t did not make the most of some favourable conditions created by the release of political prisoners and the junta's attempt to apply its "liberalisation" experiment.'³ The press, including the pro-regime papers, contributed to this hopeful atmosphere by proclaiming 'the end of the 21st of April'.⁴ The attempt by Markezinis to capitalize on this apparently positive climate to advance his 'experiment' was indicated by the interviews he started giving to the foreign press. During the short time he was in office, Markezinis kept at least part of his promises: for instance, he issued a directive to his Minister of Justice that 'no journalist is to be prosecuted for criticising me in the press or for writing anything against my government'.⁵

A number of people had the impression that the relaxation of policing was a sign that the dictatorship was backtracking because of the people's opposition and reaction and that it would now be possible to press for more concessions. As Mitsos recalls:

> No matter our lack of trust [in] ... Papadopoulos, we believed we should take advantage of the regime's openings ... [E]ven when the Markezinis government was formed, which had his backing, we were thinking 'it's basically the same, but we shouldn't reject it beforehand; we're on the right track, let's keep up the struggle'. We knew Markezinis wouldn't go far with democratisation, but we were sure that no matter how far he would go in the end, it was good and we should make the most of it.⁶

One way or another, in the late summer and early autumn of 1973, civil society was contemplating, as were some opposition politicians, that the 'experiment' offered a real window of opportunity for a reduction of oppression, though perhaps not for an outright transition to a full democracy. Even the KKE was concerned by the attitude of 'prudent realism' towards the regime, which seemed to be winning over some people: '[T]here was a real danger that the political forces and a part of the people's movement might be tricked ... and give credit to the opportunistic view that "since we cannot do away with the junta outright, we need to rely on what we can have now and then aim at gradual later changes."⁷ The deterioration of the economic situation – with a high balance-of-payments deficit and rising inflation (which had begun in late 1972) – was not yet widely felt in the country. Even before the Markezinis government was sworn in, at the end of the summer, there was a 12 per cent increase in salaries to compensate for inflation, and Markezinis introduced some anti-inflation policies in October to remediate the situation. Moreover, the consequences of the oil crisis would not be felt during Markezinis' period in office. The final favourable point to note about the economic scenario is that the government did not have to face a major strike. In general, it was noted that for most of that year 'politics was absolutely predominant, pushing the economy to the background'.⁸ Yet, Greeks failed to realize that the regime hardliners were as reluctant as ever to give up power and were in fact preparing a reaction: the focus was on Papadopoulos rather than on Ioannidis and his scheming hardliners. As Mitsos admits, 'we knew of some frictions within the regime; but we never thought that they could get as far as they did'.⁹

Nevertheless, opposition groups were bracing themselves for a new round of conflict with the regime, which was made easier with the liberalization measures, since 'the temporary relaxing of the policing by the Markezinis government provided the chance for a rapid [rise in] … organized resistance'.¹⁰ The first incident to cast a serious doubt on the 'Markezinis experiment' occurred on 4 November, after the memorial services for the fifth anniversary of the death of ex-Prime Minister Papandreou. Intelligence about possible trouble had reached the police before that date, as Markezinis recalls.¹¹ Indeed, many gathered in and around the Athens cemetery shouting anti-regime slogans, cheering the politicians present at the ceremony and, eventually, demonstrating in the centre of Athens. The police stopped them, and violent clashes followed; some policemen even fired live ammunition in the air, with many civilians and policemen wounded and seventeen demonstrators arrested. Although by the afternoon 'order' had been restored, the 'experiment' had taken a blow: it was the first time that unrest on such a scale had been witnessed in Athens since Markezinis had taken office.

The politicians, in turn, found an opportunity to discredit the Prime Minister in the eyes of the people and abroad. Greek and international newspapers and media judged that little had changed as a result of a new cabinet being formed and that the regime was as violent as ever. For instance, the BBC reported that same evening that 'the hopes of the Greek regime for a peaceful transition to parliamentary democracy took a serious blow today ... [T]he first crucial test for Mr Markezinis' government proved that in reality the chances of a compromise between him and his opponents are less than ever before.'[12] A British diplomat in Athens, reporting to the Foreign Office, presented a more nuanced view:

> There is evidence that some of the violence was premeditated ... The Government themselves have been at pains to avoid laying the blame for the demonstration on the shoulders of the 'old politicians' ... [nevertheless] they ... must be aware that in private at least the old politicians never cease talking of carrying on the 'struggle' against the 'dictatorship' with the aid of students and organised labour ... The demonstration was not in any way a threat to the Government. It does not seem to have created the kind of mass sympathy which the treatment of the students aroused and has not enhanced the Opposition's image. At the same time it has done nothing to improve the prospects for the elections.[13]

A few days later, the trial of those arrested provided another opportunity for politicians like Kanellopoulos to publicly denounce the brutality of the regime and, of course, accuse the Markezinis government of having acted precisely like its predecessors would have done. Markezinis would not have the opportunity to counter this accusation, since by the time the trials were ending he had to face a new and far more difficult situation: on the afternoon of 14 November, the Polytechnic campus was about to be occupied by students.[14]

The Polytechnic events: The students and the people

The three-day student uprising against the government in the Polytechnic and its subsequent brutal repression is considered to be proof that behind the 'experiment' smokescreen was lurking the same dictatorship that the people loathed, and that nothing had actually changed. The claim that it was because of the Polytechnic events that Markezinis failed (as if his 'experiment' was not already on the verge of collapsing because of the hardliners' reaction), as well as interpretations by regime apologists which present the students as manipulated by certain politicians aiming to discredit the 'experiment' or even by hardliners aiming to expose it as a prelude to a return to 'anarchy and chaos' if Markezinis was allowed to proceed, all neglect an element that is important in assessing a transition from authoritarianism. Indeed, in such a complex and precarious situation as the one Greece faced in November 1973, *fortuna* can influence the process and, as different groups and interests clash, may well produce an outcome that no one intended at the start.

One of the first social groups to note the easing of policing was the students, who not only felt encouraged to speak freely, but were also psychologically emboldened to push their agenda more decisively. As Chrissafis Iordanoglou, then member of the KKE-es 'Rigas Feraios' student youth, put it, 'the opportunity that the "liberalisation" gave to the student movement greatly defined its tactics with regard to the antidictatorial struggle ... [E]ven the most limited mobilization, even the smallest demand was taken as a challenge against the regime.'[15] Even before November, student committees had presented the Minister of Education, Panayotis Sifnaios, with a list of their demands, which included repeal of the February decree on mandatory military service, extension of an exemption to those already drafted, changes to the timing of examinations and, most importantly, the timing of student elections. The minister presented his response to these demands to the students' representatives on 1 November, granting all but the one concerning their elections, which he said would take place after 15 February – that is, after the general election. This turned out to be one of the Markezinis government's biggest blunders: by insisting that the student elections be held after the national elections the government caused friction that was to have unexpected results. Grigoriadis was left 'to wonder how men as politically expedient as Markezinis did not understand that they should avoid at all costs any dispute with the students, if they wanted a smooth way to parliamentary elections'.[16] From the first days of November the atmosphere in the faculties of Athens was tense and students began discussing their demands and considering how best to respond to the government. The minister's intransigence was all that was needed to escalate the situation. Tension had already been on the rise since the incidents at the Papandreou memorial services and the ensuing trials. Ironically, there is some indication that, as Markezinis said to Barkman, Papadopoulos had agreed with his plan 'to purge the administration gradually [of] ... elements that had been appointed by the "revolutionary regime"' and that 'the government commissioners [retired military officers] at the universities would be removed'.[17]

On 14 November the students' protests grew larger in and around the Athens University faculties. Incited by a false rumour that Polytechnic students were being attacked by the police, many students in the Athens Law School decided to join the Polytechnic protestors.[18] Later the same day the decision to occupy the campus was taken, but not without much controversy and argument among the students and the political parties' youth organizations. Most of the parties' student groups were sceptical about such a step, while it was initiated and supported by the independent anarchist or leftist groups. For instance, the KKE-affiliated students were taken by surprise, as the party cadres 'were unprepared for this form of struggle ... and thought of disengaging the students from the Polytechnic campus and turning the protest into broader anti-dictatorial demonstrations [in] ... various directions'.[19] A radio station was set up to broadcast the students' demands, and a Coordination Committee was formed to supervise the occupation, cater for the students inside and represent them in the talks with the academics and state officials. From this point on, the course of events inside and outside the Polytechnic, as well as in the Markezinis government and among the opposition across the political spectrum, took an unpredicted course, which still remains puzzling and to a certain extent confusing.[20]

The decision to occupy the campus reflected the overconfidence of the students and their ungrounded optimism about the prospects of such a venture, a view not shared by the official left-wing organizations, who did not trust such spontaneous actions.[21] The main instigators, the leftist and anarchist students, were totally opposed to negotiation, denouncing the liberalization as a farce and refusing even to engage with Sifnaios.[22] Notwithstanding that as far as the students were concerned this was simply an anti-dictatorial protest rather than a serious challenge to the Markezinis government,[23] the course of the events over the next few days gave its participants a false hope that the protest could go well beyond its original scope, up to the point of bringing down the regime: the 'flavour of spontaneity' that prevailed 'left no space for correct predictions and for the drawing of a line of action with clear political perspectives'.[24] According to Iordanoglou,

> ... the Rigas youth had conceived of the occupation of the campus as a means of a strategy of pressure and guerrilla warfare against the regime ... [O]ur intention therefore was to hit and pull back on time, before things got to a point of frontal confrontation with the regime [which we did not believe we could win] ... What we failed to reckon with, as we were young, was that a great mass of angry people cannot be controlled.[25]

The next day, 15 November, the protest grew in numbers, and the cry 'bread–education–freedom' was heard through the streets around the campus. Although this slogan also referred to the economic and educational conditions, the political demands were the dominant element in the demonstrations, as Mantoglou notes: '[T]he main reason of the uprising were the anti-dictatorial and anti-imperialist feelings and not the students' problems or economic issues ... those had a secondary role ... [A]ll slogans were of a political nature.'[26] And the Dean of the Polytechnic noted that 'there were no substantial demands or issues dealing with the students. There was only one demand: that Papadopoulos goes.'[27] And as the official statement by the Polytechnic Coordination Committee, broadcast on its radio, indicated, the students had come to realize that:

Our problems related to the democratisation of education ... cannot be solved without a change of the present political situation. The immediate end of the tyrannical regime of the junta and the establishment of people's sovereignty is of primary importance for the solution of the people's problems ... [This is] tightly linked to national independence from foreign interests that have been supporting tyranny in our country for years.[28]

On the first day of the events, the police sought to end the occupation by force: Chief Constable of the Athens Police Christoloukas met with Polytechnic Dean Konofagos and asked his permission for the police to enter the campus. Konofagos refused to allow 'an intervention against hot-blooded students discussing their elections'. Later that day both Education Minister Sifnaios and Head of the Greek Police Daskalopoulos agreed with Konofagos' decision, claiming that such an operation would lead to bloodshed, 'which was what the students were after'.[29] After a meeting with Papadopoulos and Sifnaios, Markezinis agreed on the free movement of people to and from the campus. Indeed, on the second day of the occupation 'the Police mysteriously vanished. No attempt was made either to disperse the crowds or to halt the supplies of money, food and medicines pouring into the School, or to jam the student radio. The crowds grew larger.'[30] Markezinis later recalled what he described as the 'strange slowness' of the police in the early stages of the events,[31] and added that 'it was a mistake of the police to delay their intervention and not to close the Polytechnic on time as they did with the University of Athens'.[32]

The contradiction between what Markezinis agreed on that day and what he wrote later about the handling of matters by the police indicates that government officials had not yet realized that the situation was slowly but steadily deteriorating, despite the warnings by Athens Chief Constable Christoloukas that it would eventually get out of hand if steps were not taken soon. This has left many wondering why action was not indeed taken sooner, since the police would have found it relatively easy, in these early stages of the affair, to repel the demonstrators. For Kanellopoulos, as he would testify during the Polytechnic trials two years later, there was something suspicious about this hesitation to act.³³ It is true that the government underestimated the challenge posed by the Polytechnic students, dismissing them as a bunch of troublemakers, and were oblivious to the deeper causes of the unrest as well as the growing momentum of the protest and the potential it had to sweep way Markezinis' meticulously planned election timetable.³⁴ Papadopoulos appeared unperturbed by the escalation of the demonstrations on the second day, reassuring Dimitrios Roufogalis, head of the Greek Central Intelligence Agency (KYP), that 'nothing serious will happen'. Commenting to Sifnaios about the damage the students were doing to the Polytechnic and the neighbouring area, he remained calm: '[L]et them do their worst – break and burn whatever; we have the money to rebuild everything anew.'³⁵

On the same day the Minister of Education asked the Dean's opinion about the issue of the university asylum – the banning of police from entering the campus – and was informed that police intervention might lead to bloodshed, as by that time the students in and around the Polytechnic numbered around 2,000. Later the government issued a statement confirming its decision to respect the asylum. The police had already left the Polytechnic area and people could move freely to and from the campus. The students in the Polytechnic, in turn, seemed to draw the wrong conclusions about how far their protest could go. Encouraged by the initial evident success and support for the occupation from many Athenians, and motivated by their 'romantic utopianism',³⁶ which led them to believe they were the main historical agents of a decisive change in Greek politics, they overestimated their influence and believed that their demonstrations could ultimately bring down the regime. According to one participant, 'this enthusiasm shows that the students were, more or less, cut off from the existing climate outside the Polytechnic, from the position and the possibilities of the people. They even started talking about the possible formation of a government.'³⁷ It was at this point that the students appeared to suffer their first setback. Although there had been an early wave of sympathy for their cause, the ongoing demonstrations and some of the more radical pronouncements began to alienate some of the more conservative Athenians. As Barkman noted, 'at first the city population sympathised with the demonstrating youngsters and were appalled by the violence the police had used against *ta paidia* [the kids]. Later these sentiments changed when the extreme leftist slogans and the needless destructions became known which brought back memories of the civil war.'[38] The anti-regime protest had began to transform into a social revolutionary call from some of the students, which set them apart from the anti-dictatorial and pro-democratic spirit of the majority of the people. As Mitsos recalls:

> We were out on Patission Avenue [adjacent to the Polytechnic campus] protesting, holding the traffic, giving flyers to passers-by and drivers... [A]t some point we started hitting the windows of buses and cars shouting 'brothers, get out and join us; join our struggle to bring down the junta.' But we were getting almost no reply; hardly anyone would join us... I could see instead their stiff faces looking at me as if saying 'we are on your side, we like your effort, but do not go too far'. To me this came as a shock, as I thought that the people were firmly on our side.[39]

Furthermore, the people feared the repressive apparatus of the state, which was still active despite the temporary retreat from the Polytechnic area. Andrews recalls a demonstration in front of the Greek National Museum, not far from the Polytechnic campus, which dispersed rapidly at the sight of a few policemen on 15 November.[40] Clearly many Athenians did not share the revolutionary fervour most of the students clustered in the Polytechnic.

Nevertheless, some workers and peasants from the nearby area joined the occupation, as the students relaxed their control of who was entering and who was leaving the campus. This free movement of people allowed some more extreme individuals to enter the campus, shouting or writing slogans of a leftist-anarchist nature, which went beyond the scope of the students' protest.[41] Along with these interlopers, a number of regime security personnel entered the Polytechnic. This fuelled subsequent theories that these were groups of agitators under the direction of the regime's secret services, whose aim was to present the protest as the work of 'anti-national extremist anarchist elements' in order not only to justify further violence against the students, but also a shift of the political transition process in an authoritarian direction. At that time it seems that this attitude was particularly popular among the 'official left' organizations. The January–February 1974 edition of the KKE students' organization *Panspoudastiki*, in an article that acquired notoriety over the next few years, 'outspokenly castigated three hundred and fifty students of the revolt as *agents provocateurs*'.[42] During the Polytechnic trials two years later it was proved that some agents of Ioannidis' ESA and members of the KYP had indeed entered the campus. However, their influence on the course of the occupation and the demonstrations was much less significant than many have believed. The radio station transmissions could certainly not be called 'extremist' and, as Kanellopoulos has observed, during this period 'all extremist slogans [that were] incompatible with the democratic spirit, were rejected by the majority of the students'.[43] These developments allowed for mass participation by non-students in the demonstrations late on the second day of the occupation, which renewed the hope that events might be moving towards some sort of pro-democratic breakthrough soon.[44] The change in attitude of the people seemed to be encouraged by the initial inertia of the police around the Polytechnic area, leading to a sudden increase in participation in the demonstrations. The apparent awakening of many people's anti-dictatorial feelings and appetite for protest was unprecedented, even if the Papandreou and Seferis funerals are taken into account. As Andreas Papandreou acknowledged, 'without the response and support of the people, the November uprising would have been but a mere student demonstration'.[45] Andrews has remarked more caustically that 'years of collective boredom had given way to a few minutes of individual responsibility'.[46] The utopian optimism of the moment is also vividly captured in the words of Mitsos:

> We never thought that something bad might come out of all this; neither did we contemplate the outcome of our demonstrations. We were living for the day, excited by the unexpected success of our protest

and we were to an extent overtaken by the dynamics it had created. We did not cease to believe that we could push Markezinis to further democratic concessions and that was all. Our goal was not the revolution; it was the leftists that were pushing things that way.[47]

Also, politicians like Kanellopoulos and Mavros did not miss the chance to attack Markezinis. They both visited the Polytechnic campus and made statements praising the students and denouncing the violence and hypocrisy of the regime. This was a serious blow to Markezinis, for whatever his intentions might have been, he now had to deal with accusations that he supported the repressive measures of a hated regime and that the change he was promising was but a sham.

For the students, what turned out to be the final day of the whole affair – Friday, 16 November – dawned with the feeling – 'one of the major paradoxes in recent Greek political history', as Kornetis notes – 'that this would be the event that would bring down the regime'.[48] The Coordination Committee 'was encouraged by the Polytechnic professors to continue with the occupation until Saturday so that Markezinis [would agree] ... to more substantial compromise'. According to the KKE report, the conviction of most of the students on campus was 'let us stay here for one more night and leave tomorrow'. Although by the afternoon the committee had received information about a police plan to attack the Polytechnic, a strange optimism prevailed and a belief that 'they will not attack [us] ... here [on campus]'.[49] It is indicative of this climate of revolutionary optimism among the students that, as Konofagos notes, 'a communiqué of the Coordination Committee spoke of the need for national unity and cooperation with all parties that were against the dictatorship in a paragraph which was omitted from the final draft due to leftists' reaction'.[50]

For the government, that Friday started with great concern, since it 'was reduced to a secondary role and its president was but a mere spectator of the events'.[51] Markezinis was scheduled to give his press conference the following day and present his plans regarding the forthcoming general election, but he could not possibly do that when the demonstrations were inevitably monopolizing the attention of journalists. He was also acutely conscious of what he described as a 'curious "coincidence": the escalation of demonstrations was happening at the same time as I announced that I would call a press conference [on the elections]'.[52] A meeting was held in Markezinis' office involving Vice-President of the Republic Anghelis; Vice-President of the government; Minister of Education Sifnaios; Minister of Public Order and Defence Therapos; the Chief of the Greek Police; and government spokesman Zournatzis. They were joined later by Papadopoulos. Their main concern at the meeting was how to put an end to the demonstrations with as little trouble as possible. After some discussion it was decided that the police should intervene in three phases: in phase one they would clear all the paths around the Polytechnic and force the demonstrators assembled there to disperse; in phase two they would cut off the students occupying the campus; and in phase three they would take control of the Polytechnic and clean up the campus after giving the students a 30-minute warning to evacuate.[53] It was understood that the police would not use firearms, and after some discussion even the proposal to use tear gas was dropped. Papadopoulos presumably advised the Chief of the Athens Police to allow space for the demonstrators to protest on the streets around the campus, 'though not to let them go as far as Constitution Square [the centre of Athens]'.[54] However, before the plan was put into action, a sudden surge of demonstrors around the Polytechnic in the afternoon and early evening paralysed the police. Within a few hours the tension mounted spectacularly to a point unimaginable just the day before. Markezinis notes that 'the discussion of that morning had been leaked and those who had an interest in the continuation of the turmoil, as they saw that I was doing business as usual, decided not to waste any more time'.[55] The attacks on the Athens Prefecture and Ministry of Public Order buildings took the police by surprise and they now responded to the waves of demonstrators with the use of truncheons and tear gas.[56]

It was at this point that firearms were used for the first time by the police and that victims were reported. Although the police were ordered to fire into the air, so as to avoid casualties, this was not what happened.

According to the evidence of a police witness, the police fired some 24,000 rounds that day and sharp-shooters were reported to be firing into the crowds with the deliberate intention of causing civilian victims.[57] Late in the evening the Chief of the Greek Police asked for the intervention of the army, as he said his forces were inadequate to contain the demonstrators.[58] However, this request was made orally, without a formal written document, which would only be officially submitted to the army the following day, by which point the main incidents were over.[59] Papadopoulos personally decided to cover the police by deploying armoured units, calculating that the psychological impact that their appearance on the streets would have on the demonstrators and the students clustered in the Polytechnic would induce them to leave the campus. Although no more than a handful of tanks were initially sent in, the forces that finally arrived in Athens city centre were on an impressive scale.[60] The coordination and organization of the operation was undertaken by an army colonel, thus bypassing the police.[61] Public buildings that had been attacked earlier were now placed under military guard, the Polytechnic campus was surrounded by troops and isolated, and the demonstrators were driven from the city centre. At the same time, armoured and Special Forces units started moving towards the Polytechnic area, preparing to storm the campus. The students inside made desperate attempts to make contact with the soldiers through the radio, urging them not to shoot at civilians. After midnight, negotiations opened between the students' committee representatives and military officers about evacuating the campus without further trouble, but to no avail, as the officers were not prepared to grant the students the amount of time they asked for to carry out the evacuation. Eventually, at about three o'clock on the Saturday morning, a tank commander, carrying out the orders of an officer acting on his own initiative – he had received no request from the police demand or written military order – crashed his vehicle into the main gate of the Polytechnic, allowing policemen and soldiers to storm the campus. The cruelty with which the students were treated was typical of the operating methods of the ESA, while the enraged policemen engaged in excessive violence against the demonstrators, even when they were brought to hospitals for treatment. It has been noted, though, that the soldiers were much more restrained in handling the students than were the police.[62] By dawn the Polytechnic was under complete military control.

The Polytechnic events were over, but in some parts of Athens demonstrations and clashes continued to be reported and people killed by sharpshooters' fire or ricochet bullets. On the morning of 17 November, martial law was declared throughout the country by the President of the Republic, Papadopoulos. Later the same day he delivered what was to be his last message, blaming the events that had just happened on 'an organised minority', proof, he claimed, 'of a conspiracy of the enemies of Democracy and of political normality, which intend to fatally block the implementation of the creative programme' that had started in the summer.[63] The same day, Kanellopoulos and Mavros were placed under house arrest, while government spokesman Zournatzis visited the Polytechnic and presented evidence to the press of the damage the students were supposed to have caused to the infrastructure of the campus, such as the buildings, lab equipment and so on. However, this 'evidence' was later challenged by Dean Konofagos, who claimed that 'most of it [the damage] was done after the occupation so that Zournatzis could [influence] ... public opinion in Greece and abroad'.[64] Zournatzis' task was never going to be easy, as indicated by a dispatch from the British ambassador which blamed the government for mishandling the situation by bringing the army in:

> The Athens garrisons did not have a competent leadership, were badly trained and incapable of suppressing demonstrations. It was decided to send tanks when the infantry would have been more suitable. They opened fire indiscriminately ... Had the authorities acted from the beginning with effectiveness and determination, there might not have been bloodshed.[65]

Yet such remarks fail to note the link between the Polytechnic events and the inner-regime struggle between Papadopoulos and Ioannidis, in which the deployment of large military units was not in fact related to the uprising but rather indicated a desperate (and, as it proved, futile) attempt by Papadopoulos to reshuffle the cards in the army in order to block an Ioannidis coup.

During the entire episode, Markezinis was totally sidelined; his son-in-law recalls that he was nervous as he had no information about what was happening in the Polytechnic and wanted no blood to be shed in the suppression of the demonstrations. In his memoirs, Markezinis asserts that he had less information about the operation than *New York Times* journalist Mario Modiano, from whom he learned the details of the evacuation of the Polytechnic and that, to his relief, 'there were no victims during the intervention of [the] armour'.[66] In his private notes, Markezinis excuses his acceptance of the imposition of martial law on the grounds that, had it not been declared, 'there would [have] be[en] extensive anarchist demonstrations making a large-scale military intervention necessary and there might have been hundreds of victims ... [whereas] had martial law and censorship been applied before, it would be impossible to see the disturbances taking the scale that they did'.[67] Nevertheless, worse was to come for him: three days after the end of the events, while visiting the Ministry of Defence to speak before the TV cameras and in front of the army commanders 'not on what had happened but on what was to happen henceforth', insisting on sticking to the elections timetable, Markezinis made a blunder that was to haunt him for the rest of his political career. He said that he assumed responsibility for the military suppression of the uprising, despite the fact that defence and public order issues were not within his jurisdiction but rather the President's; congratulated the armed forces 'on having successfully and bloodlessly put an end to the insurrection'; and concluded with a phrase that would also make him culpable for supporting the violence: 'We [Papadopoulos and himself] will bring our mission for full normalisation of the political situation in Greece to a successful end ... [T]hose interested in achieving the opposite will fail. The enemy of the nation and of democracy will not pass!'[68] Markezinis has claimed that this statement reflected his concern about the need to reach the election date with as little disruption as possible, which was in the national interest. At the same time, he was also anxious to appease the military, who were alarmed by what they saw as 'a communist comeback'. This proved to be a lethal blow to Markezinis' credibility as the agent of democratization, for when he spoke of the 'enemies of [the] nation and democracy' most people automatically thought of the students and the violence they suffered, particularly at the hands of the police. After this conference, few believed that Markezinis could 'guarantee full civil and political rights for all Greek citizens ... and preclude the reintroduction of another authoritarian regime'.[69] It remained a political stigma for him after 1974, as it irrevocably identified him with the dictatorship and with Papadopoulos, of whom he appeared to be a mere puppet. Even his opponent Kanellopoulos testified in the Polytechnic trials that he was 'of the opinion that Mr Markezinis and his government knew nothing about the bloody events ... [T]he government had no authority on military and public security issues. For that reason I could not possibly explain, even today, why Mr Markezinis, just a few days later, assumed responsibility for what he had nothing to do with.'[70] The Greeks would not 'forgive and forget' his stance after the restoration of democracy. His last public appearance as Prime Minister would become Markezinis' best remembered one, given that it occurred at the same time that Athens was counting its victims.

When all the disturbances had ended, the official number of lives lost was given as eighteen; later the number of confirmed deaths rose to twenty-four.[71] The number of hospitalized wounded rose to 366, of whom sixty-one were members of the police, according to the report by Christoloukas. However, many of the wounded did not go to hospitals due to fear of being arrested or abused by the police. It is therefore safe to assume that the number of wounded was considerably higher than the official figure.[72] The number of arrests rose to 866, only about 50 of whom were Polytechnic students.[73] The fact that the ESA were leading the investigations and were again on the streets of Athens in large numbers signalled the subtle but obvious comeback of the regime, at a time when the main voice of opposition in civil society had been crushed. It was vindication of Gill's observation that in such a transition, 'despite concessions at the edges, the essential [dictatorial] power structure remains intact.'[74] According to Mitsos, 'the suppression had come as a slap on our face; it was like we had hit a wall. We were dismayed, thinking [of] ... the impasse that lay ahead of us ... because we all knew that we were the losers of this fight, but also that this could not be repeated for a long time. The regime had won, and we were totally incapable of doing anything about it.'[75] In contrast to Markezinis' interpretation of the government's role, those involved in the occupation blamed their failure on the lack of a proper plan of action. One of the participants said two decades later that

> ... the students had no plan whatsoever: they set forth an insurrection the results of which they could not know, against an enemy [whose limit of action] they did not know ... [T]hey overestimated their own strength ... [S]ince they did not [take into] account ... all [this], there was a head-on clash, which should not have [happened] ... [I]f they had [had] a plan, they ... [would] have backed down at the appropriate moment, but they did not; and thus they lost.[76]

As Androutsopoulos asserted, 'Between the 25th of November and the 23rd of July there was not one single incident of challenge to law and order ... [T]he trouble-makers of the Polytechnic days realised that the times were not opportune for a repetition of those events, and the self-proclaimed stars of resistance had disappeared.'[77]. Mitsos paints a bleak picture of the students' movement in the months that followed the suppression of the uprising:

> For months afterwards, it was the same [as in] ... the aftermath of the Polytechnic suppression: disappointment and despair was in the air, as well as a feeling of total incapacity to do anything about the situation ... I was concerned for my friends who were wanted and were hiding from the police ... [T]hose people now in power were the real die-hards, they were not joking.[78]

The irony is that, in its early days, the coup met with the same relief and, to a certain extent, enthusiasm of the people as it was by the politicians. Shocked by the bloody repression of the Polytechnic protest, many

Greeks viewed the coup 'as a first hopeful sign of the army putting things in order ... and opening the way to a hopeful civilianisation and normalisation'.[79] The ensuing suppression of all dissidence and the authoritarianism practised by Ioannidis and the ESA, as well as the rapid collapse of the dictatorship because of the Cyprus fiasco, dashed all chances of the active participation of civil society in the actual transition, in which the people were reduced to the role of spectators and cheerleaders.

The political implications of the events: The regime and the opposition elites

Post-1974, the Polytechnic events have been a favourite subject of conspiracy theories on behalf of Markezinis and regime apologists, who try to blame their unexpected start, sudden escalation and bloody suppression on forces and interests external to the students, who are considered innocent or naive victims of some well-prepared plots. The actual starting point of these explanations is the first day of the events. Some in the government believed that the instigators of the occupation were not only oblivious to student issues, but in fact people working for sinister interests outside Greece that sought the collapse of the *reforma* and found here the opportunity to discredit the 'experiment' and plunge Greece into chaos. Konofagos was surprised to hear Minister Sifnaios, on that first day of the occupation, say that the students were 'naive victims of external forces' who were taking advantage of their passion to fuel an uprising. To the question of precisely which forces these were, Sifnaios simply said that it was all contrived by some people in France and Italy, without being more specific.[80] Papadopoulos also seemed to believe that the instigators of the Polytechnic episode were based abroad.[81] In the words of Kornetis, 'Papadopoulos demonstrated a great lack of understanding of the real situation as he sought scapegoats by identifying outsider groups as responsible for the student unrest.'[82] It is a common theme of these theories that they fail to identify which individuals or groups were the masterminds behind the events and their escalation, thus adding to the aura of conspiracy which many blame for the course that Greek politics followed at this time. The truth is that from the start the Polytechnic occupation became the focus of political calculation of both the Papadopoulos–Markezinis partnership and the opposition leaders. On the first day of the episode, Kanellopoulos issued a strong statement of support for the occupation of the campus: 'I declare my moral solidarity [with] ... the Greek youth [in] ... its struggle for a full victory of academic and political freedoms and of human rights which have been so cynically violated in the last few years.' Both he and Mavros visited the campus and encouraged the students to continue with the occupation and even to escalate their demands.[83] This was the opposition's best chance to present the Markezinis government as simply a continuation of the dictatorship under a pseudo-democratic mask. This attitude is common in cases of democratic transition: the encouragement of civil society to press for concessions from the regime as a means of achieving a more inclusive democracy, with free and fair elections as the starting point. The stance of the politicians during the Polytechnic days, however, has attracted criticism from regime apologists on the grounds that not only did they not intend to contribute anything positive to the 'experiment', but that apart from discrediting the *reforma* of Markezinis, their approach only resulted in further radicalizing the regime hardliners and their followers in the army, who saw the demonstrations as a reincarnation of the communist/anarchist threat against which the the army had intervened in 1967.[84] Indeed, for most mid- and lower-ranking officers, the events removed any doubts they may have had that the old devils of political unrest and 'communist subversion' were about to be unleashed under the 'Markezinis experiment'. The memories of the civil war and the turmoil of the 1960s, which renewed the military's sense of themselves as the protectors against an 'anti-national insurgency', were more than enough to align the officers with what Ioannidis was preparing.

Ironically, the Polytechnic uprising owed its inception and development to the softer approach to policing initiated by Papadopoulos and

Markezinis. Kyrkos argues that 'without the liberalisation of 1973 there could never have been the Polytechnic uprising'.[85] As there is no other indicator of the attitude of the people (e.g. opinion polls) to the *reforma*, the uprising is believed to reflect civil society's feelings through its most sensitive element, the youth. It is interesting that the main slogan of the uprising was 'down with the junta', proof that, in terms of political communication, the Markezinis government had failed miserably to convince the Greeks that this administration was *not* a continuation of the dictatorship and that it *was* committed to holding free and fair elections. At the same time, it is also notable that a popular motto of many students was 'EAM–ELAS–Polytechnic', presenting the student insurrection as a continuation of the left-wing National Liberation Front and National People's Liberation Army resistance organizations of the German occupation period and the early civil war years, thus directly linking it with the heroic and glorified past of the left in Greece.[86] However, this emphasis on a connection with EAM–ELAS alienated some of the initial support that the students had attracted from middle-class Athenians, but the most negative reaction came from the military, for whom these two organizations were anathema, convincing not only the hardliners but also many previously neutral officers that the old demons of 'communist subversion' were emerging once again. These developments played right into the hands of Ioannidis and his fellow conspirators. A traditional conservative view of the Polytechnic uprising, as presented by Averoff, emphasizes the supposed extremism of the demonstrators and the leftist slogans which scared many officers into rallying behind Ioannidis and tolerating his coup, which ultimately brought a 'worse dictatorship' into power with all the consequences that flowed from it. In an interview with the magazine *Epikaira* in May 1987, Averoff offered his analysis of events:

> As soon as the Polytechnic uprising took root, following Leninist tactics, it got manipulated by the KKE ... [T]hen the democratic mottoes turned to communist ones. Had this not happened, the Polytechnic uprising might have brought the dictatorship down. Instead, it empowered it ... because this led many junior officers (more or less disappointed by the regime) to rally around Ioannidis who was

preparing and imposed his own coup but could not do so until then. It was a worse dictatorship ... [M]any officers thought 'if just when it is becoming clear that we are heading for democracy there is an open effort to turn this into communism, then why should we allow this to happen? If power is to be instituted by [a] people's mandate, then it is fine. But if it is to be [the] power of the reds by violence, we must act.'[87]

Apart from the attitude of the military and the plans of Ioannidis, the rapid escalation of violence on the last day gave grounds for speculation about a premeditated subversion by Papadopoulos and Markezinis, who supposedly manipulated the students' uprising for their own purposes. According to Woodhouse, these clashes 'showed signs of skilful planning and direction'.[88] It is at this point that focus needs to shift to the plans and goals of Ioannidis. It has been confirmed that Ioannidis was in the vicinity of the Polytechnic on the 17th, something that cannot have been coincidental.[89] Many have since claimed that the escalation of violence on this day presented him with a 'golden opportunity' to present the demonstrations as 'communist/anarchist extremism' thus serving as a pretext for his imminent coup, which, as noted earlier, had originally been scheduled for a date between 20 November and 10 December. To further his plans, it is also argued that Ioannidis used numerous agitators in and around the Polytechnic as well as among the demonstrators.[90] A more plausible interpretation is that Ioannidis needed the escalation of violence in order to prove to those officers who were sceptical about a coup that he was right in claiming that 'law and order' had been seriously compromised by the 'experiment'.[91] The fundamental question remains as to whether Ioannidis actually needed an excuse for his coup, conscious as he was of the distaste that most of the younger hard-line officers had for Papadopoulos and the 'experiment' anyway. At most, he exploited the events to further destabilize an already troubled situation.

Whatever the plans of Ioannidis might have been, the stance of Papadopoulos also needs to be explained, especially the shift in his attitude from initial indifference to, in the end, deciding to impose martial law. Some have hypothesized that either he was aiming to get rid of Markezinis, whose 'experiment' had already stalled, and introduce another plan for his *democradura* under a new Prime Minister, or he was looking for an excuse to bring back martial law and re-establish the dictatorship. To advance his plans, he then allowed the demonstrations to escalate beyond the point where they could be managed by the police, thus requiring the deployment of the army.[92] However, this fails to explain in what way and with which actors Papadopoulos could proceed in the first case, that is, who would agree to join Papadopoulos after the Markezinis fiasco? In respect of the second scenario, a reversion to authoritarianism would make Papadopoulos a hostage to the hardliners and completely discredit him with the Greek people and the international community.[93] In short, he had to stick with Markezinis, to whom he pledged in one of their last meetings that 'whatever happens we shall remain inseparable until the end'.[94] It is therefore more plausible to conclude that, as even the KKE's report claims, Papadopoulos was seeking to present his democratic credentials to the opposition and the world as a reliable statesman who did not waver in his commitment to democratization.[95] This is accepted even by Papandreou, who claimed that 'the regime, knowing and fearing that closing the ring [on the Polytechnic] would harm its image of a new "democracy" and would thus sentence the experiment to failure, let the situation become a hostage to fortune'.[96]

Another theory presents Papadopoulos' reaction as a last desperate attempt to pre-empt the Ioannidis coup, which he feared was coming but did not know when, by calling martial law. In this scenario, Papadopoulos needed the army's intervention so as to mobilize the military units that would move to and within the Athens suburbs, putting them on alert in the hope of frustrating Ioannidis' plans. Although there is no clear evidence of Papadopoulos' intentions, a number of sources confirm that the declaration of martial law on the morning of the 17th did not make things easy for Ioannidis. In the Polytechnic trials, Ghizikis said that the ensuing state of siege was a hindrance to the plans of Ioannidis, as many army units were transferred to Athens and put on alert. Androutsopoulos agrees that the coup was made more difficult by the deployment and movement of military units within the Athens region.⁹⁷ None the less, these efforts ultimately failed due to Ioannidis' meticulous organization of the coup.

Finally, the role of the opposition politicians Kanellopoulos and Mavros must be considered. Markezinis believed that the Polytechnic episode witnessed a convergence of interests from two opposite positions. On one side, the hardliners wanted to put an end to his government and the *reforma*. On the other side, the ex-politicians, with Kanellopoulos and Mavros in the forefront, sought to discredit his 'experiment' and prevent elections at any cost. Was this convergence deliberate? Markezinis does not clearly answer this question, but seems to hint that it was a natural consequence of the attitudes of the groups concerned. He certainly had no doubt that 'the escalation of violence in the Polytechnic had the goal of cancelling the press conference'.⁹⁸ Theodorakopoulos also aligns himself with the opinion of regime apologists: '[T]he students had played straight into the hands of Ioannidis [sic], who looked upon the coming elections with a jaundiced eye. So had the irresponsible statements of Kanellopoulos and Mavros, two vain self-seeking men.'⁹⁹ This implies a plan that evolved in those crucial few days which had as its goal the fall of the Markezinis government and the halting of the 'experiment'. This conspiracy theory has gained some credibility from the observations of the British ambassador on these events:

> It is not yet clear what part if any the former parliamentary opposition has taken in the organisation of the demonstrations or to what extent they are responsible for the direction these have taken. However they have openly encouraged the students, knowing that this could lead to violence, and in private claim credit for what has happened. They have made use of the students in pursuing their deliberate policy of trying to provoke the government into repressive action which would put an end to the Markezinis programme. They have in large measure got what they wanted and must now accept responsibility for their actions ... At the same time, those hard-line elements who were opposed from the start to democratisation have been presented with the opportunity to say 'we told you so'.¹⁰⁰

Konstantopoulos fully endorses that conspiracy theory:

> The instigators of the trouble in the Polytechnic made three mistaken calculations: 1. That Markezinis would resign thus causing a political impasse and chaos; but he did not. Instead he agreed on the declaration of martial law. 2. They did not think that the declaration of martial law was possible. They thought the President would not proceed to such a decisive action; but he did. 3. They thought that a large scale popular support [for] ... the demonstrations was possible, convinced by their illusions; but the public keeps afar from revolutions and bloodshed. Because of those three mistakes the revolt failed.[101]

Ironically, this article was published on the 25th, the day of the Ioannidis coup. It is also worth noting Makarezos' views on Karamanlis and the Polytechnic. In his alleged letter to Makarezos after the Ioannidis coup, Karamanlis blamed the Polytechnic events on the 'old politicians' failure to condemn the extremism of the demonstrators around the Polytechnic on the 16th, having given their blessing to the demonstrations earlier, thus helping escalate tensions. Makarezos also remarked that Karamanlis did not think much of the Polytechnic uprising, as he didn't take part in its celebration and he also called the first transition election on the first anniversary of the events, that is, 17 November 1974. In fact, Karamanlis made no statements about the uprising at all.[102] The silence of the leader of the right and main protagonist of the actual transition to democracy, as well as the left-wing character ascribed to the uprising, reinforced by the absence of centre or right-wing student organizations, pushed much of the traditional right wing towards a cautiously critical if not entirely negative view of the Polytechnic uprising, thus allowing the various left-wing parties ample space to endorse and exploit it post-1974. As Averoff proclaimed, 'I deeply and sincerely honour the initiative of the young people who started this [the uprising]. But I am not willing to support the institutionalisation of a false myth based on dangerous slogans and non-existent "many victims."'[103]

The Polytechnic uprising is an example of the detrimental effects that a combination of unpredicted random events (*fortuna*)[104] can have on a delicate and tentative process such as a transition from authoritarian rule, especially in the context of a regime still going strong and refusing to give ground to civilian rule. The fact is that, as Ghizikis said in the Polytechnic trials, 'the Polytechnic events can best be described as something that cropped up out of chance but did serve the purpose of another plan that was premeditated'.[105] This is the most accurate description of the difficult and complex situation the Markezinis government had to deal with, which it did in a very clumsy way from the start (by not granting the students' demand for elections) to the finish (by accounting for the 'enemies of democracy'). The possible exploitation of the uprising by Ioannidis, and Papadopoulos' hasty reaction to it with the declaration of martial law, took the situation beyond the control of Markezinis and his government and significantly contributed to the initial sense of relief and welcoming of Ioannidis' coup by many people who simply did not understand what it was really about. The diverse range of actors and goals in the Polytechnic events further illustrates the complexity of the situation: there were the students, themselves divided by party affiliation and ideology; Markezinis, single-mindedly obsessed with the interview he was preparing and side-lined almost from the start, though charged with the bloodshed too because of his infamous conference; the opposition politicians, trying to discredit the 'experiment' and thus supporting the campus occupation; Papadopoulos, at first hoping to get some democratic credit for allowing the demonstrations and occupation, but then using the escalation as a pretext to check Ioannidis' moves in the army; and finally, Ioannidis himself and his exploitation of the events for his coup.

The Polytechnic events have also been used in democratization literature as an exemplar for a transition from authoritarianism that can move into reverse. According to Huntington, 'a limited opening could raise expectations of further change that could lead to instability, upheaval, and even violence; these, in turn, provoke an antidemocratic reaction and replacement of liberalizing leadership with standpatter leaders'.[106] As for the ideological aspect of the uprising, a lot can be said, since it can be linked to the post-1974 (re)presentation of both the dictatorship and the events themselves. As Kornetis points out, 'the Polytechnic was memorialized as the major act of resistance during the seven years of authoritarianism, thus serving as one of the founding myths of the post-1974 Greek Republic. In many respects, the Polytechnic was used to whitewash the lack of systematic dissent against the dictatorial regime of the colonels.'[107] Mitsos considers the uprising 'a constitutive moment in modern Greek history, one that cannot be obliterated or downgraded by any means on the basis of what followed'.[108] In general, the left-wing idealization of the Polytechnic insurrection as the event that brought down Papadopoulos fails to appreciate that 'by themselves, students do not bring down regimes'.[109]

In the minds most prone to conspiracy, the Polytechnic events also have a connection with the international dimension of the 'experiment', as its main protagonist himself has made this association: Markezinis claimed that the Polytechnic served as 'the pretext for Ioannidis and his group to topple Papadopoulos, [at] *America'*[*s*] *suggestion*, and install a new tyrannical regime that led to [the] Cyprus tragedy'.[110] The fact that in one of the first works published after the events, just two years later, Grigoriadis felt it necessary to devote considerable space to analysing and criticising many of the conspiracy theories about the Polytechnic uprising relects an ideological conviction, which has long outlived the actual *Metapolitefsi*, that there was more to this episode than met the eye. Among the theories that Grigoriadis considers is one that links the uprising to American interests that were eager to topple Papadopoulos at any cost, thus (ab)using the Polytechnic students – and the CIA – to that end.[111] The widespread acceptance by many Greeks – not all necessarily regime apologists – of a link between the uprising and a decision by the Americans to topple Papadopoulos and stop the 'experiment' before it could fully develop reflects both a superficial reading of history and a readiness to make a scapegoat of foreign influences.

6

The Americans Yet Again? The International Factor and the 'Experiment'

It was not the Polytechnic uprising that brought me down; rather, it was Kissinger.

Markezinis, interview in *Kathimerini*, 21 February 1993

Disillusionment has grown from our previous association with the Papadopoulos regime, intensified by the widespread belief that the CIA was involved in the November 25 coup and that the United States favours the present regime.

Foreign Relations of United States, Vol. XXX, 'Action Memorandum: US Policy toward Greece'

The failed *reforma* of Papadopoulos and Markezinis had an international dimension which has either been almost neglected since or overexaggerated in conspiracy theories by apologists of the regime. According to the latter, the main instigator of the failure of the 'experiment' and of the hardliners' counter-coup was the USA, the reason for that being the refusal of Papadopoulos and Markezinis to grant the Americans' request for facilities for the US Navy and Air Force, which was of critical importance in their support of Israel during the Yom Kippur War of 1973. One theory has it that this refusal enraged US Secretary of State Henry Kissinger, who triggered the toppling of the Greek government agents close to the regime – Ioannidis and his hardliners. Some scholars still accept this version of events.[1] Apart from the obvious instrumentalist interpretation of US–Greek relations that this theory is based on, the plausibility of which needs to be checked against the available facts, the international dimension to the failed transition is also connected to the European Community, whose support Markezinis attempted to attract for his 'experiment' as well as, to a lesser extent, the Cyprus issue and its legacy for the short-lived *reforma*. In order to properly understand the international context of the 'experiment', consideration has to be given to the foreign relations and policies of the regime from its inception until 1973 as a prelude to an account of the elites' and counter-elites' manoeuvring during the short-lived Markezinis government.

The 1967 'wrong coup' and the US

Speculation about American interference in the 1967 coup 'has penetrated deeply into Greek society, and has ... also taken root in the Greek "psyche"'.[2] It is widely believed that such a transformation towards authoritarianism in Greece could never have succeeded without US support, if not inspiration, given the position of the country in the Western world during the Cold War and the influences exerted by the Americans in Greek politics in the late 1940s and early 1950s. However, there is little hard evidence to substantiate such a thesis. Although US intelligence services were well informed about the main conspiratorial factions behind the coup[3] and the US Embassy had concerns about the real possibility of EK winning the elections to be held in May, desirous of at least limiting any winning margin, both the Embassy and the State Department were also opposed to the prospective of a military coup which, however, they expected to be launched by the Generals. The State Department had indeed instructed its ambassador, Philips Talbot, 'to make clear to all parts that a deviation from democratic norms would not be tolerated by the US administration.[4]

According to witnesses and reports, both the US ambassador in Athens and the head of the CIA mission in Greece, as well as his deputy, were taken by surprise on the morning of 21 April.[5] Weiner notes that 'the colonels had taken the CIA by surprise. "The only time I saw [CIA head] Helms really angry was when the Greek colonels' coup took place in 1967,' said the veteran analyst and current-intelligence chief Dick Lehman.[6] And, as Deputy Secretary of State Department George Battle recalls, 'we had enough indications that we should expect a coup, we knew of a plan for a coup. But we had not been forewarned about the coup that actually happened ... [E]ven if we [had known] ... that it would happen, I do not know what we could have done.'[7] According to some reports, the coup was much more welcomed in the Pentagon than in the State Department.[8] Nevertheless, US officials in Athens were cold towards the colonels, to the point that they had Pattakos say to Talbot, 'just have in mind that we are on your side whether you like us or not.'[9] In the first days after the coup, Talbot cabled Washington with the suggestion that US policy towards the new government should be 'fairly starchy'. Nevertheless, many American diplomats had considerable reservations about how far a negative reaction to the regime should go.[10] American diplomats were also anxious about the chaos that would presumably prevail in Greece if the colonels' regime should suddenly collapse.[11] It should also be borne in mind that the coincidence of the Six-Day War in the Middle East provided an excellent opportunity for the regime to confirm to the US its pro-NATO credentials while using the Arab–Israeli conflict as a protective shield against any outside initiatives that might destabilize it in those difficult first days.[12]

Therefore, once the coup did prevail, there was little the US could do if it did not want to seriously upset the balance of power in the Eastern Mediterranean and on NATO's southern flank. There were basically two options for the American foreign policy makers: either press the colonels to withdraw, making way for a transitional government, by such means as the suspension of military aid, the recalling of the US ambassador and the issuing of anti-regime statements in Washington; or maintain a neutral position, not granting recognition to the junta but at the same time not publicly denouncing it, in the hope that this might lead to the restoration of constitutional order. This was what Woodhouse described as the 'support of toleration'.[13] However, as far as Greeks were concerned, this toleration looked more like complicity in the dictatorship, if not the instigation of it. This feeling is reflected in most reports and analyses of the attitudes of the Greek people towards the US[14] and was accentuated by the ruse applied by the colonels themselves, who 'encouraged their wavering colleagues by propagating rumours of American complicity in order to secure wider support. Officers who looked to the United States for signs of active disapproval were disappointed and therefore discouraged to oppose the military regime.'[15] In the interregnum between April and the failed counter-coup in December, the US supported King Constantine's attempt to overthrow the colonels. The King himself visited Washington in September, when he obtained President Johnson's agreement to his move.[16] The failure of his December counter-coup, however, and the fact that the colonels were now on their own, created a situation that the Americans could not ignore: they had to accept the situation and deal with the regime.

The regime and the international factor: European isolation and US support

The US administration was reluctant to exert significant pressure on the regime, since it served American strategic interests in a way that would be hard for a civilian government to do without facing serious questions, if not opposition. US military interests in the region included maintaining its bases on Greek soil 'in a relatively unencumbered style', as well having 'unrestricted military transit and overflight rights over Greek territory and seas for American and NATO forces'. America's diplomatic and economic interests primarily concerned maintaining Greek–Turkish relations at a friendly level so as not to endanger the cohesiveness of NATO's southeastern flank; in relation to the Cyprus issue, the search for a solution that 'would not endanger America's presence in the Greek–Turkish territorial nexus'; and finally, the maintenance of a positive climate for American investment and trade in the country.[17]

All these foreign policy goals were met during the dictatorship years, which made it quite difficult for any groups who wanted the US administration to use its influence on the colonels to step down. It is generally accepted that the military regime was very accommodating to American interests. In this respect the colonels were much like similar regimes, which, 'lacking adequate domestic popular support, would be more dependent on outside powers for a semblance of legitimacy, if not for their outright survival. The greater this dependency, the greater would be their willingness to solicit external interference and to offer the best possible terms to their external supporters.'[18] However, as a first step in pushing the regime towards a restoration of democracy, the US administration announced in the summer of 1967 an embargo on heavy weapons supplies to Greece. This would include artillery, tanks, combat aircraft and certain types of warships. The embargo, however, was partly lifted in the spring of 1968 and became inoperative in 1969, although it remains debatable whether it actually harmed the regime's arsenal.[19]

The victory of Richard Nixon in 1968 marked a turning point in US-junta relations, as his administration 'was far more supportive of the Papadopoulos government than the Johnson administration'.[20] Although he initially succumbed to pressures at home, only appointing a new ambassador a year after the departure of Talbot, while the US Embassy remained closed for a month at the end of 1969, a record period,[21] the appointment of Henry Tasca as ambassador signalled a radical change in American relations with the regime. In fact, from 1969 until 1973 the US would be the regime's most reliable supporter: apart from lifting the arms embargo, it signed numerous military and trade treaties and cynically abstained from any diplomatic effort to isolate the colonels or pursue them on alleged abuses of human rights. Last but not least, American pressure for the restoration of democracy would be limited. In Stavrou's opinion, US spokesmen adopted the cynical principle that 'we deal with governments as they are, and we do not care what their political system is', which in practice meant little pressure was put on the regime to make democratic concessions.[22] This cynical attitude was also expressed by US Admiral Elmo Zumwalt, who 'regarded the junta in Athens as an opportunity for closer ties between Greece and the US, rather than as a stumbling block. Once the junta took over, from a military point of view we were more secure in Greece. In the 1970s, we didn't think about [the morality of doing business with the junta] at all.'[23] There were many exchange visits between Greek and American diplomatic and military delegations,[24] culminating in the visit of US Vice-President Spiro Agnew (who was of Greek ancestry) to Athens in October 1971. This was considered a great diplomatic success for the regime at the time, confirming the presumed unconditional support of US and rumoured to be the prelude to the signing of a US–Greek homeporting facilities agreement, which had been sought by America for some time. Again, a report on this particular matter by the Congressional Sub-committee for European Affairs, drawn up in April 1972, highlighted the clash between democratic principles and diplomatic interests, stressing the danger of allowing military and strategic calculations to prevail over political values – a major problem in US policy making in respect of Greece.[25] Yet, as long as the regime seemed to serve US interests, political values were sidelined in preference for diplomatic and strategic gains.

It was not quite as simple as that, though. There are indications that not everything was harmonious in relations between the US and the regime, which began to show signs of taking a relatively independent course from the US after 1970. The turning point in that year was the death of Foreign Minister Pipinelis. He was succeeded by Papadopoulos, who applied his own, distinctive approach to the regime's foreign policy. He gradually made openings to the Soviet bloc and to non-aligned countries (relations between Greece and the Soviet satellite states were not as cold as one might expect, given the anti-communism of the regime),[26] as well as recognizing communist China in 1973 (making Greece only the second Western country after the US to establish diplomatic relations with the People's Republic). Greece had been prompted to normalize relations with its Balkan neighbours in the 1960s in the context of the emerging spirit of detente and the West's new, more flexible, bridge-building policy towards the East, but no concrete moves had been made by 1967, and it was the dictatorship that applied a new policy in this area.[27] Moreover, during this period, Greece began to buy arms from countries other than the US, and in 1973 refused American military aid for the first time since 1947. It also initiated a rapprochement with the EEC, beginning in 1972. At that time the EEC 'provided 55% of Greece's total imports and took 61% of its total exports'.[28] Those foreign policy moves, according to some (mainly pro-regime) accounts, made some US policy makers consider alternatives for the future governance of Greece. For example, George Georgalas, advisor to Papadopoulos and Peripheral Director of Crete at the time, recalls that during Agnew's visit to Crete he was approached about taking 'part in an "anti-Papadopoulos government"' along with other members of the regime.[29]

Nevertheless, and despite any reservations America might have about him, Papadopoulos signed an agreement in January 1973 for the homeporting of the 6th US Fleet in Greek territorial waters for a period of five years, which had been a long-time goal of the US administration. According to Woodhouse, 'the various ports around Athens could now be called "the American Navy's largest home port of in Europe"', and that this was perhaps the junta's 'finest hour'.[30] However, by the summer of 1973 a US National Intelligence report observed that

> In this regime's early years in power, the appearance of US support was more important to Papadopoulos than it is today. The regime no longer sees such a compelling need to accommodate US desires. There will be frictions arising from the proposed major expansion of US military facilities in Greece.[31]

The most explicitly anti-regime attitude was adopted by European countries, which repeatedly expressed their opposition to the dictatorship, resulting in a long period of isolation of Greece from its European nexus and the suspension of Greece's treaties of association with the EEC. The country also lost the benefit of a considerable development loan from the EEC, which was withdrawn in October

1967 because of the political situation. The message was clear: only if Greece returned to democracy would it be accepted into the process of European integration. Yet, by that time Greece had already absorbed a large part of the loan before it was withdrawn, and in the next few years the regime proved that it could find alternative sources of funding for guaranteeing short-term prosperity and economic growth, with much of the finance coming from Western European sources.[32] The relevance of the EEC and Western Europe in general to the restoration of democracy in Greece therefore relates more to the political than the material and economic sphere.

In most West European and Scandinavian countries, committees were set up to lobby their governments to adopt policies of non-cooperation with the regime while expressing solidarity with the Greek people. This relentless anti-regime stance culminated in the dramatic withdrawal of Greece from the Council of Europe in December 1969 after its delegation faced serious accusations of human rights abuses including the use of torture in prisons.[33] The governments of many NATO countries also tried to have the Greek issue discussed at various meetings and summits, only to meet with the stubborn refusal of the US to cooperate.[34] For a number of years no Western European official visited Greece, which now experienced, in Averoff's words, 'an international isolation such as we have not had since 1920–22'.[35] European solidarity on this matter, however, was a facade, for as Woodhouse points out, individual states 'typically displayed a greater interest in promoting their economic agendas and self-interests vis-à-vis the largely untapped Greek market than in denouncing human rights abuses by the regime in Athens'.[36] In 1972, signs of a change in European attitudes towards the dictatorship began to appear, with France taking the lead. In February of that year its Deputy Foreign Minister, Lipovski, became the first member of a European government to visit Greece since 1967. His visit concluded with Greece ordering weapons and equipment from France.[37] Other Western European countries were also interested in selling arms to Greece, confirming Treholt's jusgement that

[T]he many powerful verbal reactions [of European countries] have not been followed up on a practical political level with regard to matters such as a boycott of trade, investment and military cooperation, the essential preconditions for the survival of any regime. It seems quite clear that an attitude of strong moral condemnation has not been an obstacle to close co-operation in many fields ... Moral indignation has never been allowed to affect the self-interest of the countries involved.[38]

The change in European attitudes would become more obvious in 1973. At the start of the year, as the UK ambassador noted in his annual report, the regime's main problem in foreign relations was the EEC:

There is little prospect of the present Greek Government coming up with anything which the EEC ... could accept as adequate evidence of a change of heart, and less still of their accepting of their own volition constitutional changes leading to anything which anyone in the West would seriously call democracy ... The Community has in its gift something which the regime badly wants and needs.... So long as the present regime remains in power substantially unchanged ... Greece's present political stagnation and isolation from Europe will continue.[39]

As Pesmazoglou points out, the Mediterranean policies of the EEC, as well as giving preferential status to other developing countries, stressed the need to upgrade EEC-Greek relations: there was widespread fear of the danger of marginalizing Greece, which could be relegated to being just one of the many Mediterranean partners of an enlarged Community.[40]

Cyprus and the dictatorship

Another crucial issue that had a bearing on both the internal affairs and external relations of the regime was Cyprus. The uneasy coexistence between the Greek-Cypriot and Turkish-Cypriot communities that had been restored on the island by the 1960 independence treaty was frequently interrupted by violent clashes, which had brought Greece and Turkey to the brink of armed conflict on more than one occasion in the early 1960s. Such a crisis occurred again in November 1967. After negotiations, an agreement was reached, as a result of which a Greek division that had been sent to Cyprus three years earlier by the Papandreou government was now withdrawn to mainland Greece at the end of the month. This provided only a temporary calm, however, as radical nationalist elements in Cyprus and Greece pledged themselves to achieve *Enosis* (union) between the two countries, to which Cypriot president Archbishop Makarios was opposed. It has been suggested that US policy regarding Cyprus was dictated by its desire to obtain naval and radar facilities on the island that could be used to monitor Soviet naval activity in the Mediterranean, as well as keep a close eye on the Middle East, especially after the 1967 Six-Day War. This has led some to argue that there was a convergence of interest between Greek hardliners, anti-Makarios Cypriots and the US government in removing the Archbishop from office, even by means of a coup. However, while there is no hard evidence of collusion between the US and anti-Makarios elements in Greece and Cyprus,[41] there was certainly a conspiracy by Greek and Greek Cypriot army officers against Makarios, accusing him of dropping the idea of *Enosis* as a possible option to resolve the Cyprus question. They were joined by the ex-leader of the anti-colonial struggle General Georgios Grivas, who had become a virulent opponent of Makarios and had returned to the island from mainland Greece in late 1970. Tension between Makarios' supporters and opponents, as well as between the two ethnic communities, was now reaching dangerous levels.

In March 1970, an attempt was made against Makarios' life. Most of the regime leaders, as well as extreme nationalist officers, would have been glad to have had Makarios toppled and *Enosis* declared, but Papadopoulos was reluctant to follow such a radical path. He appeared to favour a settlement between Greece and Turkey that would restore peace to the island, informing the Turkish daily *Millet* in an interview in 1971 of his belief that 'the two countries should convince our communities [in Cyprus] that we are not disposed to spoil the relations between us and quarrel for their sake; consequently they should settle their differences'.[42] According to Haralambis, this opposition to the plans of the ultras 'was a sign of the strategy that the dictatorship under Papadopoulos was not willing to follow'.[43] Papadopoulos has been accused of being part of a US-inspired conspiracy to bring down Makarios, therefore 'it was necessary for him to neutralise Makarios, as a step to a permanent settlement of the Cyprus issue, which would be his contribution to the attempt of the US to calm the Mediterranean'.[44] However, there is no proof of such a plan; on the contrary, despite many conspiracies against him, Makarios did not in fact face a Greek-inspired attempt to overthrow him between 1968 and 1973. In any case, Papadopoulos 'could not risk the consequences of a coup in Cyprus'.[45]

In early 1973, Makarios gained another five-year term as President of Cyprus, but had to face significant opposition from other Cypriot bishops, who accused him of abusing his religious and secular power, as well as from the Cypriot National Guard and Greek officers stationed on the island. There were frequent skirmishes between pro- and anti-Makarios groups, and in August a plan for a coup against Makarios was revealed in the press.[46] Papadopoulos spoke on the radio a few days later, expressing his concern about the situation and calling on the pro-Grivas groups to stop undermining Makarios.[47] A US National Intelligence report in July remarked that

> [Papadopoulos] helped to keep the Cyprus situation from breaking into flames, even though some of Papadopoulos's colleagues incline toward drastic initiatives. No Greek government is likely to be more moderate over Cyprus than the present one ... Under the rigidly controlled political conditions in Athens, political figures cannot make headlines by inflammatory declarations on Cyprus. Papadopoulos has made it perfectly clear that Greek–Turkish hostilities over Cyprus would be in the interests of neither country.[48]

The Markezinis government and the international factor

The first sign of a positive stance on Papadopoulos' *dictablanda* by foreign states came with his declaration of the 'Republic' in June. As Woodhouse notes, 'the foreign reaction to the constitutional upheaval was surprisingly favourable. Nowhere was any question raised of ... de jure [recognition] of the new Republic.'[49] Early in the summer, the British ambassador argued that it was in the interests of both the UK and the EEC to offer cautious support for the admittedly slow and limited progress towards democratization that was now underway:

> If the regime fulfill their timetable for elections and if these provide an opportunity, even if only a limited one, for the expression of popular will, then British interests may lie in supporting within the community the unfreezing ... of the Association agreement. Meanwhile, Britain and Western Europe are more likely to preserve their interests here ... by a quiet policy of wait-and-see rather than by public expressions of skepticism about the intentions of the Greek Republic and its masters. The July Plebiscite met, as expected, with the criticism of almost all foreign governments and their diplomats in Athens as rigged and only to a limited extent representative of the will of the people.[50]

The US report noted previously (from June) listed the criteria that Western democratic states would expect Papadopoulos to commit himself to, in relation to the 'free and fair' elections, including the

> ... [a]bsence of restrictions on the formation of political parties; absence of restrictions on personal participation in such political parties as are organized; complete lifting of martial law in the Athens area; freedom of the press to discuss fully all relevant aspects of plebiscite and election issues; release of numerous persons opposed to [the] regime whose 'crime' is that they wanted democracy in Greece; willingness to permit free observation of campaigning and discussion during [the] periods preceding [the] plebiscite and [the] elections.[51]

The US, however, appeared more interested in Greece's strategic partnership with NATO than in its democratization, as Acting Secretary of State Rush reported to President Nixon that the persecution of anti-regime officers after the failed coup 'raises questions as to future Greek effectiveness in NATO. It introduces a divisive issue in NATO, after a period when the "Greek question" has eased off.' At the same time, Rush doubted 'whether Papadopoulos intends to, and is able to, honor his pledge to hold elections in 1974' and acknowledged that the US would not have a clear picture of the way things were going in Greece until Papadopoulos started working out the election process.[52]

The British embassy also put the July plebiscite under scrutiny, observing the process in 30 selected polling stations in the Athens suburbs and in the countryside. A report on the voting process spoke of fraud:

> [Evidence shows] that rigging the result by one means or another ... was widespread, but also, incidentally, that the difference between the published results for the urban centres and those for the countryside does not stem from a higher level of government support in the latter, but from the amount of coercion applied and the degree of rigging that could stably be carried on.[53]

Even before Markezinis took office, he attempted to fashion a positive international image by giving interviews to various, mainly European, media. His son-in-law also claims that Markezinis received an invitation to visit the USSR from the Soviet leader Brezhnev which, if true, would not only have been the first time a Greek PM was invited to Moscow, but also a spectacular development in Greece's foreign relations in the setting of the Cold War.[54] There was little doubt that Markezinis' media strategy and increased public profile was principally designed to impress the EEC, and in this respect it might be considered a success, as Europeans generally seemed to adopt a less adversarial attitude towards the Greek regime. Markezinis had previously had close links to some European leaders, such as Germany's ex-Chancellor Adenauer, which was undoubtedly of value to him, and European diplomats even began to sound guardedly optimistic about the Greek Prime Minister. Barkman was of the opinion that 'it would be wise for Greece's NATO partners and the EC member states to adopt a cautiously positive attitude with regard to this development and that businesslike contacts with the new Greek government on a ministerial level should not be excluded'. He also felt that the government declaration exuded 'a positive, decisive and pragmatic spirit'.[55] A British diplomat reported that

> The so-called Markezinis experiment is the most encouraging development in Greece for some years, not least in the evidence it provides of the limitations on Papadopoulos's power. While it may well founder for reasons beyond our control it could stand a better chance of leading to a more acceptable form of government in Greece if it were to be given greater support from other governments than it has received so far ... If we can go some way towards supporting Mr Markezinis, on the grounds that there has already been positive progress, without creating strong criticism in Parliament, there appear to be sound reasons for doing so.[56]

Likewise, another British diplomat reported that the US embassy appeared positive about the experiment:

> Mr Tasca indicated his approval of Papadopoulos' decision to ask Markezinis to form a government. He thought that foreign countries should, as far as possible, give Papadopoulos encouragement ... [H]e was critical of [the old politicians'] generally unconstructive attitude and said he doubted whether even Karamanlis now was of much importance. [He said that] Dr Kissinger would now send instructions and that they would be in the direction of non-intervention in Greek internal affairs ... Mr Tasca's disenchantment with the regime has passed out and ... he has recommended to Washington that Papadopoulos should be given a fair wind and allowed time to carry through his constitutional programme.[57]

As soon as Markezinis took office, he was inundated by messages of goodwill from abroad: congratulations from US President Nixon and his ambassador in Athens, Tasca; the UK ambassador Sir Robin Hooper bore a warm message from PM Edward Heath; and the West German ambassador brought a similar message from Chancellor Willy Brandt. Tasca suggested to the US State Department the drafting of a welcoming statement on the formation of Markezinis' government, in which the Department would 'wish President Papadopoulos and Prime Minister Markezinis every success in this endeavour' and which could be 'expanded to take into account any praiseworthy statement Markezinis makes regarding elections'.[58] The *New York Times* noted that 'for the first time after six and a half years Greece has a government relieved from the military and an efficient politician, appreciated even by his political rivals, as Prime Minister'.[59] Miller argues that the prospect of free elections under a Markezinis government 'reawakened Tasca's dream of carrying Greece back to democratic government through the mediation of Papadopoulos'.[60] Among those who sent congratulations to Markezinis were a number of non-aligned and Eastern bloc leaders, such as Tito of Yugoslavia, Boumedienne of Algeria and Ceausescu of Rumania. Markezinis was always keen to open up Greece, and the Western world in general, to non-Western and non-aligned countries,[61] and was also supportive of detente between the Western and Eastern blocs, occasionally expressing quite radical views on the need for US–Soviet rapprochement. As to the Soviet attitude to the 'experiment', the previously cited US State Department telegram expected Moscow to 'sit back, let Papadopoulos' normalization plans run their course, and urge [the] broadest possible (i.e. communist or more realistically communist front) participation in an effort to exploit [the] return to political processes and so enhance [the] Soviets' own long range interests'.[62] On 10 November it was announced that Rumanian President Ceausescu was to visit Greece between the 21st and 24th of that month, which would be the first visit by a Warsaw Pact leader to Greece. It was cancelled, however, due to the Polytechnic disturbances.[63]

For the short lifespan of his 'experiment', Markezinis was quite active in the field of foreign policy, and in particular on the issue of Cyprus. It is hardly a coincidence that the first (and last) non-Greek statesman he met with was Archbishop Makarios. Grigoriadis notes that with the formation of the Markezinis government, the subversive activities of the pro-regime elements were brought to a end.[64] On 6 November, Makarios stopped over in Athens for a few hours on his way to Malta. Markezinis welcomed him and they had a long talk, at which for the first time no military leaders were present. As Grigoriadis concludes, 'it seemed that the Markezinis government was opening a new phase in ... Greek–Cypriot relations. But perhaps this was one more reason for the forces preparing [their] ... subversion not to allow it to last long.'[65]

Again, Papadopoulos' intentions would have aroused suspicion if not objections from the Europeans as to just how democratic his reforms might be. Nevertheless, the EEC still expected the duo at the head of the government to live up to their promises. And yet, the negative reaction of the opposition did not go unnoticed in the diplomatic circles of Athens and added to the reservations that some diplomats were expressing about the viability of the 'experiment', something that worried Markezinis, who was conscious of the 'non-responsive attitude of many European governments to his openings'.[66] For instance, a British diplomat in Athens in early November remarked on the attitude of the opposition, that 'hesitant politicians should be encouraged to try out the Markezinis experiment not in order to demonstrate that it is a sham, but in order to see whether it is, or can be turned to, a reality ... If this opportunity for politicking is passed up, another may not occur in their active lifetimes.'[67] However, this opinion was not shared by all British diplomats in Athens. According to Nafpliotis, the head of the British Foreign Office's Southern European Department, Goodison, 'based on the Greek PM's radically democratic moves after the 20 September meeting, was favouring a more encouraging and less cautious attitude towards Greece'. The British ambassador in Athens, Hooper, on the other hand, 'no doubt influenced by the reluctance of the vast majority of the opposition to participate in future elections or give Markezinis the benefit of the doubt was of the opinion that Britain should stick firmly to the line that the Greek government should be judged by its actions, not its promises'.[68] Because the 'experiment' was so short-lived, it has been speculated that 'depending on the degree of participation in the elections and on the democratic quality of the process, the EEC could accept a post-electoral upgrading of relations with Greece, thus supporting the new, even limited democracy, but at the same time pushing it to a gradual further liberalisation'.[69] Markezinis, for his part, had the major goal of restoring 'the Treaty of Association with the EEC to full operation, but that would become possible only after the conduct of "impeccable elections"'.[70]

But Markezinis was not the only one who was seeking support from the EEC. As Whitehead correctly states, 'the enlistment of international support will be a high priority for many of the parties engaged in the transition process'.[71] At the same time, the ex-politicians tried to discredit the *reforma* in the eyes of the world with critical statements and interviews, as they were doing in the domestic arena in order to influence Greek opinion (which they were successful in doing). Here they ignored the warnings they had received from European ambassadors, Barkmann, for example, recalling that Kannellopoulos had been given this message. Europe's diplomats also cautioned the Greek opposition that their negative attitude made no sense as long as there was no alternative to Markezinis, which did cause a few of the politicians to pause for thought.

Barkman recorded in his diary that just a few days after the formation of the Markezinis government, he had a visit from Mavros, who had recently returned from a trip to Western Europe and 'was afraid that the European Community would consider reviving the Association Agreement with Greece'. He added that the Markezinis government and the one that would be installed after the elections 'would be nothing but a tool in the hands of Papadopoulos' and feared that 'a more forthcoming attitude of the EC after the elections would probably be unavoidable'.[72] Still, as Barkman also noted, the European Community ambassadors in Athens, at one of their tactical meetings, had agreed that 'the leaders of the ERE and the Centre Union would not act in the best interests of Greek democracy if they were to abstain from the general elections. For once the political process is started, even imperfectly, it will gather momentum and the dictatorship will be destroyed, unless another coup d'etat should prevent this from happening. Kanellopoulos and Mavros are asking more than can be realistically obtained – and most of us have told them so.'[73] There is no noticeable difference in the US attitude towards the opponents of the government, as the British ambassador reported to the Foreign Office that 'like us the Americans are irritated by the irresponsible and unconstructive attitude of most of the opposition'.[74]

The Yom Kippur War and the 'experiment'

In terms of the international context, the 'Markezinis experiment' could not have started its life in less auspicious circumstances. Just the day before he took office on 7 October, the Yom Kippur War broke out with a joint Egyptian and Syrian force attacking against Israel. In the first few days, an Israeli collapse seemed inevitable, but the Israeli army, recovering from the initial shock, halted the Arab advance, counter-attacked and invaded both countries, reaching the Suez Canal before the end of the month and stopping about 100 km from Cairo. The United Nations, concerned by an escalation in tension between the US and the USSR, imposed a cease-fire on all the belligerents and prevented a further deterioration in the international climate. However, it could not stop the oil shock and the international economic recession.

At the outset, the Americans urgently needed to supply Israel with weapons and material to prevent the feared collapse of its army. For this reason they had to use their bases in Europe to operate an air bridge for the constant flow of supplies. However, they met with blanket refusal by the European states to allow them the use of their airspace. The Greek government also denied the Americans use of Greek airspace and territorial waters. Just days after he had taken office, Greek Foreign Minister Christos Palamas said 'the friendly relations of Greece with the Arab countries exclude any participation, either direct or indirect, in actions against them … [T]he Greek sea and air space is not to be used for any action that has to do with the war situation in the Middle East.[75] On 21 November, he handed to Markezinis the US demand for use of the airfields of Eleusis near Athens and Souda in Crete by the US Air Force. Markezinis said he would resign if the demand was accepted. Papadopoulos agreed and is reported to have called the Americans 'gangsters'.[76] However, eventually the US Navy and Air Force did make use of Greek airspace and bases, with the official government said to have been sidelined by certain high-ranking officers, such as the head of the Hellenic Navy, Admiral Arapakis. In his memoirs, Arapakis records a meeting with US Admiral Zumwalt, in which he agreed to allow the US fleet the use of its facilities in Greece, especially their big base at Souda. Arapakis added that the government was not aware of this arrangement, and Markezinis later recalled his surprise when he received a thank-you note in November from the commander of US forces in the Mediterranean.[77] The government had been totally outflanked by one of its own commanders (it appears that no one in the army was aware of Arapakis' initiative either). The official position of the Greek government in relation to the war was one of full neutrality, following Markezinis' statement after taking office that 'many ties connect us with the Arab countries, but nothing divides us from the state of Israel, which has also the right to have a place under the sun'.[78] Only what was already covered by the homeporting agreement of January would be operational in these circumstances. Any amendment to this agreement could only be authorized by the cabinet that would take office after the elections. Kissinger has confirmed this position in his memoirs, mentioning Palamas' announcement on 13 October that '"US bases have nothing to do with the Arab–Israeli war" (October 13 happened to be the start of our all-out airlift)'.[79] However, the US administration acknowledged the help it received from the Greek government:

> Publicly, the former Greek government under President Papadopoulos adopted a slightly pro Arab posture during the recent war ... The government was, however, privately helpful to the United States in a variety of ways ... [T]hey allowed us use of Souda Bay airfield, to a

much greater extent and for different purposes than is called for in our bilateral agreement. Souda Bay proved vital to the U.S. Navy for re-supplying the Sixth Fleet. Moreover, the Greeks placed no restrictions on: (1) the Sixth Fleet's access to Greek ports; (2) the activities of the U.S. Naval Communications Station at Nea Makri; (3) the USAF facility at Iraklion, Crete.[80]

Furthermore, as a State Department dispatch to the US Embassy in Athens acknowledged, extensive use of Greek facilities by the US Air Force in order to resupply Israel 'would seem directly to contradict [the] G[overnment] o[f] G[reece]'s recent restatement on [the] use of Greek facilities … Greece might be placed in an extremely awkward position vis-à-vis [the] Arab countries if any degree of regularity or frequency replaced sporadic, occasional landings.'[81]

It was this attitude of the Markezinis government that supposedly turned the Americans strongly against him and Papadopoulos. There is some evidence that a high-ranking US diplomat in Athens openly expressed his aversion to the Markezinis government, saying at one meeting that 'the Markezinis government must go; and, also, Papadopoulos must be removed. We [the Americans] want neither him nor Markezinis.'[82] Markezinis has accepted the view that his overthrow was due to US opposition to his government. In his interview 20 years later he said that Kissinger 'had asked me to give him the bases for operations in Crete. Because he thought the war would go on. I did not want us to have anything to do with that.'[83] He even admits in his memoirs that he tended to believe that 'had it [the Yom Kippur War] been forecast or anticipated, it is very difficult to imagine that the US would tolerate the political change in Greece, as the future Prime Minister had openly expressed himself against the plan of homeporting of the 6th US Fleet'.[84]

However, Markezinis seems to overlook the fact that many other governments denied the Americans the use of their naval facilities and air bases at that time, none whom faced subversion or conspiracies orchestrated by the US, although State Department spokesman Robert McCloskey stated 'that the absence of full support for US Mideast policies put in doubt the entire meaning of European security, while the statements of his superior, Henry Kissinger, went even further, declaring that he was "disgusted".[85] Moreover, the line that Markezinis was following accorded with the pattern of many interim governments: 'to defer major foreign policy decisions until after the first elections had been successfully held'.[86] Even if it was true that the Americans were not over the moon about Papadopoulos and Markezinis, this alone would not have been enough for the 'experiment' to collapse in the way it did.

It is not easy to support the conventional wisdom on the role of the US in the failure of the 'experiment', and to see in the government's attitude during the Yom Kippur War the crucial factor that turned the Americans irreversibly against the Papadopoulos–Markezinis partnership, as many regime apologists have since claimed. As Tovias has pointed out, 'the most tactical dimension in American decision-making was whether to let democratisation ... follow its own course or to intervene at the margin to accelerate it or on the contrary slow it down, according to the USA's set of priorities'.[87] But there is insufficient evidence to prove that this was the case in Greece in 1973. Even at the time, a British diplomat doubted the US-inspired coup scenario:

> Several American press reports have been carried here alleging strong criticism in Washington, particularly from the Pentagon, which singled out Greece among NATO allies as uncooperative. According to these reports, the Americans had put pressure on the Greeks to allow overflights, and were particularly annoyed that Soviet transport planes had used Greek air space without this provoking any particular Greek riposte. There appears to be no truth in this allegation ... Palamas denied that American aid to Greece was given in the expectation of Greek support of American policy towards Israel, as was suggested by remarks made by President Nixon in July 1972 'that aid to Greece was the only viable way to save Israel'.[88]

The only available CIA report at the time of Markezinis mentions 'solid opposition from the military' to a potential legalization of the Greek Communist Party by Markezinis, as well as that regime dissidents (naming only Aslanidis) 'might become part of an anti-Papadopoulos opposition' without being specific on what kind of opposition that would be.[89]

At this point there appears to have been a shift in US policy towards the *reforma*. Markezinis could not fail to note that relations between Kissinger and ambassador Tasca were 'not good', something that Murtagh confirms when commenting that 'according to a US lawyer who investigated the link between Ioannidis and the CIA on behalf of the Congress, "there was a falling out between Henry Tasca and the junta, and between Henry Tasca and Secretary of State Henry Kissinger"'.[90] It appears, however, that Tasca made an effort to lay his own 'bridge' between Markezinis and Kissinger, as he was reportedly planning to travel to London in order to arrange a meeting between the two men. Again, the hardliners' coup put paid to this initiative.[91] Tasca was also supposed to have realized the threat posed by Ioannidis to the 'experiment': in March 1975 he said that 'Ioannidis was no good from the start ... [A]ll my reports from November 73 clearly indicated he was a big setback [sic] ... but both the US and NATO chose to downplay them.'[92]

In any case, it is certain that a number of US officials were aware of the conspiracies in the army against Papadopoulos. For instance, as early as July, an American general who was attending military manoeuvres asked his fellow attendee Admiral Arapakis what he thought about the Markezinis government and Greece's path to the elections. When Arapakis said it could develop smoothly, the American responded '[W]e shall see what Ioannidis has to say about that.'[93] Furthermore, again according to Arapakis, Ioannidis was boasting two months before November 1973 that 'some Americans' – of unspecified identity and office – were advising him to intervene and depose Papadopoulos; he added, however, that he resisted their 'advice' – at least for the time being.[94] There is also a report about a meeting between Ioannidis and CIA agent James Potts, who had served in Greece in the past and who tried to convince Ioannidis to stage a coup against Papadopoulos.[95] If all this is true, the question remains as to why the US was interested in seeing the *reforma* fail before the supposed opposition of Papadopoulos and Markezinis to their requests. Psicharis argues that 'there is certainly some truth in the opinion that the Americans knew at least by 1972 that Ioannidis could at any moment overthrow Papadopoulos', but his next assertion, that 'they encouraged him in the action of the 25 November', is without foundation.[96] As for Ioannidis, Murtagh presents an extract from a classified State Department analysis of the 1974 Cyprus crisis, according to which 'the CIA station [in Athens] was unable to contain its enthusiasm for Ioannidis ... [S]uch was Ioannidis' closeness to the CIA and distaste for diplomats [that] ambassador Henry Tasca was bypassed by Ioannides when he wanted to deal with Americans. Instead of using diplomatic channels, Ioannides dealt direct with the CIA.'[97] The Greek ambassador to The Hague also supposedly showed to Palamas a confidential letter to EEC Commissioner van der Stoel, according to which the replacement of the Markezinis cabinet was necessary for the protection of the US forces in Europe.[98] As Woodhouse concludes, 'it does not follow that the ClA had [a] role in the coup of November 1973 which brought Ioannidis to his dominant position. The myth of the omnipotent CIA dies hard in Greece, but it is nevertheless a myth.'[99]

There is also an argument popular in some left-wing milieus that the Polytechnic events caused the collapse of the 'experiment' because the US started seeking alternatives to the current government when it realized the extent of the people's opposition to Markezinis. On 21 November, KKE's radio station, the *Voice of Truth*, was reporting rumours that 'in the backstage of the Pentagon, the CIA and NATO a new government under Karamanlis and Anghelis is being prepared'.[100] And Rodakis claims that 'Ioannidis acted on US orders ... [as they] wanted stability in Greece [through] ... the civilianisation [process, which would suit] ... their plans in Mediterranean and in Cyprus ... [O]nce this proved impossible it proceeded to [back the] Ioannidis coup so as to keep [the] Greek people in line.'[101] Papandreou also wrote that 'the regime reacted [to the demonstrations] with panic, led the situation to a slaughter and lost its prestige in the eyes of the armed forces and the USA.'[102]

A number of authors suggest that the Americans, and especially Secretary of State Kissinger, operated on the basis that a Turkish invasion of Cyprus, which would lead to the partition of the island, would be preceded by a coup against Makarios; thus the road would be open for the US to establish bases in Cyprus. Woodhouse, for instance, mentions that

> Ioannidis was considered to be the best person available for the solution of the two intertwined problems that were a source of concern for the then American administration: one was ... Greek–Turkish relations, and the other was the Cyprus issue. Ioannidis was well aware of the Cyprus issue, as he had served there in 1964. He was also cynical enough to be able to negotiate with the Turks regardless of ... Greek nationalist feelings.[103]

The prevalence of such ideas in Greece has made it akin to a self-fulfilling prophecy: because it actually happened it is assumed that this was what the Americans had planned all along. However, one thing can be said almost with certainty: Papadopoulos, despite his repeated disputes with Makarios, was never personally implicated in a conspiracy against the latter, while the enmity of Ioannidis towards the Cypriot President is well known. Furthermore, Markezinis has claimed that 'had my government not been overthrown, one thing is certain: that there would never have taken place the disaster in Cyprus'.[104] Even diehard opponents of Markezinis agreed with that claim. For example, Mavros told Markezinis in 1975 that in his testimony to the Public Prosecutor during the inquiry into the Cyprus episode he had stated that 'if Markezinis could [have done so], he would certainly have prevented it [the anti-Makarios coup of July 1974]'.[105] Like the political elites, foreign governments and diplomats appreciated Markezinis' efforts after he had been removed from power. On the day of the coup, the Danish Foreign Minister spoke for many of his colleagues when he observed that 'all hope for democratisation which had appeared in Greece is now gone'.[106]

British diplomats analysed the international dimension of the 'experiment' much more accurately, recognizing that its failure was largely due to the lack of support that Markezinis received from foreign governments and those governments' failure to heed to his warnings about what an alternative to his administration would be like.[107] In his first report in 1974, the British ambassador shared the pessimism of his about what he called 'the gloomy future of Greece':

> What is to come is still unsure. The Government is a collection of nonentities. Behind it and, as far as can be seen, controlling it, stands a somewhat nebulous group of officers – sometimes dignified by the title of a 'revolutionary council' – in which revolutionary purists contend for power with moderates who still envisage a deal with the old politicians. The balance of forces is still uncertain.[108]

A US State Department report produced less than ten days after the coup basically agreed with the British assessment:

> Although the present regime controls the armed forces, it lacks a broad popular base. As it attempts to deal with pressing domestic problems such as inflation, student unrest, and public demands for liberalization and political participation, it will face [the] need to make [a] choice between [the] move to [a] constitutional base or, increasingly, authoritarian rule. Over the long run the result may well be political polarization, leading to instability and setting the stage for yet another coup, again most likely from within the military.[109]

Markezinis had spoken with foresight when had told *Le Monde* that 'if I fail, power will pass into the hands of a Greek Gaddafi, who will not have oil reserves at his disposal to make things better for his country'.[110] Similarly, a British Foreign Office report on the day of the Ioannidis coup pinpointed Cyprus as a potential nationalist card that the new regime might be tempted to play:

> [The] new Government poses immediate problems for its allies not only in NATO but also in Cyprus. What will be [the] policy of [the] new Government is anyone's guess. Let's hope that it will pursue some wisdom i.e. to avoid any step which could lead to a confrontation with Turkey. Let's hope also that Turkey will not try to take advantage of any faux pas by [the] new Greek Government to divert Turkish public attention from their internal problems by exploiting [the] Cyprus issue at this particular moment.[111]

Furthermore, as Tasca observed in February 1974, 'the Greek Armed Forces have become a symbol of repression, tyranny, and disarray. Their association in their present state and posture with NATO and the U.S. remains ominous for our future security interests in Greece.'[112]

Ultimately, whatever the connection between the 'experiment' and the international factor in these events, international influence did 'not dictate or determine the timing, type or outcome of the transition process'.[113] The fact that the presumed American reaction to Papadopoulos' and Markezinis' refusal to allow the use of Greek bases was considered to be proof of interference and subversion is symptomatic of a conspiracy-obsessed interpretation of history and politics and a failure by many Greeks to distinguish fact from fiction. In blaming the US for his downfall, Markezinis was attempting to obscure his own shortcomings – not in his dealings with the Americans but in his handling of the hardliners, the ones who really toppled him and who intended to serve no one' interests but their own.[114] If Greece was a 'penetrated country' in terms of foreign influence (in the case of the 'Markezinis experiment', the influence of America), allowing it to manipulate domestic affairs to a certain extent, such 'penetration' is not to be found in a coup already planned and intended to serve purposes other than US or Israeli strategy in the Eastern Mediterranean Sea.[115] The fact is that Markezinis 'and Papadopoulos had not done badly in [attracting] ... international recognition [to] ... the "experiment", to[wards] which most states appeared much more positive than many would [have] imagine[d] at the time'.[116]

One final point to note about the supposed link between the 'foreign factor' and the 'experiment' is that since 1974 it has been gradually woven into the agreed interpretation of contemporary Greek history, a dominant feature of which is pervasive 'anti-Americanism'. The US memorandum cited at the start of this chapter correctly predicted that the disillusionment and anti-American feeling of Greeks '*will grow as long as we are seen to be identified with unpopular rule and will erode the principal long-term force holding Greece close to the United States*'.[117] This analysis has been borne out in regular repetition of the omnipotent and popular myth of US interference in Greek politics, propagated in countless books, films, journal articles and TV documentaries, and as practised various forms of activism in post-1974 Greece. Ironically, in probably the most representative ritual of this form of activism, demonstrators march to the US embassy on the anniversary of the Polytechnic uprising every November to protest against American intervention in Greece – unaware that Markezinis, whose experiment was fatally undermined by the celebrated Polytechnic events, would have totally agreed with them on the major cause of his downfall: the American factor. It is this reinterpretation of the events of November 1973 that has become one of the constituent myths of the *Metapolitefsi* that actually happened.

7

Concluding Thoughts: The 'Markezinis Experiment' between Oblivion and Myth

In today's Greece, the claim that Markezinis could have brought democracy in 1973 is not a politically correct statement.
Achilleas Mitsos, interview with the author

Myth acts economically: it abolishes the complexity of human acts, it gives them the simplicity of essences, it does away with all dialectics, with any going back beyond what is immediately visible.
Barthes, *Mythologies*, p. 143

What was the 'Markezinis experiment' and why did it fail?

The per se controversial nature of a regime-initiated transition has marked the 'experiment' from its very beginning. No such venture is a simple task, given the multiple variables that affect this delicate process. Burdened by the disdain of collaborating with a discredited and unpopular regime, anxious to acquire the legitimacy of the opposition elites, entangled in a subtle though ruthless power game, tricked by his own delusion that his good intentions would be appreciated yet totally ignorant of the real extent of the conspiracy of the hardliners, as well as totally taken aback by the students' reaction, Markezinis saw his 'experiment' collapse in seven weeks. Papadopoulos, believing that he could do away with the last remnants of his opponents in the regime and keep a firm grip on the army, dazed by six years of uninterrupted though anything but unchallenged rule, hoping to lure the politicians into initially a limited democracy then reluctantly accepting some (though never properly defined) compromise, at Markezinis' insistence, on his presidential powers and the holding of elections, believing that he was close to the fulfilment of his dream of becoming uncontested head of state before retiring in glory, saw his vision crushed by his praetorian in just a few hours. It is no wonder that the short lifespan of the Markezinis venture, as well as its inglorious ending with the Polytechnic bloodshed and the 'worse dictatorship' that ensued, have helped establish a superficial interpretation of the 'experiment' in Greece: that of a cheap scam by Papadopoulos and his puppet to perpetuate their rule under a mask of pseudo-democracy. A thorough and comparative critique of this self-fulfilling conventional wisdom, however, shows a number of flaws and reveals a different image of the 'experiment': that of a failed transition from authoritarian rule. This analysis is founded on two elements.

First, the 'experiment' was a *transition from authoritarian rule*. It encompassed almost all the features of such a situation described in the now classical work of O'Donnell, Schmitter and Whitehead. In the summer and autumn of 1973, all the ingredients for a transition existed in Greece – and perhaps to a greater degree than in other cases of successful democratizations. For a start, all political prisoners had been released and for the first time in many years there were none in the country except for a few who had been in prison before 21 April 1967. Then, martial law was lifted throughout Greece and, with the ending of censorship as well, there were some personal press attacks on Papadopoulos for the first time since the dictatorship was imposed and as early as the period before the July plebiscite. Greece was now enjoying the first proper thaw in the dictatorial ice, something that had its reflection in civil society too, with people for the first time since 1967 beginning to voice opinions without the fear of immediate arrest, public mocking of the dictators becoming an everyday thing and students making demands directly to the Minister of Education. That period between August and October 1973 was a total contrast to the preceding six years – and totally unexpected given the person who was at the top.

Opposition leaders could now publicly criticise Markezinis and Papadopoulos without fear for their personal freedom, and they were consulted by the Prime Minister about the elections to be called, the same Prime Minister who was openly talking about the need for legalization of the KKE – for the first time since 1947. It was anything but over for the regime, despite the attitude of some hardliners. Nevertheless, it looked as if something more than simply a *dictablanda* was in the offing: Greece seemed to be on the track to what might be substantial political change – certainly not the *democradura* that Papadopoulos had in mind at the start of the process.

Sadly it was not to be. This is where the *failed* transition comes into play. This is because, as O'Donnell and Schmitter have pointed out, 'those factors which were necessary and sufficient for provoking the collapse or self-transformation of an authoritarian regime may be neither necessary nor sufficient to ensure the instauration of political democracy'.[1] Below the hopeful surface of a thaw in the dictatorship there were the hardliners, regrouping and preparing to react against Papadopoulos and Markezinis. From the war of attrition in which all factions had engaged for six years, Papadopoulos seemed to emerge as the clear winner. Nevertheless, the Ioannidis coup was punishment for Papadopoulos giving up the ascetic military life for the pleasures of the many offices he had amassed, as well as for reoffering political power to the same political class which the regime was supposed to have swept away for good in 1967.'

In that sense the November conspirators claimed that they were the original revolutionaries of 1967, in contrast to the counterfeit ones like Papadopoulos who were only interested in their own material wellbeing and sinking in their vanity. It was significant that the conspirators' first statement was about the betrayal of the ideals of 21 April through Papadopoulos' electoral venture and an assurance that the new regime would be a genuine continuation of the 'Revolution'. This narrative is challenged by Papadopoulos' apologists who claim that the 'Revolution' ended the day that Markezinis was sworn into office.[2] The complex game of outwitting and outmanoeuvring each other between Papadopoulos and Ioannidis ended with the victory of the latter, who, however, had too limited a view of the political realities to appreciate that his machinations would trigger the countdown for the death of the regime he had served so passionately. As for Markezinis, his naivety about being able to deliver the elections he had planned and his lack of control of the state were truly stunning. The fate of his 'experiment' confirms that a transition from authoritarian rule does not necessarily imply the restoration of democracy. It is a process that can be frustrated and even reversed, leading to the restoration of authoritarianism instead. However, we need to explain why things fell apart so quickly.

The main reason for the failure of the 'experiment' appears to have been the nature of the regime, which had three parts to it: first, the exclusively military character of the dictatorship; second, the divergent goals of the heteroclite groups of which it was constituted; and third, the incapacity of its leading group to create and sustain any viable links with Greek society that would facilitate its successful transition to some form of democracy.

The first feature was evident from the very beginning. The authoritarian regime was imposed by some military factions who were unrelated to the political and social context and totally cut off from any other organization or interest group in Greece. It put an end to a democracy which, notwithstanding its acute crisis, was still a functional and inclusive polity facing problems created by the post-civil war polarization and institutional shortcomings, but which sought reconciliation with the elites and a rebalancing of the institutions. It was the unthinkable that came true at a time when so few people expected or even believed it to be possible, except those who dared to put into action their dreams of freezing the political and social processes in the country. Despite their humble social origins and economic status, which in fact made them see themselves as representative of the average Greek; despite their ideas about social progress, family values, religious piety and national independence, ideas which to their minds necessitated their intervention, the 1967 insurgents were a totally alien force in a country struggling to rid itself mostly from what they represented. The colonels and their supporting factions believed in their cause and were determined to carry out their perceived 'mission' of putting an end to what they considered to be a decadent, inefficient and corrupt political system, which would make way for their own visions. But what were those visions?

The second feature of the collapse of the 'experiment' has not received sufficient attention in the post-1974 era: the divergence in goals between the many juntas that collaborated to bring about the dictatorship. This factor was accentuated by the personality clashes and ambitions among the regime factions and their leaders. These clashes also highlight the fact that for many of those involved, the dictatorship was simply a means of either acquiring and maintaining the pleasure of high social status and professional and economic benefits or of restoring their corporate predominance over society – the welfare of society at large was not a consideration. This 'social autism' was not, however, shared by others, notably Papadopoulos (and, to a lesser extent, Makarezos), who did have plans to transform Greece's social and institutional structure to meet the needs of a long-term military influence in the country. However, such ideas proved to be either too vague and abstract to be applied in the complex setting of a society like Greece or too ambitious to be taken seriously by enough of those involved in the enterprise.

Consequently, the third reason for the handicapping of the 'experiment' was the inability of the colonels – or at least of those of them who did have such a plan in mind, most notably of Papadopoulos – to establish some form of political organization or group which could serve as the basis of a future pro-regime party. The two attempts at this – the 'Consultative Committee' and the EPOK – which quickly failed indicate that the scale of the task was too great in the circumstances. By 1973 this failure had created an impasse: the regime was strong enough to continue through sheer use of military force but at the same time too weak to transform itself into any form of polity other than what it was originally – a military dictatorship. Sensing the signs of change in the society and under international pressure, Papadopoulos and his entourage now turned to the politicians whom they had ousted six years earlier, and especially ironically to one of their least popular representatives – Markezinis. For the dictator, this was intended as a ruse, but gradually it became clear that a transition to the pseudo-democracy he had in mind would not fool or satisfy anyone – not even Markezinis. And then came the moment of his weakness and a window of opportunity for a proper and more inclusive transition from authoritarianism to democracy.

Here lies the crux of the failure of the 'Markezinis experiment': the fact that few at the time realized the extent of Papadopoulos' weakness which offered an opportunity to seriously engage in a process of negotiation with him which might have led to a Greek version of the '*reforma pactada*' that would see Spain achieve its own democratic transition four years later. As Mitsos admits, 'we had no idea such a thing was possible; none of us had imagined what would happen in Spain with Suarez – that a dictatorship could give its place to a democracy in such a peaceful way'.[3] However, the contingency of the whole venture needs to be stressed: there is no credible proof – only opinions or guesses – that Papadopoulos really meant to concede more to the opposition and Markezinis and accept his eventual retirement and replacement (probably by Karamanlis), with a radical amendment to his 1973 constitution that would facilitate a transition to democracy in Greece. Papadopoulos' position at the time did not allow him as much room to manoeuvre as he had done in the past, but he seemed to have a choice of two courses of action: either (if elections were called and depending on their fairness and outcome) accept a process that would gradually marginalize him and lead to an earlier retirement than he had planned, or move to a strict authoritarianism that would have divested him of all support other than that of the hardliners, whose puppet he would have become. Given the political developments of the autumn of 1973, there can be no definite answer to the question of what might have been – the abrupt end of the 'Markezinis experiment' by force of arms has led to both democratic opponents and regime apologists focusing simply on the intentions of Markezinis and

Papadopoulos rather than engaging in a substantive political analysis of the situation. Indeed it is possible to trace two potential paths that a would-be Greek *reforma* might have taken had it not been put to death by the diehards, based on the similar experiences of Spain and Turkey, which occurred four and ten years respectively after the 'experiment' and which produced two substantially different outcomes.

A counter-factual venture: What if the 'Markezinis experiment' had succeeded?

The answer to the above question has to be tentative given the danger of simply resorting to speculaton, which has been supported by Papadopoulos apologists since the 1974 transition – the 'opportunity missed' thesis. Given the counter-factual nature of the question, one is naturally drawn to a judgement on the intentions of the major protagonists rather than to a definitive analysis of the outcome of the 'experiment'. And so the controversy persists, as there is no answer to the question 'Could Greece have become a democracy had Markezinis been allowed to call elections in late November/early December 1973?'

The 'Spanish scenario'

In the Spanish scenario, the first possible outcome would have been the one that Papadopoulos apologists claim was the latter's intention from the start: the restoration of democracy – albeit a democracy that would have been, at least initially, far less inclusive than the opposition expected and the majority of people wished for.

The similarities and differences between the two cases need to be pointed out. After the death of Franco and given the internal crisis facing the regime in Spain, doubts had been raised as to whether a radical transformation was feasible, especially considering the anti-democratic credentials of both King Juan Carlos and Adolfo Suarez, the Prime Minister of the transition.[4] The opposition accepted the bitter truth that the regime was too powerful to bring down other than by negotiation on the terms of the elections,[5] and showed self-restraint when faced by the Franquista hardliners who sought to reverse the transition both before and after the first elections of June 1977. This effort failed before the elections due to the deceptive tactics that Suarez and the softliners employed, when they led the diehards in the army to believe that they would not legalize the Communist Party. When this did happen, along with the simultaneous calling of snap elections, reactionary elements within the regime and the army were left with no time or space to plan a coup.[6] Furthermore, the presence of Juan Carlos had the opposite effect to that of Papadopoulos in Greece: to the Spanish military, the King was a symbol of national unity and thus any move against him as head of state, under whose aegis the transition was happening, was unthinkable.[7] The final matters of the post-transition settlement were resolved after the first elections, with the ratification of a new Spanish constitution, release of all political prisoners,[8] agreement on economic policies to be followed and confirmation of the regions' semi-autonomous status (especially Catalan devolution). The reaction of a hardliner faction who tried to turn back the political clock by storming the parliament building in February 1981 and capturing all cabinet members and MPs was decisively opposed by the King, whose reaction frustrated the attempted coup and effectively ended the military threat to democracy.

If the 'experiment' had taken the Spanish path, one could argue that, at least in the initial phases of the transition, with Papadopoulos as the strong man holding extensive presidential power, it is inconceivable that Greece would have attained the level of quality of democracy it actually did after 1974. Nevertheless, the processes and dynamics that democratic transition and consolidation entail could have been made to work against Papadopoulos' omnipotence. The key issue in this case would be an agreement between the democrats – Markezinis not necessarily excluded from the equation – to challenge the constitution of 1973 in the new parliament, pressing for an amendment to curtail the presidential powers as soon as possible. In a scenario in which

Markezinis' party had lost the elections and the democratic opposition's coalition had won, this process could have been accelerated from the beginning of the new parliamentary term; but even in the event of his own victory, Markezinis had pledged to begin the amendment process – though it might have been slower in that case. With such an agreement, the constitution would be amended, turning Papadopoulos into a mere spectator of an irreversible shift of authority from the President (himself) to the executive and legislative branches of government. Along with the amendment, the new democracy would have had to face the issue of permanently neutralizing the military threat, something that would have had to be dealt with on an ad hoc basis depending on the balance of power after the elections as well as the pressure from civil society for democratization. The end of that road might well have been Papadopoulos' resignation from the presidency, handing over to a figure who enjoyed a consensus of the democratic groups (most probably to Karamanlis), and the start of the consolidation of democracy in Greece, with a new government emerging from the elections under the amended constitution and proceeding to sweep away the dictatorial heritage in the armed forces, the police and the civil service.

The 'Turkish scenario'

There are two issues that complicate this idyllic image of a 'clean' democratic restoration. The first one is the reaction of Papadopoulos to the process of reequilibration that might have followed the elections. Can one assume that he would have been content to permanently retire from power? As noted above in various testimonies and analyses, Papadopoulos was tired after six years of intensive inter-regime plots, behind-the-scenes clashes with rival factions and politicking. Given that his initial plan to restore a supervised 'democracy' under his own prerogative proved far too ambitious, and bearing in mind his less secure position as a result of the politicians' stance and the Polytechnic uprising, one could argue that Papadopoulos would have agreed to a gradual withdrawal from the political stage and a chance to enjoy the fruits of his six-year rule, basking in his own self-image as the mastermind of the 'democratic transition'. Again, much would have depended on the outcome of the elections, the bargaining positions of the relevant parties and the general dynamics of the post-transition political landscape. It is possible that he would not have left the political stage immediately, refusing to retire in shame. However, he could still have guaranteed for himself a happy retirement free from any concern, including impunity for his role in the 1967 coup, which would have been an outrage for the many who suffered physical and verbal abuse under the dictatorship.[9] The democratic opposition would also not have found it easy to reconcile themselves to an 'honorary retirement' for Papadopoulos. But as far as the man himself is concerned, an 'honorary retirement' did have its attractions, as long as he did not appear to be acting in panic or under pressure from the opposition. It would be the first post-dictatorial government to inherit the hot potato of his (and all other 1967 plotters') immunity.

The 'Turkish scenario' probably fits what was in the mind of Papadopoulos from the beginning. Indeed, he was *trying* to achieve what the Turkish military and regime leader Kenan Evren *did* achieve ten years later. The introduction of a constitution with numerous clauses on the role of the military in political structures and institutions, tight control of political parties and elections by a National Security Council and restrictive regulations on participation in trade unions, civil organizations and freedom of press[10] all echo the effort of Papadopoulos in the summer of 1973 to turn the *dictablanda* into *demoradura* after the plebiscite he organized. However, Evren had the unified support of the armed forces, something that Papadopoulos never enjoyed. On the other hand, the participation of Turgut Ozal's Motherland Party in the 1983 elections produced a surprise result – his victory against the regime favourite General Turgut Sunalp.[11] The 'old politicians' of Turkey, most notably Bulent Ecevit and Suleyman Demirel, protested against Ozal, portraying his victory as an act of theft against them because of the ban on their participation. They considered that they had a right to contest the elections, no matter how strict the constitution and the military supervision of politics. This episode offers an interesting comparison with the attitude of the Greek opposition politicians who rejected the offer of Markezinis based on the 'castrated parliament' argument. Such an argument becomes even more questionable when considering the victory of Ozal in such a tightly controlled election as the one that took place in Turkey in November 1983. This is a reminder of the contingency factor that comes with democratic transitions once the electoral game is open to participation, and the fact that, no matter what the extent of electoral manipulation might be, elections can still lead to surprising opposition victories or at least a strengthening of opposition parties to enable them to apply greater pressure for further democratic reforms. The case of Turkey seems to give some credibility to a 'missed opportunity' analysis of the 'Markezinis experiment' – but only if one crucial factor is ignored.

This is the second and more important point that blurs the image of a possible democratic transition in 1973, and it concerns the question of the reaction of the military. Would they tolerate such a process of change after the planned elections? Again, the military-as-institution might have negotiated with the politicians certain changes to the constitution regarding the role of the army in politics, and a basis might have been found for a gradual and permanent withdrawal of the army to the barracks – though this would not have been a straightforward process as indicated by the bargaining that took place between them and Karamanlis in early autumn 1974, when the army was in a weak negotiating position. It is plausible, nevertheless, to assume that the military-as-institution, once elections were held and a new democratic order in place, might have thought twice about reverting to its old habits of conspiracy and subversion, which would have taken Greece back to the tormented condition of the pre-1967 years. Yet this scenario would still have a window of opportunity open to the army to become a praetorian body that would exert a certain institutionalized influence over Greek politics, which would undoubtedly have come close to what the restrictive constitution of Papadopoulos was aiming at – and which would be experienced in Turkey for many years after 1983. Again, the key factor in determing the outcome would be the balance of forces after the transition elections, which of course leaves us in the realm of mere historical speculation.

If the above picture can be assumed for the military-as-institution, it is much more difficult to assess the role of the hardliners. The extremism of many junior officers was always a potentially critical factor for the transition. How would they accept their submission to civilian rule, especially given the resurgence of most of the pre-1967 political elite they so much loathed, and with so many of their leaders either still serving in the army (Ioannidis) or free and available for advice on possible further reaction based on their know-how about coups (e.g. Ladas, Aslanidis)? It is reasonable to assume that, even if they were not to react immediately to the process of transition and the ending of military supervision of politics, they would have definitely been a cause for concern and uneasiness in the new democracy, burdened with the memories of 1967 and lacking, at least in the beginning, the institutional basis to face a potential new threat. Thus it appears inevitable that the consolidation of democracy would have been seriously compromised and that hard-line officers could only have been dealt with by taking some radical steps, such as forced retirements or at least transfers far from Athens and other units in large urban centres. Again, the question of the officers' reaction is open to speculation and would again have depended on the post-election balance and deals between the military hierarchy and the politicians. The factor of agency is also important, in respect of both the hardliners and the democrats. This issue would cast a heavy shadow on the new democracy, with a reaction similar to the coup attempt in Spain in February 1981 a distinct possibility.

Irrespective of which scenario materialized in Greece post-1973, it would have taken a considerably longer time than it did in 1974 for democracy to consolidate itself and become inclusive and immune from the threat of praetorianism in the army and/or from an extremist right-wing political party claiming to be the voice of the 'Revolution' in the post-dictatorial political arena. This is a possibility that

Diamantouros identified in 1986, remarking that with the eventual success of the *reforma* 'democracy would not have been immediately restored, and the regime would have cleared a critical hurdle in its search for a broader base of support, and would have gained a minimum degree of wider acceptance that was the sine qua non of its viability in a form other than sheer repression'.[12] Moreover, another sensitive matter would have had to be deferred to a more convenient time in the future: the punishment of the 1967 coup instigators as well as of those who carried out torture on behalf of the regime in the ESA and the police/gendarmerie, first and foremost Ioannidis himself. The ethical issue of leaving unpunished those who had committed human rights violations for six years because of the fear of triggering a reaction from pockets of regime nostalgics in the armed forces would burden the new democracy for an indefinite time. Along with the issue of cleansing the armed forces and civil service of dictatorial elements, these would be thorny problems inherited by the post-transition polity and, if not tackled within a reasonable period, would undoubtedly disillusion many people and radicalize others, becoming part of the political agenda and polarizing political debate.

Everything comes at a price, even more in the case of a transition from authoritarian rule. Greece enjoyed a rapid transition in 1974, in contrast with the slow and tentative process that the 'Markezinis experiment' would inevitably promise. As noted earlier, apologists for Papadopoulos and Markezinis point out that the price for abandoning the 'experiment' was the Cyprus tragedy and the burden it placed on the Greek body politic and society. This, however, is an a posteriori evaluation and fails to take into account that in 1973 very few would have foreseen the regime would end its life in the way it did in 1974, not because of an internal crisis or reaction but because of a foreign policy adventure. Yet again, having the hardliners in the saddle was a destabilizing factor, as quite a few have recognized, Markezinis included (in his interview on 'the Greek Gaddafi'). But the main problem that Greece faced in 1973 was the lack of a viable political alternative: either the regime would collapse, leaving a gaping wound, or there would have to be a compromise on the quality of the ensuing democracy, at least initially, to facilitate a peaceful transition. As Gillespie concluded, if 'liberal democracy is the most important immediate political goal'[13] for the political elites, they were faced with a hard choice. Arguably, it was the tactics of Papadopoulos and Markezinis that decided the outcome of the 'experiment', which already faced a hostile environment. As Vanhanen has observed, 'the less favourable structural conditions are for democracy, the more the success or failure of democratisation depends on the skills of political leadership and on the strategies chosen by them, although beyond a certain point no strategies may be enough to overcome the obstacles of unfavourable social conditions'.[14] Even if the 'experiment' stood very little chance of success because of the hardliners, the Greek elites in 1973 still failed to create the conditions that would have overcome the nature of the dictatorial regime or to effectively take advantage of some of the existing albeit limited opportunities for a successful *reforma* that would, at least to some extent, have satisfied the democratic expectations of the people while at the same time steering the country away from adventures such as the Cyprus imbroglio. The tragic and shameful collapse of the dictatorship in the summer of 1974 would also stigmatize the 'experiment' and sentence it to an undeserved disdain.

Oblivion and a posteriori interpretation: The legacy of the 'Markezinis experiment'

In sharp contrast to that harsh judgement, and by an irony of history, in the time between the aftermath of the Ioannidis coup and the actual transition of July 1974 the defunct 'experiment' began to attract some a posteriori appreciation as indeed an opportunity missed, and its main instigator recognized as a man of principle. On the same day of Androutsopoulos' inaugural speech, Arapakis could not help comparing the new Prime Minister to Markezinis who, 'despite his mistakes, was generally a decent man and [whose] … cabinet included many honourable personalities'.[15] Three months later, at an official dinner in the US embassy, Tasca was heard saying that Markezinis was 'too good for Greece'.[16] Even Iliou admitted in an interview in *Le Monde* in May 1974 that 'the Markezinis government was the only solution for Greece and it was a pity that it did not succeed',[17] Karamanlis told Palamas that he deplored the failure to seize the Markezinis opportunity.[18] Yet the Markezinis government and the failed *reforma* would soon be accused of serving as a smokescreen for the dictatorial regime. Due to a lack of a historical perspective and objective assessment of events related to the 'experiment', as well as to its ideological use post-1974, the Markezinis initiative has variously been identified with 'the junta', ridiculed as a sham typical of its masterminds' clumsiness and used as a posteriori proof of the people's dynamic opposition to the dictator's ruse which brought him down along with his puppet. The inglorious collapse of the junta in July 1974 due to the Cyprus tragedy irrevocably associated the regime with treachery and national catastrophe. In this context not only would no one be held accountable for not cooperating with Markezinis but, on the contrary, such cooperation would be a stigma on anyone who tried to justify it. On the other hand, Papadopoulos' declarations of his intentions were taken at face value by his apologists, proof of his pro-democratic attitude, and accordingly eulogized, in marked contrast to the 'old politicians' who were denounced for not cooperating with Papadopoulos and Markezinis, thus missing the chance to democratize Greece and spare it the Cyprus trauma. The catalytic intervention by the US is often invoked by the people who dismiss the idea of foreign interference in the 1967 coup yet completely endorse this type of analysis of the November 1973 one. Both these interpretations lack insightfulness into the nature of the regime that was supposed to be self-transformed, as well as analytical depth on the interest of the actors involved (or perhaps not involved) in the transition game. Indeed, a truly impartial study would have taken note of both the difficulties in reforming a regime which stubbornly refused to reform itself and the pursuit of individual objectives by the various political and military actors with an eye on their post-transition future.

Let us start with the final act: 'the Polytechnic events discredited the "liberalization experiment" that had aimed at a long-lasting authoritarian state with a democratic façade'.[19] This has been the received political wisdom on the period in question in Greece since 1974 and especially post-1981. The Polytechnic uprising became a constitutive myth of what in Greece characterizes the core of the period of *Metapolitefsi*: far from being a mere change of regime, it represents a political paradigm shift – the change from one generation and political class in the country to another, brought about by the rise of PASOK in the late 1970s and early 1980s. The younger generation of people who were called to administer the political and administrative apparatuses of the state, the civil service, the universities and the state-controlled media needed a new narrative that would convincingly portray that generation's critical contribution to the democratization of Greece and arouse the support needed for PASOK and the parties of the left to gain a long-term ideological hegemony in the country, presenting themselves as the continuation of that democratization effort. The idolization of the students' uprising as being at the forefront of the presumed mass resistance to the dictatorship was of primary importance to the rising Greek political elites, as it offered them the constitutive 'myth' they needed and which, to use Barthes's aphorism, 'gives them a natural and eternal justification . . . a clarity which is not that of an explanation but that of a statement of fact'.[20] The Polytechnic uprising served the 'myth' of resistance to the junta, with the students in the vanguard, defying the regime's tanks and fighting for democracy until they were crushed by the crude and blind force of the dictator, none the less gaining a moral and political victory by their courageous action. This heroic narrative of the 'junta vs people headed by the students' thus served the needs of the new political class after 1981. It is no coincidence that one of the first acts of the Papandreou government after its landslide victory in the October 1981 elections was to establish 17 November as a day of official celebration and commemoration of the Polytechnic uprising at all levels of education and in the civil service. In this effort PASOK and the left were ironically and unintentionally aided by the Greek right. The

New Democracy Party did not direct particular focus on the Polytechnic episode in its political discourse after 1974, thus leaving the space free for PASOK and the parties of the left to exclusively endorse the uprising and build their ideological hegemony upon it, claiming that they were the political heirs of the forces in Greece which had resisted the colonels and promoted democratization. The opinion of Averoff on the Polytechnic events, dominant in the Greek right for a number of years, was itself stigmatized as 'extreme right wing' – almost as an apologia for the bloody dictatorial regime and its methods. It would take the rise of Constantine Mitsotakis to the leadership of New Democracy for this 'extremist' attitude to give way to a more nuanced one, nevertheless still rather embarrassing for the conservatives when faced with the uncompromising self-confidence of the left's discourse on 'the people's struggle that dealt the junta a crucial – though not fatal – blow in November 1973'. There was no place here for an evaluation of the 'Markezinis experiment' beyond dismissal as a scam by the junta. To accept the idea of a transition 'experiment' from authoritarianism in the autumn of 1973 as something genuine and worth reference would drain the 'resistance/Polytechnic' narrative of its political meaning.

If the narrative of PASOK and the left in the *Metapolitefsi* was one of the people's struggle against the junta, the conservative narrative was that of the leader who successfully brought back democracy to Greece and saved the day from the imminent threat of war with Turkey. Karamanlis was 'the restorer of Greek democracy', in the words of his main British hagiographer, the man who assumed the premiership amidst the chaos left by the junta on its shameful collapse and not only successfully managed the peaceful transition to democracy but also restored stability to the Aegean region and put Greece back on track in the European integration process, which was finally accomplished in May 1979. Karamanlis was to become the patriarch and the personality of reference of the Greek right, with a prestige that extended far beyond the limits of his newly-founded New Democracy Party, transcended partisan affiliation and ideological conviction. One of the most popular slogans of the November 1974 elections was 'Karamanlis or the tanks', drafted by the famous composer (and anything but a right-winger) Mikis Theodorakis. The founding conservative myth of the *Metapolitefsi* therefore had a personality focus from the beginning. Needless to say, there was no space at all in this discourse of the 'one man saviour of Greece' for Markezinis. If any credit for the restoration of democracy was to be given to Markezinis for his *reforma*, then the whole post-1974 agency-centred, right-wing narrative would collapse. Therefore, although some conservatives viewed the 'experiment' with a degree of sympathy, following Averoff's line of thought, it was the Kanellopoulos line that finally prevailed. The new right-wing political class discredited and ostracized Markezinis, and his *reforma* was again identified in its collective memory as an inseparable part of the junta's life and times, a squalid attempt to legitimize that regime at the expense of the people's desire to see proper democracy restored – a task which only Karamanlis was able to achieve.

It is also true that Markezinis was often his own worst enemy and provided his opponents with political ammunition to use against him. In addition to his infamous remark about 'the enemies of the nation and democracy who will not pass', which failed to keep the military in line, he also shattered his credibility as a democratic statesman who really meant what he was saying when he assumed the role of apologist not only for himself in relation to his inconclusive transition in 1973, but also for Papadopoulos. Thus, he invited the accusations of being a spokesman for the junta, despite the fact that he and his ministers were acquitted of all charges concerning the Polytechnic massacre in 1975. Markezinis revived his Progressive Party in the late 1970s, and made a last effort to play a role in politics as he had done in the 1960s, but to no avail: in his final run at the polls in the 1981 elections, many Progressive Party candidates were drawn from the cabinets of Papadopoulos.[21] After Markezinis retired from politics in 1982, a number of his former cabinet members and some members of his party joined the extreme right-wing EPEN (National Political Union), which made its first appearance at the polls in the European elections of 1984. In sum, Markezinis made it easy for both the right and the left to further discredit his 'experiment' and present him as a political continuation of the unpopular junta in the post-1974 Greek political climate of a sweeping shift to the left. It is no wonder, then, that any attempt to portray the 'experiment' as a failed but genuine attempt at transition from authoritarian rule would be stigmatized as an apologia for the dictatorship and disrespectful to the victims of the Polytechnic uprising.

It would be quite some time before different, less ideological and more analytical approaches to the 'experiment' began to appear, offering an alternative interpretation of the events of that tormented year. In one of the first of these studies, Barkman would offer one of the most balanced (but also 'politically incorrect', according to Mitsos) judgements on Papadopoulos' intentions, impressed by what he was supposed to have conceded to Markezinis:

> It will probably never be known whether Papadopoulos really wanted to lead Greece back to democracy or whether, if he did, he would have been capable of doing so . . . He was incapable of the politician's arts of maneuver and persuasion, and he never succeeded in building up political support or winning much more than at best a grudging acquiescence in his rule. The one man who would accept office at his hands was dogged by misfortune. For all that, and whatever one may think of that strange, unpleasant, complex little man, history may yet judge that it was his misfortune – if not necessarily his country's – that the treachery of his own most trusted follower deprived him of the opportunity to undo the harm he had done to Greece.[22]

For all Markezinis' faults and shortcomings, it should be acknowledged that, as Mitsotakis would accept more than 40 years later, he was 'a very efficient man who was ill-treated by the historical conjuncture, although he was not a supporter of the junta'.[23] He was also the only protagonist in the events of 1973 who had a clear agenda from the beginning to the end of his involvement, an agenda which he never had the opportunity to fully develop, along with his post-elections plans which he presented to foreign diplomats and which were more radical than they had anticipated.[24] Notwithstanding his slowness and single-mindedness in handling the negotiations with the politicians, as well as his fatal inertia and apparent adherence to the agenda of Papadopoulos during and after the Polytechnic events, the aphorism of Theodorakopoulos that 'history will probably be kind to Markezinis, because no one tried harder to serve his country at a historic moment'[25] seems a fair judgement of the man who was unpopular and highly unsuitable for the demanding task of transition. The fact that nobody else accepted the challenge of the 'experiment', that very few supported it and that only the military hardliners took it seriously shows how limited were the chances of success for the 'Markezinis experiment' in the way it was conceived, advocated and evolved.

The narrative of the people's resistance to the junta, culminating in the Polytechnic events, was used to exonerate the vast majority of Greeks for their six-year passivity vis-à-vis the colonels. It is important to bear in mind that the power of the 'Polytechnic myth' was even reflected in some extreme political activities post-1974. For example, the notorious terrorist group that chose the date of the bloody suppression of the uprising for its name had the deliberate intention of exploiting the 'myth' of the Greek youth's 'unfinished revolutionary struggle of 1973', which was carried forward from the dictatorship into the democracy years as an unfulfilled imperative of social revolution.[26] Finally, it is notable that the alleged link between the 'experiment' and US interference in Greek politics, as propounded by apologists for the regime, meets its left-wing equivalent in the famous protest march organized every year on the anniversary of the suppression of the uprising from the Polytechnic campus to the US embassy in Athens. It is here that, for a number of Greeks (not necessarily of the same political affiliation on the conventional right–left spectrum), the conspiracy myth of American intervention and the heroic narrative of the people's anti-junta resistance converge. The Greek people almost unconsciously still remember the 'Markezinis experiment', although not for what it actually was – a shattered attempt for a *Metapolitefsi* that could not possibly have been.

Notes

Introduction

1. The word denotes the self-transformation of an authoritarian regime.
2. For the best account of developments leading to the 1909 coup, see Dertilis 1977 and Papakosmas 1981. For an analysis of the role of military interventions in the inter-war years, Veremis 1997 offers the most interesting account.
3. For an account of those forms of transitions, see Share 1987; see also the comments of Linz and Stepan 1986 on redemocratization initiated from within the regime.
4. Huntington 1991: 127–8.
5. Przeworski 1988: 70.
6. Huntington 1984: 214.
7. Casper and Taylor 1996: 5.
8. O'Donnell and Schmitter 1986: 17.
9. Haggard and Kaufman 1995: 12; see also O'Donnell and Schmitter 1986: 17.
10. Huntington 1991: 122. See also Casper and Taylor 1996: 5, where they speak of the regime elites obtaining 'guarantees of continued influence' by exiting from direct control.
11. Rustow 1970: 345. See also Huntington (1984: 212): 'almost always, democracy has come as much from the top down as from the bottom up; it is as likely to be the product of oligarchy as of protest against oligarchy'.
12. Linz and Stepan 1996: 144.
13. Rustow 1970: 353.
14. Schedler 2001: 14. See also Eisenstadt 2000 on the factor of miscalculation.
15. Etzioni-Halevy 1993: 32.
16. Pridham 1991: 1.
17. O'Donnell and Schmitter 1986: 19.
18. Pridham 1991: 4.
19. Rustow 1970: 348.
20. Sorensen 1993: 61.
21. Di Palma 1990: 34.

1 From 'Difficult Democracy' to the 'Wrong Coup'

1. For an excellent account of the structure and characteristics of ERE, see Meynaud 1974.
2. See Kazakos 2009: 158 for a critique to the post-civil war attitudes of the left.
3. The conditions under which the referendum took place were quite favourable to overt state intervention, leading to a 64 per cent vote in favour of the restoration of the monarchy. There have been allegations that the results were pre-determined – not unusual in a country with a long history of manipulated referenda and elections. For an account of the institutional aspect of that referendum, see Alivizatos 1983.
4. Theodorakopoulos (1976: 121) notes that the Royal Family fervently believed 'that they were the guarantors and personification of the state. This attitude was tolerated and actually encouraged by servile politicians in return for royal favours and patronage.' The apogee of royal intervention in politics was the appointment of Karamanlis as premier in October 1955, when Papagos died.
5. This situation was exacerbated by the conspicuous – and provocative – luxury lifestyle of the Royal Family.
6. In the words of Voulgaris (2013: 42), it was a 'para-constitution' forming 'a parallel – if not blatantly anti-constitutional – legality'. See Koundouros 1978: 129–31 for a detailed account of all the laws and decrees passed during the civil war and continuing to apply after its conclusion.
7. As Meynaud (1974: 71) notes, this system 'allowed to the authorities the manipulation of the political geography of voting by an *ad hoc* transfer of army units during the elections . . . It has been proven that . . . the right wing had largely benefited from conscript votes . . . Officers have various means to influence the voting of the conscripts under their command.'
8. This definition is from Alivizatos 1983: 536.
9. See Featherstone 1987; Genevoix 1973.
10. The best account of these elections is in Meynaud 1974: 110–14. After the elections, Karamanlis was accused of being the mastermind behind the fraud. However, this is untrue: the apparatus of the state had spun out of his control. Favouring ERE was the only constitutional way to act in their interest; should this fail, the road to a coup would be open. Kanellopoulos (1975: 48) admits that 'members of the Junta used to say that they helped ERE in the elections of 1961'.

11 Demertzis 2000: 117.
12 Veremis 1997: 241.
13 See Voulgaris 2013: 60–1.
14 Kazakos 2008: 168
15 Haralambis 1985: 83.
16 Rueschemeyer et al. 1992: 16; see also Huntington 1991.
17 Legg and Roberts 1997: 50.
18 Alivizatos 2012: 377.
19 A detailed account of this attempt is in Alivizatos 1983, 542–54; Hatzivassileiou 2010: 389–92; Haralambis 1999: 83 calls it 'an attempt ... [at] political rationalisation'.
20 Haralambis 1985: 121; see also Theodorakopoulos 1976: 133 for an acute criticism of the various EK partners' 'common desire to leave the opposition benches'.
21 Kanellopoulos 1975: 74, for instance, is certain that Andreas Papandreou 'had indeed links with some officers (which politician in Greece has not made this mistake!) but there was no serious or concrete evidence brought against him for that matter'. Zacharopoulos (1972: 24) agrees that although ASPIDA did exist, 'what its actual purposes were has not yet been made absolutely clear. One theory has it that its members were chiefly disenchanted with the slow pace of promotions, low pay, and [the] declining status of officership in a peacetime society.'
22 As Theodorakopoulos (1976: 160) notes, 'there were daily fist-fights, slanderous attacks by Deputies on their colleagues who, when not fighting, engaged in hurling nationally and morally harmful charges and counter-charges at each other'. He also records (158) an incident he attended: an attempt to pay off a Deputy to switch affiliation from Papandreou to the 'Renegades' for a price ranging from $8,000 to $15,000 – a vast amount by Greek standards of that time.
23 On those fruitless negotiations, see Passas 1980. He argues that, had Karamanlis accepted the invitation, the officers involved in the conspiracy would have thought twice about going ahead with a coup.
24 As Murtagh (1994: 105) notes, 'opinion polls, corroborated by secret surveys carried out by the CIA, predicted an overwhelming victory for George Papandreou and everyone knew that would [also] mean the return to office ... of his son'.
25 Haralambis 1985: 201; see also Legg and Roberts 1997: 52.

26 According to Kanellopoulos (1975: 141), 'only if there were major turmoil would we apply the article 92 of the Constitution on the declaration of [a] state of siege'.
27 Woodhouse 1982: 22.
28 Meynaud (2004: 245); he speaks of 'overproduction of military academies' in the civil war years.
29 See Mouzelis 1978: 206 for the report of Panourgias.
30 See Veremis 1997: 154.
31 Zacharopoulos 1972: 24.
32 See Alivizatos 1983: 269–70.
33 Danopoulos 1991: 30.
34 Zacharopoulos 1972: 25; see also Alivizatos 1983: 260–1 on the military's self-imposed image as defenders of the nation and anti-communism in contrast to the unreliable politicians.
35 As Legg and Roberts (1997: 170) note, by the late 1950s 'given the instability and inefficiency Greece's traditional political world, the Greek military viewed itself as the one institution whose corporate interests were identical to the interests of the whole nation. This meant that the military had not only the ability but the will and at times, the responsibility to intervene in domestic politics'.
36 See the analysis of Moskos 1988 on this matter.
37 As Meynaud (2004: 289) points out, the 'Nasserite' officers were conservative though 'disillusioned by the established institutions to the point of believing in the necessity of structural changes in political life at all costs'. It is not coincidental that this group of 'Nasserites' would dominate the 1967 regime and contribute much to its crisis and to the fall of Papadopoulos/Markezinis. For now, suffice to say that Papadopoulos himself was saying after the 1961 election that 'there will come a time when he would rule Greece like Nasser' (Rodakis 1975: 107).
38 Taken from Karakatsanis 2001:162.
39 For more details, see Zacharopoulos 1972: 30. He mentions the complaints of officers that 'after 1961 it became increasingly difficult to appear in public in uniform without facing the possibility of verbal abuse. On occasion, even young children would go up to an officer in uniform, shout Fascist at him and run away playfully'. Also, the future chief insurgent Pattakos himself notes in a report to the King in early 1966 that Greek officers 'have reached the limits of our patience, as we are often loathed and

hurled against and not responding in the proper way' (extract in Grigoriadis 1975A: 27).
40 In fact, in the IDEA officers' 'personal interests and goals had been connected to seemingly idealist national causes' (Stavrou 1976: 130) in a very efficient way.
41 For this failed attempt, see Stavrou 1976: 163–70, and Veremis 1997: 242–3.
42 As Zacharopoulos (1970: 25) notes, the existence of these factions within the army 'signified a general breakdown in civilian supervision and control [and] a dangerous decline in discipline'.
43 For instance, Papadopoulos voted seven times in the 1961 election, as Zournatzis admitted to the author.
44 As Zacharopoulos (1970: 25) notes, 'despite the loyal support it received from the army, the Karamanlis regime had shown very little concern for the material well-being of the officer class. This obviously contributed to an expansion of the inherent anti-political mood of professional soldiers; it was compounded by a sense of betrayal when Karamanlis decided to withdraw from active politics following the 1963 elections'. And Hatzivassileiou (2009: 440) agrees that 'political control of the army was lost after 1963'.
45 See Meynaud 2004: 245. Also Haralambis (1985: 175) points out that 'by placing trustees in the army leadership the King thought that he controlled the army ... despite [the fact] that a series of key posts were in the hands of mid and low ranking officers'.
46 Diamandouros 1986: 145.
47 Haralambis 1985: 213. Voulgaris (2013: 70) speaks of the right-wing idea of a 'mild and controlled' authoritarian action of short duration. Theodorakopoulos (1976: 170) agrees that the Generals' coup 'was supposed to install a political government and return to a parliamentary system as soon as possible'. Kanellopoulos denies that such an idea was endorsed by himself or the ERE. Nevertheless, Stavrou (1977: 173) offers the testimony of his Minister of Defence, Papaligouras, who 'viewed a military intervention as "probable", even though it was not something [he] wished to see', and he 'called upon the officers to be ready for any "eventuality", even for a military intervention'. He also quotes a retired general of the army saying that 'the feeling that "something ought to be done" by the army to stop the intensified leftist agitation was shared by many political personalities' (Stavrou 1977: 174).

48 Mitsotakis (2017: 296) blames this indecisiveness on the King, who hesitated to give the order for a coup. In his words, 'there was no central mastermind guiding [the King's and the Generals'] moves'.

49 The ex-King himself admitted that 'we had the Generals on our side but not the Majors and the Captains ... whatever a General commands, the soldiers will do whatever their Captain orders them first' (King Constantine 2015C: 48).

50 As Meynaud (2004: 382) claims, 'the fact that most of the insurgents were transferred to key posts in the Athens suburbs gives grounds to speculation that they were used by their conspiring superiors in order to assist them in an electoral fraud or a coup under the Palace's orders'. See also Grigoriadis 1975A: 12.

51 Theodorakopoulos 1976: 170.

52 Stern (1977: 56) suggests that the Generals' coup was planned to take place two weeks before the elections. Papachelas (1999: 313) mentions a meeting of the Generals' junta on 20 April, where they concluded that a coup was inevitable and decided to communicate this to the King, asking for his opinion, and agreeing to meet again a few days later. This information was passed on to Papadopoulos and other faction leaders, who decided to move the next day. Grigoriadis 1975A: 98 speaks of plans for a coup after the first big rally of the EK in Thessaloniki that would kick-off its election campaign. See also Kakaounakis 1975A: 77; Karagiorgas 2003: 59.

53 On the 'Prometheus Plan' – the contingency plan for declaring a state of siege – which facilitated the coup, see Kakaounakis 1976; Grigoriadis 1975; Karagiorgas 2003; and Papachelas 1998. Meynaud (2004: 455) calls the colonels 'the acting spearhead of the Generals' planned coup', hence their knowledge of the operational details of 'Prometheus'.

54 Keeley 2010: 147.

55 Voulgaris 2013: 70.

56 See Keeley 2010: 150 for these conclusions.

57 Kanellopoulos 1975: 141. However, there were others who had realized what that deadlock was brewing for Greece. Businessman Ioannis Passas quotes a discussion he had in late March 1967 with the retired General Papageorgopoulos, head of the Greek Intelligence Agency. While Passas focused on the danger of dictatorship by majors and captains enraged by the political passions and the prevailing extremism, Papageorgopoulos

disagreed, insisting that 'it is all under control by the King and the Chiefs of Staff'. See Passas 1980: 521.
58 See Voulgaris 2013: 70. Korizis (1975: 102) agrees that the coup was the product of political apathy and non-participation on behalf of the people, and the selfish calculations of the political elites.

2 'Greece of Christian Greeks'

1 This is the opinion of Korizis 1975: 56–68. For a typical example of the literature classifying the regime as one of a Latin American style, see Rodakis 1975: 10–14.
2 For this discussion, see Clogg, who correctly points out that 'the populist thesis has greater plausibility than the fascist' (1970: 51). Manesis (1999: 42) describes it as 'bonapartist' because of the high level of military autonomy.
3 Clogg (1970: 53) remarks that 'the regime shows none of the radicalism which many fascist movements, at least in their early stages, have ... the coup ... came about not from instinct, but from calculation'. Haralambis (1985: 275) agrees that 'the fascist organization of society was not the strategic goal of the dictatorship'. Korizis (1975: 56) agrees.
4 Veremis 1997: 168. On the 'veto regime' type, see Clapham and Philip 1985: 8–9.
5 This is the calculation of Kakaounakis 1975A: 137–83, who gives a detailed account with names and ranks of the insurgents. Theodorakopoulos (1976: 170) accounts for 16 leaders supported by 45 officers.
6 In the words of Zacharopoulos (1970: 32–3), all the 1967 insurgents 'reached the impressionable formative years of their life and entered the Military Academy during the Metaxas dictatorship ... the civil-war experience ... accounts for the near pathological anti-communism and messianic nationalism of the protagonists of the 1967 coup'.
7 According to the analysis of Meletopoulos (1996: 52), the majority of the officers were of peasant and, to a lesser extent, petty-bourgeois origins. Theodorakopoulos (1976: 171) for his part stresses 'the peasant, puritanical, and strict religious upbringing of the plotters, their admiration and espousal of old-fashioned qualities such as loyalty, honesty and reliability'.

8 For a detailed discussion of the ideological and social leanings of the insurgents, see also Clogg 1970; Korizis 1975; Haralambis 1985; Woodhouse 1985.
9 Woodhouse 1985: 60.
10 Haralambis 1985: 252.
11 The overambitious plan of Papadopoulos appears vividly in a CIA report of early 1967, in which he is reported to have said, in December 1966, that once the 'Revolution' prevailed he planned to seek US support in order to initiate a series of social and economic steps that would neutralize the shift of some Greeks to the left. See Keeley 2002:187 and Papachelas 1998: 273. Karter (2010: 38) claims that Papadopoulos' objectives were the modernization (as he viewed it) of the national political and economic institutions, the renewal of its political personnel and the calling of elections as soon as possible thereafter.
12 Again, as Karter (2010: 38) notes, Pattakos' view was that the regime should last as long as necessary and not rush to elections, not specifying how long that 'necessary' would be. For his part, Makarezos had a more structured plan in mind: he claimed that the regime's lifespan should be from three to four years, during which time political passions would ease and the economy would get sorted; then elections should take place, in which he would have a role as party leader.
13 Pedaliu 2011: 116.
14 As Woodhouse (1985: 82) notes, 'Papadopoulos and Pattakos were, on balance, in favour of moving forward, though uncertain of their direction. A majority of their colleagues, led by Ladas, believed that only a hard line could keep them permanently in power.'
15 As Meynaud (2004: 421) points out, some officers occupied high posts in the civil service such as general secretaries of ministries, while others were simply appointed without portfolio, as 'political commissaries' alongside the civil service hierarchy. See also Woodhouse 1985: 33.
16 According to Haralambis (1985: 251–2), the junta created 800 high officer posts by retiring 400 senior officers in 1967. Meynaud 2004 states that there were 201 officer retirements in October 1967 alone.
17 As Haralambis (1985: 251–2) notes, the King's coup was precipitated by rumours that the last few monarchist officers remaining in service would be retired in December 1967.

18 For details of the failed royal counter-coup, see Kakaounakis 1975A: 221–43 and Grigoriadis 1975A: 149–92. See also Haralambis 1985; Karagiorgas 2003; Leontaritis 2010.
19 Woodhouse 1985: 32.
20 Quoted in Kakaounakis 1975A: 185.
21 Grigoriadis 1975B: 42. He counts one major regime crisis each year from 1969 until its downfall in 1974.
22 On the retirement of officers occupying government posts, see Kakaounakis 1975A: 255–7; Haralambis 1985: 258.
23 Haralambis 1985: 308. Rodakis 1975: 251 gives a number of 20,000 ESA officers and recruits. On Ioannidis' tight control of the Cadets, see Kakaounakis 1975A: 107; Grigoriadis 1975A: 181.
24 According to Theodorakopoulos, Greece was undergoing what he called 'Papadocracy'. On the Revolutionary Committee, see Maynaud 2004; Leontaritis 2010; Kakaounakis 1975A.
25 Meynaud 2004: 648.
26 Leontaritis (2010: 92) quotes Averoff's account of a discussion with the hardliner Aslanidis, who said that 'the pro-Revolution officers are not happy with Papadopoulos because he did not make a real Revolution, did not sort the King's problem and now is enjoying the company of capitalists'.
27 Woodhouse 1985: 98. For this incident, see also Leontaritis 2010; Kakaounakis 1975A; Grigoriadis 1975B; Psycharis 1975.
28 As Veremis (1997:166) notes, 'paradoxically, as Papadopoulos moved up the hierarchy of state offices, he became increasingly dependent on Ioannides to ensure the continuing loyalty of the army, and in particular that of the seven crack units stationed in and around Athens'.
29 Leontaritis 2010: 103.
30 Leontaritis (2010: 94) mentions a reference by Aslanidis in mid-1970 to the fact that 'out of thirty units in the Attica (Greater Athens) periphery, Papadopoulos controls only four'.
31 Karter 2010: 59–60.
32 Karamanlis to Kollias, 20 June 1967, Markezinis archive. See also Woodhouse 1985: 185.
33 Hatzivassileiou 2010: 472.
34 For a detailed account of the 1968 'Constitution', see Alivizatos 1983 and 2012.

35 Veremis 1997: 163.
36 Woodhouse (1982:196) for his part claims that Averoff had no illusion that the colonels would accept a return to civilian rule; nevertheless, he did not rebuff their approach in 1969.
37 Averoff letter to Ioannidis, 17 July 1973. Taken from Markezinis archive.
38 Quoted in Papadimitriou 1985: 169. The important conclusion he also communicated to Karamanlis was that the colonels 'will only fall because of a national catastrophe of some sort' (Woodhouse 1982: 282).
39 Kanellopoulos 1987: 83
40 For his discussions with Kanellopoulos, see Couloumbis 2002: 118; with Karamanlis, see Couloumbis 2002: 146; with Mitsotakis, see Couloumbis 2002: 149. On Kanellopoulos' options for democracy, see Couloumbis 2002: 165, and and on the talks with Iliou, see Couloumbis 2002: 207.
41 Barkman 1989: 48.
42 Woodhouse 1985: 96.
43 For more on these meetings and the participation of former MPs in the Papadopoulos cabinets, see Kallivretakis 2016: 245–7; Karter 2010: 87.
44 Markezinis was one of the first people in Greece to adopt liberal policies: he tried to restore the country's devastated infrastructure and secondary sector and succeeded in bringing investors to Greece from Western Europe and the US. He also restructured the banking sector and tried to expand export markets. However, his best-remembered and most controversial measure was the devaluation of the Greek currency in April 1953.
45 For the early political career of Markezinis, see Meynaud 1974; Linardatos 1986B and 1986C.
46 According to Zournatzis in an interview with the author, the reference of Papadopoulos was to Makarezos, Ioannidis and Ladas. He claimed that Papadopoulos first considered stepping down in 1969. On the meetings with Markezinis, see also Passas 1980: 539; Karter 2010: 83.
47 Karter 2010: 99.
48 On the Pipinellis Memorandum, see Leontaritis 2003; Makarezos 2010. The editor Savvas Konstantopoulos, one of the regime's theoreticians, was of the opinion that the regime should not last beyond 1972 and suggested a process of transformation leading to a 'dual power' – representative of both the regime and an elected government (Leontaritis 2003).
49 Makarezos to the author.

50 Murtagh 1994: 207. Mitsotakis (2017: 310) agrees that 'Andreas was the only person who would not collaborate with the other groups. The rest of us were always together but he kept his distance.' And Woodhouse (1982: 191) notes that Karamanlis 'was doubtful about Andreas Papandreou, with whom he had no common ground'.
51 Farakos to the author.
52 Rodakis 1975: 298.
53 Rodakis 1975: 293.
54 Farakos to the author.
55 Karakatsanis 2001: 8.
56 'Greece: Internal Situation', FCO 9/1705, 4/4/1972.
57 Theodorakopoulos 1976: 213.
58 Danopoulos 1991: 30.
59 In the words of Verney and Couloumbis 1991: 107.
60 See Konofagos 1982: 147.
61 Manesis 1999: 42.
62 Notaras 1999: 191; see also Korizis 1975: 101.
63 Yannopoulos 1972: 165.
64 Notaras 1999: 192. See also Woodhoue 1985: 36 on the issue of the fragmentation of anti-regime groups.
65 Mantoglou 1994: 156.
66 Murtagh 1994: 225. Iordanoglou (1993) claims that Papandreou's only concern was how he could 'sell himself' in the post-dictatorship setting, and believes that 'the contribution of PAK to the resistance drama was negligible'.
67 On the National Resistance Council, see Yannopoulos 1972: 185; Woodhouse 1985: 90
68 Murtagh 1994: 239.
69 For thorough consideration of the economic policies of the dictatorship, see Pesmazoglou 1972; Kazakos 2016; Psalidopoulos 2016. For a superficial pro-regime account, based on short-term indicators, see Theodorakopoulos 1976. Sotiropoulos (1999: 128) speaks of the 'paternalist, but not corporatist social policies' of the colonels.
70 See Legg and Roberts 1997: 53. Haralambis (1985: 295) agrees that 'the ideological poverty of the dictatorship was to a certain extent balanced by the rise of incomes and consumption one of the most substantial factors of passivity towards the dictatorship'.

71 Theodorakopoulos 1976: 223. Couloumbis (2002: 51) estimates that in 1971 'more people in [the] countryside [than in the urban centres] support the colonels ... overall I think 80% are against and 20% for them'. This calculation seems closer to reality, although the lack of opinion polls frustrates any attempt at a precise calculation of the actual appeal of the colonels to the Greek people. Couloumbis' opinion remains the consensus view in Greece today.
72 Yannopoulos 1972: 175. Theodorakopoulos (1976: 220) quotes a foreign journalist writing in February of that year that 'an apathy even more resounding than order reigns in Greece'. Finally, Markezinis himself (1979: 135) recalls the 'impressive passivity of Greeks until 1973 ... aided by their economic well-being'.
73 As Kazakos (2016: 149) claims, 'while stuck to hierarchical social conceptions of duty in a changing Greece, [the colonels] needed to deal with a complex political-economic system in a rapidly diversifying society that was calling for participation and resisting their authoritarian arrangements. This constitutes one of the major causes of failure of the fake 'modernisation' the dictatorship tried to impose on the Greeks.'
74 Reluctant to be too severe on Papadopoulos, Theodorakopoulos (1976: 220) nevertheless is explicit on who was to blame: 'The army, with its new-found power, did not look kindly upon Papadopoulos's close associates nor on the members of his cabinet, who had begun to behave in a manner all too reminiscent of politicians in the past, appointing relatives and friends to influential jobs.' Legg and Roberts (1997: 53) agree that 'despite its diatribes against the bureaucratic inefficiencies and favouritism in civil governments, the military regime proved that it could match regular politicians in these matters'. And Veremis (1987: 224) concludes that the colonels 'tended to follow in the footsteps of traditional party bosses by extending their patronage to their kin and to the ever-growing number of their clients'.
75 Averoff to Papadopoulos, 5 April 1969 (from Markezinis' archive).
76 Characteristically, the most remembered motto of the dictatorship years was the 'Greece of Christian Greeks'. For more on the ideology of the dictatorship, see Clogg 1972: 51–2; Diamantouros 1986; Meletopoulos 1996.
77 Haralambis 1999: 89.

78 For an interesting discussion of individual behaviour in large groups, see Olson 197: 165–6. Korizis (1975: 102) agrees that the passivity was the result of 'selfish interest calculations' of large parts of Greek society.
79 Grigoriadis 1975B: 168–9 calls the *Symvouleytiki* a 'Little Parliament'; for Woodhouse (1985: 85) 'it was almost the only measure introduced by the junta which could literally be described as "fascist"'. See also Papadimitriou 1985: 169.
80 Theodorakopoulos 1976: 226.
81 Couloumbis 2002: 170–1. Even Theodorakopoulos agrees (1976: 223) that by 1972 Papadopoulos 'had missed the boat [of forming a party and calling elections]. The people's initial welcome, followed by apathy, had begun to turn to hate.' And Notaras (1999: 197) notes that by the end of 1972–3 'the closed conspiratorial resistance groups started opening to the masses'.
82 This illusive image appears even in the British ambassador's Annual Review for Greece for 1972, where he notes that 'there is no reason that would prevent Papadopoulos to last as long as Salazar in power or, to use a more recent example, as General Franco' (FCO 9/1709, 2/1/1973).
83 As Theodorakopoulos (1976: 225) admits, 'by 1972 there were hundreds of jokes going around about the Colonels'.
84 Mitsos to the author.
85 Manesis 1999: 43.

3 The Early Liberalization, January–September 1973

1 Clapham and Philip 1985: 14.
2 Whitehead 2002: 34.
3 Makarezos 2010: 114; Gill 2000: 169.
4 Zournatzis to the author.
5 Markezinis (1979) recalls a meeting with Pattakos in early 1973 in which the latter expressed serious concerns about the economic situation in Greece.
6 Markezinis (1979: 148) mentions a chat he had at a party with hardliner Aslanidis in early January; the latter told him that the inter-regime rift that led to the August 1970 crisis had only been dealt with superficially.

7 See Verney and Tsakaloyiannis 1986 for statements by Papadopoulos and Pattakos, made in December 1972 and January 1973 respectively, stressing the regime's decision to keep Greece firmly aligned with the EEC.
8 In the words of Voulgaris 2001: 27. For an account of the dictatorial policies in the higher education sector, see Papazoglou 1975; Mantoglou 1995; Kornetis 2013.
9 For this report, see Papazoglou 1975: 71.
10 Accounts of the February–March 1973 events are given in Papazoglou 1976; Mantoglou 1995; Kornetis 2013.
11 'One hundred students bullied the other four hundred, clustered in the Law School, to make this event look like a demonstration of large numbers of students' (quoted in Papazoglou 1975: 99). Barkman (1976: 91) seems to accept that 'a small active minority of students has been instrumental in organising strikes'.
12 See Papazoglou 1975: 71.
13 On this point, see Grigoriadis 1975B. Mitsos, who was involved in the occupation of the Law School, recalls nevertheless a certain reservation by the people towards the students: '[I]t was like saying to us "we empathise with your cause but we'd better stay out of this for the moment."'
14 On this report, see Grigoriadis 1975B and Papazoglou 1975. Barkman (1989: 92) also wrote on 9 March that the 'troubles at the universities are by no means over and might well become a matter of great concern for the regime'.
15 Papazoglou 1975: 104. It is interesting that Papadopoulos believed that 1973 and 1974 would be 'critical years'.
16 For more details on the aims and character of EPOK, see Karter 2010: 81.
17 US Secretary of State to USICNCEUR, Further Reflections on Greek Regime's Proclamation of a Republic, 21 June 1973.
18 For instance, both Pattakos and Makarezos rejected the idea of EPOK. Pattakos said to Karter that he was told by Averoff that even if it won a future election, this would not be accepted by any politician in Greece or by any foreign government (Karter 2010: 84–5).
19 Markezinis' private notes from his archive.
20 The full text of Karamanlis' statement is in Karamanlis vol. 7; see also Papadimitriou 1985: 29–31.
21 Kakaounakis 1976A: 348.

22 Martin to FCO, Karamanlis, 26 April 1973, WSG 1/5, FCO 9/1711.
23 The full editorial is given in Papadimitriou 1985: 555–6.
24 See Veremis 1997 for the number of officers persecuted during the dictatorship. Papadimitriou claims that the first attempts at anti-regime action started in the summer of 1968; one year later some naval officers planned the abduction of Papadopoulos during an inspection of the fleet and the sending of an ultimatum to the rest of the dictatorship leaders to step down (Papadimitriou 1985: 124).
25 For more details on the plans of the naval officers, see Woodhouse 1982; Papadimitriou 1985; Grigoriadis 1975B.
26 Rallis was also informed but in his interview with the author claimed that the officers' hopes were naive.
27 For an account of both versions of the Karamanlis–Averoff meeting, see Woodhouse 1982: 198. As Woodhouse notes, memory of the fiasco involving the King in December 1967 helps explain Karamanlis' reservations. See also Papadimitriou 1985: 310 and Karagiorgas 2003: 181. Leontaritis (2010: 136) notes ironically that Karamanlis 'would endorse the coup only if it succeeded'.
28 Papadimitriou 1985: 103.
29 As Markezinis (1994: 172–3) notes, 'the May conspiracy had considerable appeal to naval officers, most of whom were royalists'.
30 On the causes of failure of the plot, see Papadimitriou 1985: 336 and Bonanos 1986: 107. On its defeat and the ensuing arrests, see Papadimitriou 1985: 575–610 and Grigoriadis 1975B: 257.
31 Papadimitriou 1985: 639.
32 On the impact of the naval coup abroad, see Papadimitriou 1985: 504; Barkman (1989: 100) notes that 'the prestige of the regime has certainly suffered another setback, and Ioannides' position has been strengthened'.
33 Papadimitriou 1985: 553.
34 Leontaritis 2010: 141; Androutsopoulos, the future PM of Ioannidis, agrees in his memoirs (1993: 40) that blaming the coup on Constantine 'was an excuse that was found for the decision, taken weeks before the coup, to depose the King'. Papandreou (1976: 54) considers the abolition of the monarchy to have been inevitable because it was regarded by the US as 'an obsolete means of controlling Greece'.
35 This term is taken from Papadimitriou 1999: 56.

36 Huntington 1984: 214.
37 As Casper and Taylor (1996: 5) put it. For the term *dictablanda*, denoting a 'soft version' of a dictatorship, see O'Donnell and Schmitter 1986.
38 Hooper to FCO, Abolition of Monarchy, 6 June 1973, WSG 1/9, FCO9/1713.
39 US Secretary of State to USICNCEUR, Further Reflections on Greek Regime's Proclamation of a Republic, 21 June 1973.
40 For an exhaustive analysis of the 1973 constitution, see Alivizatos 1983: 291-2, 313-24; Alivizatos 2012: 426-35; Haralambis 1985: 261; Grigoriadis 1975C: 270-1.
41 Alivizatos 2012: 430. Even Androutsopoulos (1993: 42) claimed that 'the amendment of 1973 would end up in a regime of constitutional dictatorship because of the volume of powers that were in the hands of the President'. A Papadopoulos apologist agrees that Papadopoulos' plan 'was for a "guided" democracy with himself as watchdog' (Theodorakopoulos 1976: 227).
42 Barkman 1989: 106.
43 Hooper to FCO, Abolition of Monarchy, 6 June 1973, WSG 1/9, FCO9/1713.
44 Kanellopoulos 1986: 155-6.
45 Shain and Linz 1995: 56.
46 Barkman's notes on 30 June, 1989: 107.
47 In the words of Alivizatos 1983: 297.
48 Kanellopoulos 1987: 153-4.
49 Kanellopoulos 1987: 168.
50 Interview with Mitsos.
51 See Grigoriadis 1975B: 271-2 for this matter.
52 Rallis, interview with the author.
53 See the SEB Bulletin of 15 July calling for a 'yes' vote 'as a guarantee of stability, social peace and economic development', in Haralambis 1985: 288.
54 Markezinis 1994: 176-7.
55 Barkman 1989: 105.
56 Barkman 1989: 113, with the numbers for Athens. Theodorakopoulos (1976: 228) claims that the plebiscite 'took place under surveillance by the foreign press corps and diplomatic observers' but fails to note that this happened only in the large urban centres, while in the countryside the fear of the police resulted in a higher 'yes' vote.

57 Hooper to FCO, Greek Referendum of 1973, 1 September 1973, WSG 1/9, FCO 9/1714.
58 Haralambis 1985: 292.
59 According to O'Donnell and Schmitter (1986: 17).
60 Hooper to FCO, Greek Referendum of 1973, 1 September 1973, WSG 1/9, FCO 9/1714
61 In the words of Veremis (1997: 166), the officers were sensitive 'not only to the problem of promotional blockages, but also to the charges of ineptitude and corruption made against the regime, which served to discredit the military as a whole. Complaints of one-man rule and electoral manipulation were coupled with acute resentment by some senior officers of the President's recent overtures to old-time politicians to participate in the parliamentary elections promised before the end of 1974.' Theodorakopoulos (1976: 225) concurs: 'charges of nepotism and corruption abounded by early 1973, mostly put out by disgruntled army officers'.
62 Bonanos 1986: 102-3. The most fervent regime supporters were also called 'Khaddafists' due to their admiration for the Libyan dictator. The similarity with the 'Nasserites' of the previous decade is more than striking. See also Barkman 1989: 106, who refers to them as 'purists' or 'Spartans'.
63 Hooper to Cornish, The Hardliners, 30 August 1973, WSG 26/1, FCO 9/1716.
64 Kakaounakis (1976A: 361) and Karter (2010: 71) agree on this decision by Ioannidis.
65 See Grigoriadis 1975C: 12.
66 Characteristically Pattakos is said to have remarked early that summer that 'the military are against the holding of elections and the keys to the army's control have slipped [out] of Papadopoulos' pocket' (Karter 2010: 97).
67 Makarezos 2010: 114; also interview with the author.
68 On the protracted negotiations, see Markezinis 1979; Passas 1980; interview with Zournatzis.
69 Barkman (1989: 107) calls Markezinis an 'old man in a hurry' who wanted to be 'the statesman who would lead Greece back from an anomalous situation to democracy' and stresses his commitment to resign, should the regime block the road to elections. He also correctly calculated that Papadopoulos' room for manoeuvre would gradually decrease after the referendum, making it easier to get more concessions from him.

70 On this point, see the recollections of Markezinis' son-in-law (Helmis 2006: 63).
71 'If seventy or eighty per cent [of the parties] agree on the constitutional amendment, who can veto it?' was the argument of Markezinis (1979: 274).
72 This is the line of argument of Passas 1980; Zournatzis and Michalopoulos 1999; also interview with Zournatzis.
73 O'Donnell and Schmitter 1986: 9.
74 Woodhouse 1985: 112. Barkman (1989: 116) agrees that 'Papadopoulos may acquire the image of one who keeps his given word and sincerely wishes to end the revolutionary regime. At the very least he confirms the impression – prevalent even among his fiercest opponents – that he is not a fanatic, but a relatively moderate, reasonable and intelligent, though scheming man.'
75 Denson to FCO, 28 August 1973, WSG1/5, FCO9/1714.
76 Woodhouse 1985: 121.
77 'My mistake was that I overestimated Papadopoulos' presumed control over the army when I accepted the premiership. I took the unanimous obedience of the military for granted ... [H]ad I known, I would never have accepted it' (Markezinis 1979: 205).
78 Woodhouse 1985: 121.

4 The 'Unfinished Revolution' and the 'Castrated Parliament'

1 Danopoulos 1991: 38.
2 Shain and Linz 1995: 57.
3 Veremis 1997: 166; see also Theodorakopoulos 1976: 225.
4 Both citations in Bonanos 1986: 110–12. Psycharis (1975: 16) also claims that Ioannidis' name was kept out of scandals and that he was protected from charges of sleaze and personal corruption. Appropriately, he was known as 'the untouchable' by his followers.
5 See Couloumbis 2002: 303.
6 Karampelias 2001: 377.
7 Kakaounakis (1975A: 381) claims that the younger officers were anxious that 'they would have to rig the elections for Markezinis, whose popular appeal is negligible ... and will blow whatever the Revolution has achieved'.

8 Bonanos 1986: 114-20.
9 Danopoulos 1984C: 233.
10 Grigoriadis 1975C: 31. Ladas also said, 'I am leaving office with clean hands', thus alluding to the corruption of other members of the government.
11 Makarezos, interview with the author.
12 Bonanos recalls that Ioannidis shadowed all the higher officers, himself included, with officers he trusted, as well as ESA men, who checked every move and reported directly to him. He describes himself and his colleagues as being subject to a tight though invisible 'closed circuit of supervision' (1986: 146). See also Kakaounakis 1975A: 388 and 1975B: 42. Psycharis 1975: 21 claims that Ioannidis asked his trusted officers to provide him with copies of all reports they had access to in the Military Intelligence services.
13 On Ioannidis' ruses, see Kakaounakis 1975A: 378; 1975B: 41; Psycharis 1975: 24-6.
14 Zagorianakos was an enemy of Ioannidis. For this incident, see Psycharis 1975; Bonanos 1986.
15 For this, see Bonanos 1986: 113; Arapakis 2000: 111-13; Kakaounakis 1975A: 383; Psycharis 1975: 25.
16 See Bonanos 1986: 129-31.
17 Regarding the first version, see Arapakis 2000: 111, where he claims that when junior officers learned of Papadopoulos' plans, they wanted to arrest him but were dissuaded by Ioannidis himself. Regarding the second version, see Kakaounakis 1975A: 373-6.
18 Kakaounakis 1975A: 386-7; Psycharis 1975: 25. Bonanos (1986: 131) claims the inertia of Papadopoulos totally alienated him and turned him against the *reforma*, encouraging him to get in touch with Ioannidis in early November in order to find out more about the coup he was preparing.
19 This incident is mentioned in Arapakis 2000: 110.
20 Barkman 1989: 146.
21 O'Donnell and Whitehead 1986: 11.
22 Markezinis 1994: 185.
23 See Markezinis 1994: 180-1. Woodhouse (1982: 201) claims that 'Karamanlis maintained absolute silence' on this matter. Karter (2010: 103) doubts that the two men ever met.
24 Arapakis 2000: 109.

25 Rallis to the author.
26 For extensive excerpts from Tsatsos's letter, see Karamanlis 1994: 194. This was also a problem for the EK, as Mavros confessed to Barkman (1989: 120) that 'in his party, and even more so in the ERE, there were many young politicians who did not want to wait another five years'.
27 Woodhouse 1982: 201.
28 See Arapakis 2000. Makarezos claims that Karamanlis said in his letter that 'Markezinis will not hesitate to breach his agreements, even his oaths!' (interview with the author).
29 Rallis (interview with the author) basically agreed but said that Karamanlis was sceptical about the chances of success on his return to Greece.
30 Couloumbis 2002: 273; Markezinis 1994: 187.
31 KKE 1976: 14.
32 NARA, Jackson to Secretary of State, Reported Statement by ex-PM Karamanlis, 30 October 1973
33 Helmis 2006: 168.
34 See Karamanlis VII: 197.
35 Quoted in Papadimitriou 1985: 336.
36 For instance, Rodakis (1975: 320) claims that the famous Greek ship owner Pavlos Vardinoyannis said that 'he tried to talk Papadopoulos into handing power over to Karamanlis'. Makarezos (2010: 25, 119) says he was convinced that Papadopoulos could be talked into ditching Markezinis and resigning in favour of Karamanlis. Papadopoulos' supporter Georgalas urged him to recall Karamanlis because of his broad popular support (Leontaritis 2010: 15).
37 For the full text of the article, see Leontaritis 2010: 166–7; also Grigoriadis 1975C: 39.
38 Regarding this speculation, see Markezinis 1994: 187. Theodorakopoulos (1976: 230) claims that Rallis 'was known to echo Karamanlis's wishes'.
39 For Rallis's interview in 1975, see Grigoriadis 1975C: 40. Rallis told the author that he also wanted to test whether the regime was bluffing; he was critical of the a priori rejection of the 'experiment' by the other politicians.
40 For Averoff's stance, see Grigoriadis 1975C: 39; Markezinis 1979: 286.
41 Hooper to Goodison, 16 October 1973, WSG1/5, FCO9/1714.
42 Varvitsiotis to the author.
43 Kanellopoulos, interviewed by Grigoriadis 1975C: 39.

44 Grigoriadis 1975C: 38.
45 Markezinis 1979: 268. Arapakis (2000: 108–9), though agreeing with Markezinis on Kanellopoulos' desire to become Prime Minister again, notes that Markezinis had become somewhat obsessed with acquiring Kanellopoulos' approval, even more than that of Karamanlis.
46 Barkman 1989: 110–11, 116.
47 For Mavros's discussion with Markezinis in July, see Zournatzis and Mihalopoulos 1998: 280. For his October statement, see Grigoriadis 1975C: 38.
48 Barkman 1989: 120.
49 Barkman 1989: 146. Markezinis records in his memoirs his 'intimate hope that Kanellopoulos would ask me not to run in elections, so as to provide the best proof of their fairness' (1979: 265).
50 See Diamantopoulos 1990: 355 for both citations. See also Mitsotakis 2017: 311; Grigoriadis 1975C: 22.
51 Diamantopoulos 1990: 358; Couloumbis 2002: 273.
52 For the attitude of Novas and Stephanopoulos, see Woodhouse 1985: 125; Theodorakopoulos 1976: 230.
53 Papandreou 1976: 57.
54 The excerpts from the interview are taken from a dispatch of the US Consul in Thessaloniki. See Jackson to State Department, 'Makedonia', exclusive interview with Andreas Papandreou, 23 October 1973.
55 KKE 1976: 18
56 KKE 1975: 14–15. In his interview, Farakos considered the rejection of the 'experiment' by the KKE as correct.
57 NARA, Secretary of State to US Embassy in Moscow, Political Manoeuvres on the Left, 26 October 1973.
58 Markezinis 1994, 186. See also Mantoglou 1994: 229; Haralambis 1985: 284. Rodakis (1975: 321) considers the attitude of Iliou to be 'characteristic of the confusion of the left wing ... in those days'. The KKE saw this stance as proof of 'the opportunism of the reformists' leadership [which] made them practically accept the experiment' (1975: 15).
59 Kyrkos to the author.
60 NARA, Secretary of State to US Embassy in Moscow, Political Manoeuvres on the Left, 26 October 1973.
61 Markezinis 1994: 181. See also Helmis 2006: 61; Grigoriadis 1975C: 24.
62 Barkman 1989: 120.

63 Grigoriadis 1975C: 22. See also Couloumbis 2002: 281–2, where Theodorakis judged the opinion of Alekos Panagoulis that 'Greece is a big prison' to be 'nonsensical'.
64 Interview with Georgalas; see also Leontaritis 2010: 115.
65 Karter 2010: 109. He mentions elsewhere that Markezinis' boast that, even alone, he would run in the elections and win had alienated many politicians. Markezinis had not made such brazen statements, at least not in public.
66 See Chapter 3.
67 Markezinis (1979) recalls a very friendly meeting with the leadership of the Greek Industrialists' Association before he assumed the premiership.
68 The phrase used by O'Donnell and Schmitter 1986: 25.
69 Regarding the concept of the 'electoralist fallacy', see Linz and Stepan 1996: 5.
70 Martin to FCO, The Internal Political Debate, 25 October 1973, WSG 1/5, FCO 9/1716.
71 Barkman 1989: 124–5. He also doubted that 'Papadopoulos would give up his position so easily and whether the Army would tolerate such a development'.
72 Couloumbis 2002: 284.
73 Barkman 1989: 118.
74 On Markezinis' series of interviews in the autumn of 1973, see Grigoriadis 1975C: 35–7.
75 Quoted in Grigoriadis 1975C: 37.
76 'My interviews ... [with] *Le Monde* and [*Der*] *Spiegel* had the opposite effects ... [with] many officers who were annoyed by my daring views' (Markezinis' archive notes). Theodorakopoulos (1976: 238) agrees that the prospective return of figures like Papandreou 'alienated many purist officers'.
77 Barkman 1989: 119.
78 Makarezos to the author.
79 See Makarezos 2010: 18–25 on the issue of the Karamanlis letters.
80 Markezinis 1994: 214. Couloumbis (2002: 292) claims that Makarezos showed Markezinis a poll which showed that 93 per cent of Greeks were opposed to Papadopoulos.
81 Regarding the claims by Konstantopoulos, see Leontaritis 2003: 165; Makarezos 2010: 115. Karter (2010: 112) claims that Papadopoulos was

Notes 213

worried that there would be no proper opposition in parliament but rather 'on the streets' if Markezinis ran on his own and won in the elections.

82 On this incident, see Kakaounakis 1975A: 394.
83 Barkman 1989: 122.
84 This is the opinion of Grigoriadis 1975C: 22, who claims that 'Papadopoulos' will to civilianise was sincere inasmuch as it was under his control'. Barkman (1989: 136) agrees that 'the evidence that Papadopoulos did intend, in the long term, to return to some form of constitutional government cannot altogether be disregarded'.
85 For details on the Polytechnic uprising and the 'experiment', see Chapter 5.
86 Markezinis 1979: 436; 1994: 213. See also Helmis 2006: 87; Woodhouse 1985: 143.
87 Markezinis 1979: 547; 1994: 208.
88 Woodhouse 1985: 140. Karter (2010:112) claims that the Markezinis speech 'failed to convince the military'.
89 Markezinis 1979: 454, 458.
90 Regarding the last meeting between Markezinis and Papadopoulos, see Helmis 2006: 108–11; Markezinis 1979: 479–84; Markezinis 1994: 212–15.
91 Markezinis 1979: 485.
92 Markezinis 1979: 489.
93 Grigoriadis 1975C: 28, 72; Woodhouse 1985: 142.
94 Bonanos (1986: 128–9) claims that when he failed to convince Papadopoulos of the conspiracy by Ioannidis, he decided he had enough of Papadopoulos and joined the plot.
95 For details on the preparations for the coup, see Arapakis 2000; Grigoriadis 1975C; Kakaounakis 1975B.
96 See Kakaounakis 1975B: 32. The involvement of the army in the Polytechnic events is examined in Chapter 5.
97 Makarezos to the author; Pattakos to the author: 'I immediately thought [on the 25th] that that intelligent and agile man [Papadopoulos] could [not] but have been the architect of that situation ... Ioannidis had shown six times in the past his devotion to Papadopoulos, had frustrated many conspiracies against him.'
98 Zournatzis to the author.
99 Markezinis 1994: 213; 1979: 468.

100 Markezinis 1994: 215.
101 For the full note, see Kakaounakis 1976: 48; see also Woodhouse 1985: 144.
102 Bonanos 1986: 138–9. Bonanos also acknowledges that he cannot understand why Papadopoulos did not get rid of Ioannidis 'as he was the state and could have done so if he so wanted' (Bonanos 1986: 144).
103 KKE 1976: 18.
104 Makarezos to the author. See also Passas 1980: 545 and Barkman 1989: 146 for a similar conclusion.
105 Pattakos to the author.
106 Makarezos 2010: 118. He notes further that 'the Polytechnic uprising was the coup de grace to Papadopoulos' morale and convinced him to retire in order to ... [avoid] the forthcoming storm' (Makarezos 2010: 117).
107 Meletopoulos 1996: 327. Pattakos told the author that Ioannidis informed him about a plot by junior hard-line officers to kill Papadopoulos (and not only him) should he be allowed to call elections. Kakaounakis (1976B: 57) speaks of a secret attachment to the note handed to Papadopoulos on the night of his overthrow which mentioned that the hardliners wanted to shoot him, but Ioannidis had rejected their suggestion. See also Markezinis 1979: 523.
108 On the night of his overthrow, the first thing that Papadopoulos asked the commanding officer who placed him under house arrest was 'Is this the work of Ioannidis?' (Kakaounakis 1976B: 49).
109 Georgalas, one of his closet followers, referred to Papadopoulos as 'an excellent tactician' in his interview.
110 Regarding this speculation, see Karter 2010: 116–19. Makarezos (2010: 117) reaches a similar conclusion.
111 As Bonanos (1986: 145) notes, 'Ioannidis was the perfect conspirator: taciturn, sibylic, secretive and deliberately vague when talking, hiding his own inner thoughts while trying to guess the ones of his interlocutors.' See also Psycharis 1975: 26.
112 Theodorakopoulos (1976: 236) claims that 'Ghizikis was assured that honest elections would be held within two years when he was summoned by Ioannides to accept this position.'
113 On the rumours about Androutsopoulos as a CIA agent, see Murtagh 1994. Kakaounakis (1976B: 130) mentions Georgalas' caustic comment that Androutsopoulos 'was good for collecting taxes but not for dealing with political crises'.

114 Haralambis 1985: 306; see also Barkman 1989: 140.
115 Wooudhouse 1985: 144. On the positive reaction of politicians, see Bonanos 1986: 143; Theodorakopoulos 1976: 236; Grigoriadis 1975C: 132–4. Barkman (1989: 140) repeats his remark that 'The Greeks are again reacting emotionally rather than rationally.'
116 Hooper to FCO, 13 November 1973, WSG 1/5, FCO 9/1716.
117 Kanellopoulos 1987: 225.
118 Barkman 1989: 143. Bonanos (1986: 149) ironically recalled that he was thinking that 'only Papadopoulos might have been happy when listening to Androutsopoulos' inaugural speech'. Arapakis (2000: 118) recalls his dismay when listening to the speech.
119 Interview with Pattakos. Markezinis (1994: 225) mistakenly says that Ioannidis spoke of elections, but not earlier than 1977 or 1978. See also Bonanos 1986.
120 Theodorakopoulos 1976: 237.
121 Androutsopoulos 1993: 41.
122 Theodorakopoulos 1976: 238.
123 For the full letter by Averoff, see Andrews 1989: 305–10.
124 Bonanos 1986: 153.
125 Papandreou 1974, reprinted in Papandreou 1976: 69.
126 For instance, Mitsotakis (2017: 311) notes the 'dark which Greece was plunged into after Markezinis' failure ... there was no indication of a group that could take any political initiative ... even Karamanlis was dismayed ... and started getting fatalistic about the situation'.
127 Ioannidis' speech to the naval officers, 20 February 1974; taken from Markezinis' archive.
128 Markezinis 1979: 525.
129 See Bonanos 1986 for an account of the thoughts of the Greek military as an institution during the first days of the transition. For the institutional aspect of the transition, see Diamantouros 1986; Linz and Stepan 1996.
130 The exception of Andreas Papandreou, who called the Karamanlis government 'a NATO change of guard in Athens', was negated by Papandreou himself, returning in September 1974 to Greece and endorsing the transition. Also, the calling of elections on the first anniversary of the Polytechnic uprising was resented by the left.
131 On this point, see Psomiades 1982; Diamantouros 1986; Karakatsanis 2001.

132 The best account of the failed 1975 plot is provided by Psomiades 1982. See also Diamantouros 1986.
133 Theodorakopoulos 1976: 231. See also Zournatzis and Michalopoulos 1990: 551 for the theory of the missed opportunity.
134 Farakos to the author.
135 NARA, State Department to US Embassy in Tehran, Fall of Papadopoulos, 29 November 1973.
136 Bonanos 1986: 135.
137 Barkman 1989: 125.
138 Hooper to FCO, 16 October 1973, WSG3/548/2, FCO9/1716.
139 Hooper to Cornish, Internal Political Situation, 6 September 1973, WSG 1/5, FCO 9/1716.
140 Huntington 1991: 190.
141 Barkman 1989: 145.
142 Passas 1980: 546–7.
143 Georgalas to the author.
144 Theodorakopoulos 1976: 230.
145 Tzortzis 2012: 328.

5 *Fortuna* and the 'Experiment'

1 Haralambis 1985: 287.
2 Barkman 1989: 115–16.
3 All this despite the fact that, as again the party admits, 'the "liberalisation" was not recent by mid-1973; rather, it had started ... earlier, more specifically by early 1972, with the release of exiles, the creation of the Consultative Committee etc.' (KKE 1978: 12–13).
4 For instance, the daily *Akropolis*' main headline on 2 October was 'The 21st of April 1967 is over', while that in the pro-regime *Eleftheros Kosmos* proclaimed 'There has come the moment that the 21st of April retires in history'.
5 Markezinis 1979: 263.
6 Mitsos, interview with the author.
7 KKE 1976: 14.

8 Meletopoulos 1996: 409.
9 Mitsos, interview with the author.
10 Grigoriadis 1975C: 73; Kornetis (2013: 116) agrees that 'Papadopoulos' maneuvers and his decision to proceed toward the gradual normalization of political life opened a space for the reactions of counter elites and civil society in general.'
11 'We had secret police reports that many EK politicians, as well as leftist and extremist organisations, were planning mass anti-government demonstrations in order to exploit politically the new situation' (Markezinis 1979: 398).
12 Grigoriadis 1975 C: 74. Zournatzis and Michalopoulos (1996: 528), attempting to credit Markezinis with a tolerant view of democratic change, claim that 'the Chief Constable of Athens Police fired four shots in the air, fearing he would lose control of the demonstration ... [T]he same night he was summoned by Markezinis and told that if this happened again he would lose his post.'
13 Martin to FCO, FCO 9/1716, 8 November 1973.
14 Markezinis (1979: 404) was forewarned by the Chief Constable of Athens Police that further trouble was on the way, and that he was making emergency plans for this contingency. He vaguely concludes that 'behind the events lay the political ambitions ... of those who wanted to block the way to normality', not specifying who 'those' were.
15 Iordanoglou, taken from Kyrkos's archive.
16 Grigoriadis 1975C: 77. Passas (1980: 548) agrees that granting the student demands could have averted the campus occupation and what ensued, blaming the Minister of Education. KKE's *Voice of Truth* radio broadcast of 2 November described the minister's promise of free elections as 'cheap demagogy [by] ... the regime which aims at creating a false impression of democracy'. See also Papazoglou 1983: 124–5.
17 Barkman (1989: 122) claims this was what Markezinis told him on 23 October, but there is no confirmation of this plan from any other source.
18 Kornetis (2013: 255) correctly points out that 'the fact that the Polytechnic occupation took off because of a misunderstanding exposes the importance of contingency'.
19 KKE 1976: 31. Papazoglou (1983: 127) says that 'the idea to occupy the Campus belonged to extreme leftists – Maoists, Trotskyites etc – groups'.

The Dean notes that on the 14th the 'traditional left' student organizations were pushing for a 'tactical retreat' and for leaving the campus, while the non-party affiliated students were for the occupation, in contrast to the their party-aligned colleagues (Konofagos 1982: 89–90).

20 As Kornetis (2013: 253) admits, 'when writing of the Polytechnic occupation, it can be difficult to distinguish eyewitness testimony from hearsay'.

21 It is notable that the official KKE report (1976: 18) admits that 'the party's position [insisting on the proper organization of all forms of anti-dictatorial struggle] ... was not complete, as it lacked specific instructions on the handling of unpredicted situations, such as spontaneous or semi-spontaneous peoples' outbursts'.

22 For this point, see KKE 1976: 27; Konofagos 1982: 29.

23 Papazoglou 1983: 127. The KKE's report adds that the students' movement 'did not study well its further actions ... It had made no material-technical preparations for such an event ... [T]he students operating the radio station were against occupying the campus, but the leftists were for; eventually the eight hundred or so students on campus and many staying outside gave the impression that the occupation had already started' (KKE 1976: 26–30).

24 A student of 1973 would say 22 years later that 'the students hoped that their break with the military regime would move the anti-dictatorial feelings of the Greek people ... thus causing an open social break between the junta and the people, which in turn would lead to the downfall of the junta' (Mantoglou 1995: 22).

25 Iordanoglou 1993.

26 Mantoglou 1995: 118–20.

27 Konofagos 1982: 47.

28 For the full statement, see Papazoglou 1975: 134–5. Kornetis (2012: 266) agrees that 'by extending their demands beyond university concerns, students made it clear for the first time that university issues could not be separated from society as a whole'.

29 Konofagos 1982: 35. According to his recollection, Daskalopoulos said to him 'let the students shout and shout again; in the end they will get bored and will leave the Campus' (Konofagos 1982: 40).

30 Andrews 1989: 195: Konofagos (1982: 51) found this behaviour by the regime 'puzzling' since he was sure they failed both to neutralize the

Polytechnic radio transmitter and to stop the free movement of people to and from the campus. The report by the KKE, on the other hand, considers this 'an honoring of the liberalization plan' (KKE 1976: 55). See also Barkman 1989: 127; Zournatzis and Michalopoulos 1990: 531.

31 'Even on Thursday night [15 November] I had the impression that the police officials were not taking the demonstrations too seriously' (Markezinis 1979: 416).

32 Markezinis 1979: 423. The University of Athens was closed on the 14th on the decision of its Dean and against Markezinis' advice, as the latter admits in his private notes.

33 'I cannot tell why the police allowed the demonstrations outside the Polytechnic to grow as large as tens of thousands of people . . . [I]n my opinion it was gross negligence if not malice on behalf of the authorities that let the demonstrations grow larger' (Kanellopoulos 1987: 323–8). See also Woodhouse 1985: 132.

34 According to Konofagos (1982: 61), even on the morning of the 16th, Sifnaios was optimistic that Markezinis' planned conference for the next day about preparations for the elections was still feasible.

35 Regarding the reply to Roufogalis, see Kakaounakis II: 14. For the assurances to Sifnaios, see Karter 2010: 110. See also Grigoriadis 1975C: 93, who mentions Sifnaios' suspicion that 'Papadopoulos was after some political gain'.

36 See Kornetis 2013: 322 for the implications of this attitude.

37 Quoted in Mantoglou 1995: 195. See also Kornetis for this utopian conviction.

38 Barkman 1989: 129. Mantoglou (1995: 213) quotes a participant in the occupation saying that 'the students were in collision not only with the regime, but also with parts of the Greek people . . . [M]any of their slogans did not represent the people and thus could not be accepted.' See also Theodorakopoulos 1976: 232 for a sharp criticism of the students' tactics.

39 Interview with Mitsos.

40 'Five policemen made their appearance; five thousand of us scattered. As we ran I heard somebody "wait, it's only five of them!" Five policemen only, walking rather rapidly in our direction, were enough to chase a multitude away' (Andrews 1989: 74).

41 See Papazoglou 1983: 128.

42 See Kornetis 2013: 289. See also Papazoglou 1983: 205; Konofagos 1982: 190. The KKE report of 1976 would partly amend this position, as it claimed that 'the opinion of an agitation plan does not stand an evidence trial... but it is true that the reaction's forces tried to exploit the struggle with agitations... as far as they possibly could' (KKE 1976: 31).
43 Kanellopoulos 1987: 218. Regarding the issue of *agents provocateurs*, see Papazoglou (1983: 199–200), who presents the testimony of one of them during the Polytechnic trials claiming that during the events there were about 150 agents of the KYP and ESA on campus. See also Kornetis 2013: 288–90.
44 KKE's report (1978: 35) even claims that on the morning of the 15th there was 'a cooling of the massive character of the demonstrations and of enthusiasm' among the students, and scepticism about the course things were taking, which was reversed by the expression of popular solidarity later in the afternoon.
45 Papandreou 1974, reprinted in Papandreou 1978:71. Konofagos (1982: 175) also quotes a member of the Polytechnic Coordination Committee saying that the driving force of the Polytechnic events was not the students but the people, as they were spontaneous and independent from party manipulations.
46 Andrews 1989: 82.
47 Mitsos to the author. The KKE report (1978: 39) agrees about this optimistic anticipation of democratic change, speaking of the 'illusions... [regarding] the intentions of the junta encouraged by the anticipation of Markezinis' statements' scheduled for the 17th.
48 Kornetis 2012: 270.
49 See KKE 1976: 40 on those points.
50 Konofagos 1982: 61.
51 Grigoriadis 1975C: 92.
52 Markezinis' private notes, taken from his archive.
53 For details of the plan – codenamed 'Thunder' – see Kakaounakis 1976B: 23–4; Konofagos 1982: 66.
54 See Kakaounakis 1976B: 21. Zournatzis notes that tear gas was also prohibited because of Anghelis' concern 'lest a projectile falls on the head of some student and kills them'. See also Markezinis 1994: 202.
55 Markezinis 1979: 419. It is not the first time that Markezinis failed to be more precise about the identity of those who had such an interest. Zournatzis believed that some of the higher officials in Athens police who were informed by their commander were responsible for leaking the plan.

56 According to Rodakis (1975: 356), this wave of attacks 'was a nonsense that led to a tragic mistake ... [I]f it was not an agitation, it was a show of anarchist tendencies ... [T]he attack on state buildings was a revolutionary action for which nobody was prepared.' See also Konofagos 1982: 63.

57 Woodhouse (1985: 134) claims that the orders to the police not to fire on civilians 'were not meticulously obeyed'. Barkman (1989: 128) contends that 'at no time during this operation were shots fired at people'. The report of Tsevas mentions at least one sharp-shooter firing from the Ministry of Public Order straight into the demonstrators. The number and identity of the sharp-shooters remains a mystery.

58 By that time, Konofagos (1982: 71) claims that the demonstrators around the Polytechnic numbered in excess of 100,000 people.

59 This point is stressed in Kakaounakis II: 34–5. Grigoriadis (1975C: 93–105) claims that the Attorney General was not consulted about the issue of the army's intervention. Barkman (1989: 147) mistakenly claims that it was Markezinis who called in the army. See also the Tsevas report.

60 See Konofagos 1982: 71; Tsevas report.

61 Interestingly, Markezinis (1979) says that he knew nothing about these moves.

62 On police and ESA cruelty, see, among the many sources, Andrews 1989: 84–7; Konofagos 1982: 65–75; Papazoglou 1983: 145; Tsevas report: 45. On the army's contrasting attitude, see Kakaounakis II: 37.

63 Grigoriadis 1975C: 110.

64 Konofagos 1982: 114. The KKE radio station too, on the 18th and 19th of the month, accused Markezinis and Zournatzis 'of Goebbels-like tactics, aiming at discrediting and distorting the meaning of the uprising, by presenting it as a rampage of vandals'. Two days later it accused the regime of trying to claim that the incidents were the work of a small minority of anarchists and nihilists (*Voice of Truth*, transcripts of 18, 19 and 20 November 1973). See also Papazoglou 1983: 171.

65 PREM 15/1611, 20 November 1973.

66 Helmis 2006: 84; Markezinis 1994: 203; 1979: 424.

67 Notes from Markezinis' archive.

68 Grigoriadis 1975C: 111.

69 In the words of Karakatsanis 2001: 16.

70 Kanellopoulos 1987: 322.

71 Papazoglou mentions other sources linked to the unofficial and illegal press of the time, which raise the number of the dead to 43. However, after

the restoration of democracy and during the investigations for the 'Polytechnic trials', the report by Public Attorney Tsevas rejected this figure and instead accepted the original number of 18 dead plus six more linked to the suppression of the demonstrations. See Papazoglou 1983: 176–81.
72 Konofagos (1982:119) gives the number wounded as 2,000.
73 Woodhouse (1985: 138) claims that 268 students from other faculties were arrested. See also Zournatzis and Michalopoulos 1998: 531.
74 Gill 2000: 48.
75 Mitsos to the author. Iordanoglou (1993), while agreeing that 'the Polytechnic could not be [seen as] but a major defeat', also claims that 'the regime paid a higher price for its victory than we did for our defeat... [T]he declaration of martial law signalled the irreversible end of the policy of "liberalization".
76 Mantoglou 1993: 228.
77 Androutsopoulos 1993: 48. Kornetis (2013: 288) agrees that 'no open action against the regime was recorded. Authoritarianism in its fullest form, as fantasized and practiced by Ioannidis, did not allow for any sort of student mobility.'
78 Interview with Mitsos.
79 Bonanos 1986: 139–43.
80 Konofagos 1982: 53.
81 Regarding these rumours, see Karter 2002: 113. Passas (1980: 548) also speaks of 'elements of both domestic and foreign secret services infiltrating the Polytechnic... and making the course the events took on the night of the 17th inevitable'.
82 Kornetis 2013: 236.
83 Kanellopoulos 1987: 218; Theodorakopoulos 1976: 232.
84 See the outspoken criticism by Theodorakopoulos (1976: 232), who takes the mild reaction of the police as proof of a sincere democratic commitment on behalf of Markezinis. See also Zournatzis and Michalopoulos (1996: 528), who claim that 'when the politicians realised that the occupation started by the leftists was successful they visited the campus in order to manipulate it'. They even claim that their motives were just 'to do what they could not do for over 6 years – cause a commotion and demand a new coalition government that would include them' (Zournatzis and Michalopoulos 1996: 548).

85 Kyrkos to the author. Iordanoglou 1993 agrees, while Zournatzis and Michalopoulos also reach the same conclusion, but from an opposite perspective.
86 On this point, see Mantoglou 1995: 213.
87 Quoted in Zournatzis and Michalopoulos 1998: 524.
88 Woodhouse 1985: 133. He also relates a witness's testimony that 'the students never left the area of the Polytechnic and had nothing to do with the violence elsewhere' (Woodhouse 1985: 134).
89 Regarding the presence of Ioannidis around the campus, see Woodhouse 1985: 133; Papazoglou 1983: 199.
90 This opinion is given in Grigoriadis 1975C: 117. See also Andrews 1989: 198; Barkman 1989: 147. Papazoglou (1983: 199) points to the fact that many officers who were coordinating the action between the army and the police also participated in the Ioannidis coup.
91 Androutsopoulos (1993: 49) claims that many officers supported the coup because 'there was a power vacuum and the country was living at the brink of anarchy, a first touch of which was experienced during the days of the Polytechnic events'.
92 See Kakaounakis 1976B: 9 for the first theory. Grigoriadis 1975C: 116 supports the second hypothesis.
93 According to Rodakis (1975: 347), 'Papadopoulos took advantage of the Polytechnic uprising to get a new dictatorship going' and ditched his plan for a fake democratization. This is why he did not allow the police to intervene on the second day of the demonstrations, as he intended to provoke a massacre that he could use as a pretext to reintroduce martial law. Grigoriadis 1975C: 116 mentions a statement by an Ioannidis insider who claimed that the escalation of events was a conspiracy by Papadopoulos to reverse the civilianization process. Again, this opponent of Papadopoulos does not explain why if this was the case the Ioannidis coup was necessary, since it had precisely the same goal.
94 Markezinis 1979: 436
95 The KKE (1976: 55) speaks of the government honouring its liberalization timetable. Konofagos (1982: 98) argues that the government hoped that the students 'would leave Polytechnic [of] ... their own will so [that] it would be unnecessary and illegal to send [in the] police, which was important for a government trying by all means to trumpet its faith [in] ... democracy'.

96 See Papandreou 1974, reprinted in Papandreou 1976: 68.
97 See Grigoriadis 1975C: 114–15 for the testimony of Ghizikis. See also Androutsopoulos 1993: 47. Bonanos (1986: 133) says that Ioannidis considered bringing the coup forward, as he was aware of Papadopoulos' intentions to call martial law. However, he had second thoughts on the matter, since his networks were so extensive and the information they provided so accurate that he judged he could proceed with his original plan. See also the KKE report 55.
98 Markezinis 1979: 416, referring to the conference he was about to give with details concerning the elections.
99 Theodorakopoulos 1976: 234. See also Zournatzis and Michalopoulos 1998: 551.
100 Hooper to FCO, Greek Internal Situation, 20 November 1973, WSG 1/5, FCO 9/1712.
101 *Eleftheros Kosmos*, 25 November 1973, taken from Zournatzis' archive. This agrees with Markezinis' view that the instigators of the future coup expected him to resign, but when he did not, they proceeded to oust him and Papadopoulos.
102 Makarezos 2010: 19, 49 on Karamanlis and the uprising. This silence is also noted in Karamanlis VII: 202: '[N]ot having direct knowledge of the dramatic events happening in Athens, and in view of possible uncontrollable developments ... [Karamanlis] did not consider any premature statement as useful.'
103 Averoff, in Zournatzis and Michalopoulos 1998: 551.
104 See O'Donnell and Schmitter 1986: 5 for the concept of *fortuna*.
105 Quote taken from Grigoriadis 1975C: 115. Androutsopoulos (1993: 470) partly agrees, but claims the Polytechnic events were totally irrelevant to the Ioannidis coup, noting that they were 'not a case of organised resistance, let alone a popular insurrection. It was instead a coincidental and conjunctural outburst. It was due to the mistaken government decisions related to the student elections, and started as a reaction against their timing. It is fact distorting to link it to the revolutionary action that followed eight days later. This was set for the 25th of November long before.'
106 Huntington 1991: 134, where he also mentions the Polytechnic suppression and the removal of the 'liberalising Papadopoulos by the hard-line Ioannidis'.

107 Kornetis 2013: 327. Kornetis also highlights the refusal of the students, in the trial that followed the restoration of democracy, to accept facts that would portray the uprising as 'an anarchist revolution' (Kornetis 2013: 325).
108 Interview with the author.
109 Huntington 1991: 144.
110 Markezinis 1994: 205 (emphasis added).
111 Grigoriadis 1975C: 113–14, where he refers to, and challenges, the theory implicating the CIA in the uprising.

6 The International Factor and the 'Experiment'

1 See, for instance, Syrigos (2016: 329): 'the liberalisation experiment lost the support of the US ... because of [the] refusal of the regime to allow the use of USA bases in Greece for supplying Israel'.
2 Featherstone 1987: 10. Stern (1978: 140) also accepts that 'three decades of post-war history have inspired [in] ... the Greeks a deeply rooted opinion that their affairs are [controlled] ... by foreign services'.
3 Murtagh (1994: 97) claims that 'as early as 1963 the US government was aware that Papadopoulos and two of his associates, Pattakos and Makarezos, had formed a group which began to consider the possibility of an eventual take-over of government'. And Papachelas (1998: 273) presents various CIA reports on the factions of Papadopoulos and others, the last one in early 1967 claiming that they were ready 'to proceed to a coup if the dictatorship is their only alternative to a victory of the EK'.
4 Among the rich literature on US policy towards Greece in the weeks leading to the April coup, see Murtagh 1994: 108–11; Iatrides 2009: 59; Stern 1978: 46–7; Keeley 2002:147.
5 See Papachelas 1998: 315–17. Stern (1978: 51) quotes a State Department official in Athens in April 1967 saying 'we are witnessing the wrong coup; we have been taken by surprise'. And Keeley (2002: 186) quotes Phil Stoddard, Head of Intelligence Research of the State Department on Greece, Turkey and Iran: 'we have no information on this conspiratorial group'.
6 Weiner 2007: 331.
7 Papachelas 1998: 327. It is not very clear when and how the US intelligence services lost track of the colonels. Keeley (2002: 187) claims that the

Papadopoulos group set itself in operational readiness in February 1967, and cut all contacts with any sources that could provide the CIA with reports on its moves. Leontaritis (2010: 24) provides similar information, claiming that Papadopoulos, aware of the Americans' efforts to trace the plotters' moves, advised all groups to steer clear from them. Finally, extreme rightist ERE MP Nikolaos Farmakis is said to have forewarned the US Attaché Norbert Anschutz about the forthcoming colonels' coup in early April 1967. Anschutz told US Embassy personnel about this but they all agreed that Farmakis' information was not credible and did not inform Washington. See Papachelas 1998: 276.

8 Some Pentagon officials considered the coup 'the best thing that happened in Athens since the time of Pericles'. See Papachelas 1998: 354.
9 See Tomai 2009: 85.
10 Murtagh 1994: 153. Papachelas 1999: 354 quotes head of CIA in Athens John Maury saying in 1977 that 'even career diplomats believed that an intervention, even if against a brutal military dictatorship, was unacceptable'. Goldbloom (1972: 241), while noting 'the general American contempt for the new rulers of Greece', observes that 'the Embassy and its superiors in Washington preferred the junta's rule to a possible civil war'.
11 According to Stavrou (1976: 194), 'the Americans feared that if the Colonels fell, chaos and eventually Communism would be the result'.
12 Woodhouse (1985: 40) considers the war to be 'the greatest stroke of luck for the junta'; and Murtagh (1994: 155) says that 'the US Sixth Fleet facilities in Crete were used to help the Israelis'. See also Grigoriadis 1975A: 121.
13 See Woodhouse 1982: 185; Stern 1978: 61.
14 For instance, Tomai (2009: 85) quotes a report by Talbot to the State Department that 'a large number of Greeks believe the US either helped or tolerated the coup'. Based on a sample of views from Greek citizens, Keeley (2002: 261) concludes that there was 'bitterness for the Americans [whose] ... tanks [allowed] ... the colonels [to] impose ... themselves ... [There was] a belief that the Americans knew about and tolerated the coup.' Couloumbis (2002: 33) notes that during a hearing in the US Congress 'Greek politicians [were] ... of the opinion that the USA supported the coup or, at best, knew about it and did not stop it'.
15 Veremis 1997: 155
16 According to Constantine's memoirs (2015B: 285–6), Johnson promised him political and diplomatic support in his effort to oust the colonels.

17 All quotations from Couloumbis et al. 1986: 133–4, where an excellent account of American interests is given.
18 Couloumbis et al. 1986: 144.
19 As Stern (1978: 75) notes, during the time of the embargo the colonels kept on receiving light weapons, which would be more appropriate for internal policing and suppressing riots, than modern tanks and warplanes needed for war.
20 Klarevas 2006: 508.
21 Grigoriadis 1975B: 45. The US Embassy had never previously been inaccessible for such a long period.
22 Stavrou 1976:185.
23 Murtagh 1994: 231.
24 Stavrou (1976: 183) presents a total of 58 American generals and admirals who visited Greece between 1967 and 1973.
25 See Stern 1978: 92. The report concluded that strategic and military interests were threatened when the political consequences of decisions such as the one on homeporting facilities in Greece were underestimated.
26 'As usual, Moscow was differentiating its state policy from its relations with her sister communist parties' (Woodhouse 1985: 84). Papadopoulos established diplomatic relations with Bulgaria and Rumania in 1971 and with the German Democratic Republic in 1973. Theodorakopoulos (1976: 222) praises Papadopoulos for these initiatives, describing him as 'the first post-war Greek leader to establish an independent foreign policy by increasing contacts with Eastern bloc Governments'. Woodhouse (1985: 91) argues that these openings to communist countries served 'a dual purpose: to assert a degree of independence of the United States, and also to neutralize the left-wing opposition'.
27 See Pedaliu 2011: 653, who claims that this rapprochement 'silenced most advocates of ostracizing the Greek regime from the Western family of states'.
28 Verney and Tsakaloyannis 1986: 183.
29 Georgalas to the author. He was not very detailed on why the Americans would want this, nor on who the other regime members were. Georgalas claims that when he refused to participate in these machinations, all channels of communication with American officials were cut off.
30 Woodhouse 1985: 112.
31 FRUS, Vol. XXX, National Intelligence Estimate: Short-Term Prospects in Greece, 19 July 1973.

32 On this point, see Tsingos 2001: 321.
33 For the events leading up to the 'withdrawal' of the regime from the Council of Europe, see Treholt 1972; Woodhouse 1985.
34 As Woodhouse (1985: 71) notes, 'in European capitals the US Embassies were reported to be urging restraint on the proposal to expel Greece from the Council of Europe'.
35 Excerpt from Averoff's letter of 1969 to Papadopoulos, Markezinis' archive.
36 Woodhouse 1985: 69. Tsingos (2001: 323) also notes that 'the Community members, far from actively trying to pressure or topple the Colonels from within the EC ... generally co-operated with, supported, and even courted them (albeit reluctantly in some cases) for strategic, geopolitical, and security reasons, both in their independent, bilateral relations with Greece, and within other organizations'.
37 Pesmazoglou (1999: 285) considers Lipovski's visit to Athens to be 'the point of reconnection of Greece with the EEC'. See also Woodhouse 1985: 109; Grigoriadis 1975B: 208.
38 See Treholt (1972: 225) for the arms trade between European countries and Greece during the dictatorship. Tsingos (2001: 323) points out that many of the EC countries which had voted to suspend the association agreement with Greece were helping to supply the junta with the arms which were used to impose its rule on the Greek people.
39 Hooper to FCO, Greece: Annual Review for 1972, 2 January 1973, WSG1/2, FCO9/1709.
40 Pesmazoglou 1999: 108.
41 On this point, see Nicolet 2001: 376–7.
42 Xydis 1972: 203. See also Theodorakopoulos 1976: 203. According to Stavrou (1976: 187), Papadopoulos 'aimed at a solution of the Cyprus issue in 1972 which would facilitate détente with Turkey and lessen the only perceptible external tension'.
43 Haralambis 1985: 287. It should be noted that the fiercest opponents of Papadopoulos within the regime were those pressing for *Enosis* even by violent means.
44 Woodhouse 1985: 115.
45 Haralambis 1985: 287.
46 It was almost the same plan that would be put forward one year later. For details, see Grigoriadis 1975B: 59–63.
47 See Grigoriadis 1975B: 63–4 for the whole text. See also Woodhouse 1985.

48 FRUS, Vol. XXX, National Intelligence Estimate: Short-Term Prospects in Greece, 19 July 1973.
49 Woodhouse 1985: 120. Papandreou (1976: 54) called the abolition of the monarchy 'inevitable' because it had become for the US 'an obsolete means of control[ing] Greece'. On the day Papadopoulos proclaimed the Republic, Papandreou told the BBC that 'Papadopoulos was and still is the agent chosen by the US in order to keep Greece under the dictatorship and to offer military facilities for the service [of] ... Pentagon interests in the Middle East' (Papandreou 1976: 35).
50 Hooper to Home, Abolition of the Greek Monarchy, 15 June 1973, WSG1/9, FCO9/1713.
51 US Secretary of State to USICNCEUR, Further Reflections on Greek Regime's Proclamation of a Republic, 21 June 1973.
52 FRUS, Vol. XXX, Memorandum From Acting Secretary of State Rush to President Nixon, 12 June 1973, Ford Library, National Security Adviser, Scowcroft Daily Work Files, Chronological File A, Box 3.
53 Denson to FCO, *Report on the 1973 Greek Plebiscite*, 4 August 1973, WSG1/9, FCO9/1713.
54 See Helmis 2007: 45. This information, however, cannot be confirmed.
55 Barkman 1989: 118.
56 Goodison to FCO, British Policy towards Greece, 13 November 1973, WSG 8/548/3, FCO 9/1732.
57 Martin to Cornish, 17 September 1973, Denson Report on US/Greek relations, WSG 3/304/1, FCO9/1732.
58 NARA, Tasca to State Department, Possible US Statement on new GOG, 6 October 1973
59 Markezinis 1979: 234–43.
60 Miller 2009: 171.
61 According to his son-in-law (Helmis 2007: 45), Markezinis had, in July 1973, told him that he would shift Greece's foreign policy in a non-aligned direction, not explaining how this was to be done. This is the only indication of a possible radical turn and cannot be taken at face value.
62 Secretary of State to US Embassy in Moscow, Political Manoeuvres on the Left, 26 October 1973.
63 Markezinis 1979: 394.
64 Grigoriadis 1975B: 71.

65 For the visit of Makarios, see Woodhouse 1985: 122; Grigoriadis 1975B: 71. Grigoriadis fails to be more specific about which forces were preparing Markezinis' overthrow, thus adding a flavour of conspiracy to the issue of Markezinis and Cyprus.
66 These are the words of his son-in-law (Helmis 2007: 81).
67 Baker to FCO, 2 November 1973, WSG 1/5, FCO 9/1716.
68 See Nafpliotis (2012: 196) on this difference of opinion on the question of support for Markezinis between the Foreign Office in London and the embassy in Athens.
69 Pesmazoglou 1999: 109.
70 Woodhouse 1985: 122.
71 Whitehead 2002: 9.
72 See Barkman 1989:119–20. Papandreou (1976: 72) considered that the European Social Democracy had urged the Greek 'bourgeois political world to accept the Markezinis solution'.
73 Barkman's diary note of 18 October (1989: 120).
74 Hooper to Goodison, Greece: Internal Situation, 25 November 1973 WSG 25/304/12 FCO 9/1717.
75 Grigoriadis 1975B: 45.
76 On this incident, see Markezinis 1994: 209–10; Helmis 2007: 104–5.
77 Markezinis 1994: 210.
78 Abadi 2000: 55.
79 Kissinger 1982: 708.
80 FRUS, Vol. XXX, Action Memorandum from the Director of the Policy Planning Staff (Lord) to Secretary of State Kissinger, US Policy toward Greece, 15 February 1974.
81 Secretary of State to US Embassy in Athens, Resupply to Israel, 26 October 1973.
82 See Grigoriadis 1975B:47. Passas (1980: 546) considers the negative stance of Markezinis as fatal for the *reforma*, and again, he blames the latter for dragging Papadopoulos to his downfall because of his strident anti-American position. Verney and Couloumbis (1986: 110) agree that '[the refusal] was particularly important for the USA ... [T]his created doubts in Washington concerning the Junta's reliability as an ally during any future Middle East crisis.'
83 Markezinis interview in *Kathimerini*, 21 February 1993. For Maragkou (2014: 654), this refusal was yet another example of the regime's intransigence towards the Americans.

84 Markezinis 1979: 206. He claimed (1994: 165) that 'one can better protect Greek–US relations if one says no to the Americans at some point than by saying yes all the time'.
85 Kallivretakis 2014: 108.
86 Shain 1995: 261.
87 Tovias 1991: 186.
88 Martin to Cornish, Greece and the Middle East crisis, 1 November 1973, WSG 3/304/1, FCO 9/1729.
89 Central Intelligence Bulletin, 26 October 1973.
90 Markezinis 1979: 621; Murtagh 1994: 239.
91 For this, see Markezinis 1979: 468. His son-in-law claims that Tasca said that 'had Markezinis been invited to visit Washington the course of events might have been different' (Helmis 2007: 125).
92 Quoted in Grigoriadis 1975C: 137.
93 Mentioned in Psicharis 1975: 24; also Bonanos 1986: 113. A CIA memorandum of September 1972 stated that 'if he [Ioannides] decided to go against the prime minister, the threat of a successful military coup would balloon rapidly' and that 'if Papadopoulos becomes [a] victim of a coup, it will be essentially because of [the] failure on his part to maintain a close relationship with those officers who see themselves as guardians of the revolutionary virtue (CIA Intelligence Memorandum, Papadopoulos: a Question of Survival, 25 September 1972). Two months later, another memorandum stated that a coup against Papadopoulos would succeed and pointed our two possible directions a new military regime could take: the first, under Ioannides, would be to 'probably move slowly towards constitutional government', while the second, 'dominated by younger officers in the junta would probably set up a tighter, more dictatorial regime'. The memorandum concluded that Papadopoulos would 'probably remain in office ... for another year or two ... [T]he immediate successor to George Papadopoulos will be another military government' (CIA Memorandum, Some alternatives to the Papadopoulos Regime, 9 November 1972).
94 This incident is mentioned in Arapakis 2000: 117; also in Grigoriadis 1975C: 137.
95 For this alleged meeting, see Kakaounakis 1975A: 389–90.
96 Psicharis 1975: 30. Grigoriadis (1975C: 138) agrees.
97 Murtagh 1994: 239. Haralambis (1985: 310) agrees that 'the only international support [for] ... the dictatorship of Ioannidis was the U.S. foreign policy'.

98 Helmis 2007: 116–17. Again, there was no corroborating evidence for the existence of this letter.
99 Woodhouse 1985: 145.
100 *Voice of Truth*, 21 November 1973 in Farakos' archive.
101 *Voice of Truth* transcripts of 21 November 1973 in Farakos' archive; Rodakis 1975: 368–9.
102 Papandreou 1974, reprinted in Papandreou 1976: 68.
103 Woodhouse 1985: 212.
104 Markezinis 1979: 184. Miller (2009: 185) agrees that 'as long as Papadopoulos remained in power ... Makarios could fend off the most dangerous external threat ... [After Papadopoulos' fall] a much more dangerous group now controlled the Greek Cypriot National Guard. Makarios' internal enemies rejoiced.'
105 Quoted in Markezinis 1994: 254. All interviewees accepted the sincerity of Markezinis' statement on this point.
106 See Helmis 2007: 94.
107 Gauvin to FCO, Aftermath of New Coup in Greece, 25 November 1973, WSG 1/14, FCO9/1717.
108 Hooper to FCO, Greece: annual review for 1973, 11 January 1974, WSG 1/2, FCO 9/1998.
109 NARA, State Department to all NATO Capitals, Current Situation in Greece, 5 December 1973.
110 Markezinis 1994: 245.
111 Gauvin to FCO, Aftermath of New Coup in Greece, 25 November 1973, WSG 1/14, FCO9/1717.
112 FRUS, Vol. XXX, Telegram From the Embassy in Greece to the Department of State, The Military in Greece: Dominant Political Power at the Crossroads – A Country Team Assessment, 8 February 1974.
113 Schmitter 1986: 8.
114 'They would have brought us down with or without Kissinger ... I refuse to believe that a Greek officer took orders from the US Foreign Minister to proceed [with] ... such a move' (Zournatzis to the author).
115 For the notion of 'penetrated countries', see Pridham 1991.
116 Tzortzis 2017: 76.
117 FRUS, Vol. XXX, Action Memorandum, US Policy toward Greece, 15 February1974. Emphasis in original.

7 Concluding Thoughts

1 O'Donnell and Schmitter 1986: 65.
2 It is interesting that amongst the author's interviewees, Pattakos, Makarezos, Zournatzis and Georgalas agreed that the regime had ended its life in October 1973 and that the 'Revolution' was no more. In contrast, all the opposition politicians interviewed held a diametrically opposite view, insisting that nothing had really changed – neither before nor after Markezinis took over.
3 Mitsos to the author.
4 The Spanish communist leader Santiago Carillo had predicted that Juan Carlos's reign would be brief, as he was so identified with the regime that he could not outlive it. Most political analysts believed that Suarez would either not last long or degenerate into a hardliner. The similarity with Markezinis is evident. See further Carr and Fusi 1979 for a description of the early opposition reaction to both men.
5 Secretary general of the Spanish communist party Santiago Carillo's remark that 'violent change doesn't make sense where the security forces dispose of sophisticated weapons' is indicative of the realism of the opposition. See Share 1986: 46.
6 On the tactics of Suarez regarding the military, see Aguero 1995. Interestingly, Bonanos believes that the main reason for the demise of the 'experiment' was the failure of Markezinis to pre-empt the hardliners in a similar way.
7 On this point, see Preston 1986.
8 It is significant that this happened in October 1977, four months after the transition elections. The contrast with Greece – where there were no political prisoners at the start of the transition – is striking.
9 This point also raises the question of the fate of all those who were involved in the 1967 coup, of those who profited from their collaboration with the regime and of those who engaged in torture under the auspices of the police/gendarmerie and the ESA. The prospect, at least in the early days of the new democracy, that their deeds would go unpunished was understandably anathema to many Greeks.
10 On the authoritarian Turkish constitution of 1982, see Ozbudun 2000.
11 On the 1983 elections and the reaction of the military to the victory of Ozal there is abundant literature. See especially Cizre 1997.

12 Diamantouros 1986: 153.
13 Gillespie 1990: 48.
14 Vanhanen 1992: 169.
15 Arapakis 2000: 94.
16 Helmis 2006: 130. It was not the first time that Tasca deplored the failure of Markezinis: just the previous month, he had reportedly told an American diplomat that the Markezinis government 'was the best one that Greece had in the past few years' (Helmis 2006: 125).
17 Quoted in Helmis 2006: 160. The attempt of Markezinis' son-in-law to eulogize the 'experiment' is obvious.
18 See Chapter 4.
19 Kornetis 2013: 287.
20 Barthes 1972: 143.
21 In the 1981 elections, the Progressive Party gained just 1.9 per cent of the popular vote. For a brief but accurate account of Markezinis' short post-1974 career, see Kohler 1982.
22 Barkman 1989: 138.
23 Mitsotakis 2017: 308. Meletopoulos (1996: 379) agrees that Markezinis 'took the unfair blame for a short and fruitless cooperation with the dictatorship'.
24 In a report to the Foreign Office, the British ambassador mentioned that Markezinis had allegedly said that 'if the junta knew what I intended to do, they would never have made me Prime Minister' (Hooper to FCO, FCO 9/1729, 1 November 1973). Nothing is known about the intentions of Markezinis had elections taken place, though, and the allegation that he was trying to enhance his democratic credentials by talking like this cannot be ruled out.
25 Theodorakopoulos 1976: 235.
26 Interestingly, one of the victims of the terrorists was Nikolaos Momferratos, Markezinis' Minister of Industry, who was assassinated in February 1985.

Bibliography

Primary sources

Interviews (in alphabetical order)

Grigoris Farakos, former Secretary General of the KKE.
Georgios Georgalas, regime Under-Secretary of Crete and confidant of Papadopoulos.
Leonidas Kyrkos, former Secretary General of the KKE-es.
Nikolaos Makarezos, regime leader.
Achilleas Mitsos, Professor of the Aegean University of Greece, member of 'Rigas Feraios' KKE of the Interior youth.
Stylianos Pattakos, regime leader.
Georgios Rallis, minister in the Karamanlis governments and ex-Prime Minister of Greece.
Ioannis Varvitsiotis, minister in the Karamanlis governments.
Spyros Zournatzis, Markezinis' government spokesman.

Greek Newspapers and Magazines

Akropolis
Eleftheros Kosmos
Epikaira
Kathimerini
Vradyni

Private Archives

Kyrkos's archive
Markezinis' notes, Markezinis' archive, Athens: Etaireia ton Filon tou Laou
Zournatzis' archive
'Voice of Truth' KKE Radio broadcast transcripts, Farakos' archive

Public archives

UK

Foreign Office, the National Archives (in date order)

FCO 9/1709, 2/1/1973.
FCO 9/1711, 26/4/1973.
FCO 9/1712, 20/111973.
FCO 9/1713, 6/6/1973.
FCO 9/1713, 15/6/1973.
FCO 9/1713, 4/8/1973.
FCO 9/1714, 1/9/1973.
FCO 9/1716, 6/9/1973.
FCO 9/1716, 25/10/1973.
FCO 9/1716, 2/11/1973.
FCO 9/1716, 8/11/1973.
FCO 9/1717, 6/12/1973.
FCO 9/1717, 25/11/1973.
FCO 9/1729, 1/11/1973.
FCO 9/1732, 17/9/1973.
FCO 9/1732, 13/11/1973.
FCO 9/1998, 11/1/1974.

USA

FRUS (Foreign Relations of United States) Vol. XXX, GREECE; CYPRUS; TURKEY, 1973–6 (in date order)

Memorandum from Acting Secretary of State Rush to President Nixon, 12/6/1973, Ford Library.
National Security Adviser, Scowcroft, Daily Work Files.
National Intelligence Estimate: Short-Term Prospects in Greece, 19/7/1973.
Telegram From the Embassy in Greece to the Department of State, Views of PM Markezinis, 18/11/1973.
Telegram from the Embassy in Greece to the Department of State, The Military in Greece: Dominant Political Power at the Crossroads – A Country Team Assessment, 8/2/1974.

NARA *(National Archives and Records Administration)*
(in date order)

CIA Intelligence Memorandum, Papadopoulos: a Question of Survival, 25/9/1972.
CIA Memorandum, Some Alternative to the Papadopoulos Regime, 9/11/1972.
Secretary of State to USICNCEUR, Further Reflections on Greek Regime's Proclamation of a Republic, 21/6/1973.
Tasca to State Department, Possible US Statement on new GOG, 6/10/1973.
Jackson to State Department, 'Makedonia' Exclusive Interview with Andreas Papandreou, 23/10/1973.
Central Intelligence Bulletin, 26/10/1973.
Secretary of State to US Embassy in Athens, Resupply to Israel, 26/10/1973.
Secretary of State to US Embassy in Moscow, Political Manoeuvres on the Left, 26/10/1973.
Jackson to Secretary of State, Reported Statement by ex-PM Karamanlis, 30/10/1973.
Embassy in Greece to the Department of State, Greece's Apparent New Master: Demetrios Ioannides; Some Fears, 26/11/1973.
Central Intelligence Bulletin, 27/11/1973.
State Department to US Embassy in Tehran, Fall of Papadopoulos, 29/11/1973.
Central Intelligence Bulletin, 3/12/1973.
State Department to all NATO Capitals, Current Situation in Greece, 5/12/1973. Action Memorandum from the Director of the Policy Planning Staff (Lord) to Secretary of State Kissinger, US Policy Toward Greece, 15/2/1974.

Secondary sources

Books and chapters

Aguero, F. 1995. *Soldiers, Civilians and Democracy: Post-Franco Spain in Comparative Perspective*. Baltimore, MD: Johns Hopkins University Press.
Alivizatos, N. 1983. *Οι πολιτικοί θεσμοί σε κρίση 1922–1974: Όψεις της ελληνικής εμπειρίας* (*The Political Institutions in Crisis 1922–1974: Facets of the Greek Experience*). Athens: Themelio.

Alivizatos, N. 2011. *Το Σύνταγμα και οι εχθροί του στη νεοελληνική ιστορία 1800–2010 (The Constitution and its Enemies in Modern Greek History 1800–2010)*. Athens: Polis

Andrews, K. 1980. *Greece in the Dark, 1967–1974*. Amsterdam: Adolf Hakkert.

Androutsopoulos, A. 1993. *Η μαρτυρία ενός πρωθυπουργού (The Testimony of a Prime Minister)*. Athens: To Oikonomikon

Arapakis, N. 2000. *Το τέλος της σιωπής (The End of Silence)*. Athens: Nea Synora.

Barkman, C. 1989. *Ambassador in Athens*. London: Merlin Press.

Barthes, R. 1973. *Mythologies*. St Albans: Paladin.

Bonanos, G. 1986. *Η Αλήθεια (The Truth)*. Athens: n.p.

Carr, R. and Fusi, P. 1979. *Spain: Dictatorship to Democracy*. London: George Allen & Unwin.

Casper, G. and Taylor, M. 1996. *Negotiating Democracy: Transitions from Authoritarian Rule*. Pittsburgh, PA: University of Pittsburgh Press.

Clapham, P. and Philip, G. 1985. 'The political dilemmas of military regimes', in P. Clapham and G. Philip (eds), *The Political Dilemmas of Military Regimes*, pp. 1–26. London: Croom Helm.

Clapham, P. and Philip, G. (eds). 1985. *The Political Dilemmas of Military Regimes*. London: Croom Helm.

Clogg, R. 1972. 'The ideology of the 'Revolution of the 21st of April', in R. Clogg and G. Yannopoulos, G. (eds), *Greece under Military Rule*, pp. 36–58. London: Secker and Warburg.

Clogg R. and Yannopoulos, G. (eds). 1972. *Greece under Military Rule*. London: Secker and Warburg.

Constantine, ex-King of Greece. 2015. *Χωρίς Τίτλο (No title)*. Athens: To Vima.

Couloumbis, T. 2002. *Σημειώσεις ενός πανεπιστημιακού (Notes of an Academic)*. Athens: Patakis.

Couloumbis, T., Petropoulos, J. and Psomiades, H. 1986. *Foreign Interference in Greek Politics: A Historical Perspective*. New York: Pella Publishing Company.

Demertzis, N. 1997. *Greece in European Political Cultures: Conflict or Convergence?* Ed. R. Eatwell. London: Routledge.

Dertilis, G. 1977. *Κοινωνικός μετασχηματισμός και στρατιωτική επέμβαση, 1880–1909 (Social Change and Military Intervention, Greece 1880–1909)*. Athens: Exandas.

Diamantouros, P.-N. 1986. 'Regime change and the prospects for democracy in Greece: 1974-1983', in G. O'Donnell, P. Schmitter and L. Whitehead (eds), *Transitions from Authoritarian Rule: Prospects for Democracy*, Vol. II: Southern Europe. Baltimore, MD: Johns Hopkins University Press.

Di Palma, G. 1990. *To Craft Democracies: An Essay on Democratic Transitions*. Berkeley: University of California Press.

Etzioni-Halevy, E. 1993. *The Elite Connection*. Cambridge: Polity.

Featherstone, K. 1987. 'Introduction', in K. Featherstone and D. Katsoudas (eds), *Political Change in Greece: Before and After the Colonels*, pp. 1-13. London: Croom Helm.

Featherstone, K. and Katsoudas, D. (eds). 1987. *Political Change in Greece: Before and After the Colonels*. London: Croom Helm.

Genevoix, M. 1973. *The Greece of Karamanlis or the Difficult Democracy*. London: Macmillan.

Gill, G. 2000. *The Dynamics of Democratisation*. Basingstoke: Macmillan.

Gillespie, C. 1990. 'Models of democratic transition in South America: negotiated reform versus democratic rupture', in D. Ethier (ed.), *Democratic Transition and Consolidation in Southern Europe, Latin America and Southeast Asia*, pp. 45-72. Basingstoke: Palgrave Macmillan.

Goldbloom, M. 1972. 'United States policy in post-war Greece', in R. Clogg and G. Yannopoulos (eds), *Greece under Military Rule*, pp. 228-45. London: Secker and Warburg.

Grigoriadis, P. 1975. *Ιστορία της δικτατορίας* (*History of the Dictatorship*). Athens: Kapopoulos.

Haggard, S. and Kaufmann, R.R. 1995. *The Political Economy of Democratic Transitions*. Princeton, NJ: Princeton University Press.

Haralambis, D. 1985. *Στρατός και πολιτική εξουσία: η δομή της εξουσίας στη μετεμφυλιακή Ελλάδα* (*The Army and Political Power: Power Structure in Post-Civil War Greece*). Athens: Exandas.

Haralambis, D. 1999. 'Η δικτατορια ως αποτέλεσμα αντιφάσεων της μετεμφυλιακής δομής του πολιτικού συστήματος και οι αρνητικές της συνέπειες' ('The dictatorship as a result of the contradictions of the post-civil war structure of the political system and its negative consequences'), in G. Athanasatou, A. Rigos and S. Seferiadis (eds), *Η Δικτατορια 1967-1974* (*The Dictatorship 1967-1974*). Athens: Kastaniotis.

Hatzivassilioiu, E. 2009. 'Αυταπάτες, διλήμματα και η αποτυχία της πολιτικής: Ο στρατός στην πορεία προς τη δικτατορία' ('Illusions, dilemmas and the failure of politics: The army on the course to the dictatorship'], in Gr Psalidas (ed.), *Από τον Ανένδοτο στη Δικτατορία* (*From the Unyielding Struggle to the Dictatorship*), pp. 417–42. Athens: Papazissis.

Hatzivassilioiu, E. 2010. *Ελληνικός φιλελευθερισμός* (*Greek Liberalism*). Athens: Patakis.

Helmis, G. *Ταραγμένη διετία 1973–1974* (*Tormented Biennial 1973–4*). Athens: Kastaniotis.

Huntington, S. 1991. *The Third Wave: Democratisation in the Late Twentieth Century*. London: University of Oklahoma Press.

Iatrides, J. 2009. 'Απρόθυμος Ηγεμόνας. Αμερικανική διπλωματία και η ελληνική πολιτική κρίση, 1961–1967' ('Reluctant hegemon: American diplomacy and the Greek political crisis, 1961–1967'), in Manolis Vasilakis (ed.), *Από τον ανένδοτο στη δικτατορία* (*From the Unrelenting Struggle to the Dictatorship*), pp. 51–65. Athens: Papazissis.

Iordanoglou, C. 1993. 'Comments on the tactics of the anti-dictatorial student movement during 1972–73'. Unpublished paper presented at a conference on the anti-dictatorial student movement at Panteion University of Athens, 2–4 December 1993. Kyrkos's archive.

Kakaounakis, N. 1976. *2650 Μερόνυχτα συνωμοσίας* (*2,650 Days and Nights of Conspiracy*). Athens: Papazisis.

Kallivretakis, L. 2016. 'Πολιτικοί και δικτατορία της 21ης Απριλίου: μια απόπειρα απογραφής' ['Politicians and the dictatorship of the 21st of April: an attempt for a record'], in Ίδρυμα της Βουλής των Ελλήνων για τον Κοινοβουλευτισμό και τη Δημοκρατία, *Η δικτατορία των συνταγματαρχών και η αποκατάσταση της δημοκρατίας: Πρακτικά συνεδρίου* (Hellenic Parliament Foundation for Parliamentarism and Democracy, *The Dictatorship of the Colonels and the Restoration of Democracy: Minutes of a Conference*), pp. 243–66. Athens: Hellenic Parliament.

Kanellopoulos, P. 1975. *Ιστορικά Δοκίμια* (*Historical Essays*). Athens: Hestia.

Kanellopoulos, P. 1987. *Κείμενα Παναγιώτη Κανελλόπουλου από τον αγώνα του εναντίον της δικτατορίας 1967–1974* (*Panayotis Kanellopoulos' Scripts from his Anti-dictatorial Struggle 1967–1974*). Athens: Etairia Filon Panayoti Kanellopoulou.

Karagiorgas, G. 2003. *Από Τον ΙΔΕΑ Στο Πραξικόπημα της 21ης Απριλίου* (*From IDEA to the 21st of April Coup*). Athens: Iolkos.

Karakatsanis, N. 2001. *The Politics of Elite Transformation: The Consolidation of Greek Democracy in Theoretical Perspective*. London: Praeger.

Karamanlis, K. 1994. *Αρχείο: Γεγονότα και Κείμενα* (*Archive: Facts and Documents*). Athens: Ekdotiki Athinon.

Karampelias, G. 2001. *Ο Ρόλος των Ενόπλων Δυνάμεων στην Πολιτική Ζωή της Τουρκίας και της Ελλάδας* (*The Role of the Armed Forces in the Political Life of Greece and Turkey*). Athens: Ellinika Grammata.

Karter, G. 2010. *Τα καύσιμα ετελείωσαν* (*Out of Fuel*). Athens: Pelasgos.

Kazakos, P. 2009. 'Ανάπτυξη και πολιτική κρίση στη δεκαετία του '60: Οι αιτίες του στρατιωτικού πραξικοπήματος του 1967' ('Development and political crisis in the 1960s: The reasons for the military coup of 1967'), in Manolis Vasilakis (ed.), *Από τον ανένδοτο στη δικτατορία* (*From the Unrelenting Struggle to the Dictatorship*), pp. 149–72. Constantine Mitsotakis Foundation. Athens: Papazissis.

Kazakos, P. 2016. 'Πολιτικοί θεσμοί και οικονομική ανάπτυξη: η εμπειρία της δικτατορίας 1967–1974' ('Political institutions and economic development: the experience of the dictatorship 1967–1974'), in Ίδρυμα της Βουλής των Ελλήνων για τον Κοινοβουλευτισμό και τη Δημοκρατία, *Η δικτατορία των συνταγματαρχών και η αποκατάσταση της δημοκρατίας. Πρακτικά συνεδρίου* (Hellenic Parliament Foundation for Parliamentarism and Democracy, *The Dictatorship of the Colonels and the Restoration of Democracy: Minutes of a Conference*), pp. 137–68. Athens: Hellenic Parliament.

Keeley, R. 2010. *Η Αμερικανική Πρεσβεία και η Κατάρρευση της Δημοκρατίας στηνΕλλάδα, 1966–1969* (*The US Embassy and the Collapse of Democracy in Greece, 1966–1969*). Athens: Patakis.

Kissinger, H. *1982: Years of Upheaval*. London: Weidenfeld & Nicolson.

KKE (Communist Party of Greece). 1976. *Έκθεση και συμπεράσματα για τα γεγονότα του Νοέμβρη* (*Report and Conclusions on the November Events*). Athens: KKE.

Kohler, B. 1982. *Political Forces in Spain, Greece and Portugal*. London: Butterworths.

Konofagos, K. 1982. *Η Εξέγερση του Πολυτεχνειου* (*The Polytechnic Uprising*). Athens: Boyatis.

Korizis, H. 1975. *Το Αυταρχικό Καθεστώς* (*The Authoritarian Regime*). Athens: Gutenberg.

Kornetis, K. 2013. *Children of the Dictatorship: Student Resistance, Cultural Politics, and the Long 1960s in Greece*. New York: Berghahn Books.

Koundouros, R. 1978. *Η Ασφάλεια του καθεστώτος 1924–1974* (*Regime Security in Greece 1924–1974*). Athens: Kastaniotis.

Legg, K. 1969. *Politics in Modern Greece*. Stanford, CA: Stanford University Press.
Legg, K. and Roberts, J. 1997. *Modern Greece: A Civilization on the Periphery*. Oxford: Westview.
Leontaritis, G. 2003. *Σάββας Κωνσταντόπουλος, τα άγνωστα ντοκουμέντα* (*Savvas Konstantopoulos, Unknown Documents*). Athens: Proskinio.
Leontaritis, G. 2010. *Βασιλεύς και Γεώργιος Παπαδόπουλος* (*The King and George Papadopoulos*). Athens: Proskinio.
Linardatos, P. 1986. *Από τον εμφύλιο στη χούντα* (*From the Civil War to the Junta*). Athens: Papazisis.
Linz, J. and Stepan, A. 1996. *Problems of Democratic Transition and Consolidation*. Baltimore, MD: Johns Hopkins University Press.
Makarezos, N. 2010. *Πώς Καταλήξαμε στη 'Μεταπολίτευση'* (*How We Ended Up in the Metapolitefsi*). Athens: Filippotis.
Manesis, A. 1999. 'Ο εύκολος βιασμός της νομιμότητας και η δύσκολη νομιμοποίηση της βίας' ('The easy rape of legality and the difficult legitimization of violence'), in G. Athanasatou, A. Rigos and S. Seferiadis (eds), *Η Δικτατορία 1967-1974* (*The Dictatorship 1967-1974*), pp. 37-52. Athens: Kastaniotis.
Mantoglou, A. 1995. *Η Εξέγερση του Πολυτεχνείου* (*The Polytechnic Uprising*). Athens: Odysseas.
Markezinis, S. 1979. *Πολιτικαί Αναμνήσεις* (*Political Memoirs*). Athens: n.p.
Markezinis, S. 1994. *Σύγχρονη πολιτική ιστορία της Ελλάδος* (*Modern Political History of Greece*). Athens: Papyrus.
Meletopoulos, M. 1996. *Η Δικτατορία των Συνταγματαρχών* (*The Dictatorship of the Colonels*). Athens: Papazisis.
Meynaud, J. 1974. *Οι πολιτικές δυνάμεις στην Ελλάδα* (*Political Forces in Greece*). Athens: Byron.
Meynaud, J. 2004. *Οι πολιτικές δυνάμεις στην Ελλάδα: Βασιλική εκτροπή και στρατιωτική δικτατορία* (*Political Forces in Greece: Royal Aberration and Military Dictatorship*). Athens: Patakis.
Miller, J. 2009. *The United States and the Making of Modern Greece*. Chapel Hill: University of North Carolina Press.
Mitsotakis, C. 2017. *Ο Κωνσταντίνος Μητσοτάκης με τα δικά του λόγια* (*Constantine Mitsotakis in His Own Words*). Athens: Papadopoulos.
Mitsotakis, Constantine Foundation, 2009. *Από τον ανένδοτο στη δικτατορία* (*From the Unrelenting Struggle to the Dictatorship*). Ed. M. Vasilakis. Athens: Papazissis.

Moskos, C. and Wood, F. (eds). 1988. *The Military: More than Just a Job?* New York: Pergamon-Brassey's.

Mouzelis, N. 1978. *Modern Greece: Facets of Underdevelopment.* London: Springer.

Murtagh, P. 1994. *The Rape of Greece: The King, the Colonels and the Resistance.* London: Simon & Schuster.

Nafpliotis, A. 2012. *Britain and the Greek Colonels: Accommodating the Junta in the Cold War.* London: I.B. Tauris.

Nicolet, C. 2001. *United States Policy towards Cyprus, 1954-1974: Removing the Greek-Turkish Bone of Contention.* Mannheim: Bibliopolis.

Notaras, G. 1999. 'Δικτατορια και Οργανωμένη Αντισταση' ('Dictatorship and organized resistance'), in G. Athanasatou, A. Rigos and S. Seferiadis (eds), *Η Δικτατορια 1967-1974 (The Dictatorship 1967-1974).* Athens: Kastaniotis.

O'Donnell, G. and Schmitter, P. 1986. *Transitions from Authoritarian Rule: Comparative Perspectives.* Baltimore, MD: Johns Hopkins University Press.

O'Donnell, G. and Whitehead, L. 1986. *Tentative Conclusions about Uncertain Democracies.* Baltimore, MD: Johns Hopkins University Press.

O'Donnell, G., Schmitter, P. and Whitehead, L. (eds). 1986. *Transitions from Authoritarian Rule: Prospects for Democracy.* Baltimore, MD: Johns Hopkins University Press.

Olson, M. 1971. *The Logic of Collective Action: Public Goods and the Theory of Groups.* Cambridge, MA: Harvard University Press.

Özbudun, E. 2000. *Contemporary Turkish Politics: Challenges to Democratic Consolidation.* London: Lynne Rienner Publishers.

Papachelas, A. 1998. *Ο βιασμός της ελληνικής δημοκρατίας: Ο αμερικανικός παράγων, 1947-1967 (The Rape of Greek Democracy: The American Factor 1947-1967).* Athens: Estia.

Papadimitriou, N. 1985. Το *Κίνημα του Ναυτικού (The Naval Coup).* Athens: Elliniki Evroekdotiki.

Papakosmas, V. 1981. *The Military in Greek Politics: The 1909 Coup d'Etat.* Kent: Ohio State University Press.

Papandreou, A. 1976. *Από το ΠΑΚ στο ΠΑΣΟΚ (From PAK to PASOK).* Athens: Ladias.

Papazoglou, M. 1975. *Φοιτητικό Κίνημα και Δικτατορία (Students' Movement and Dictatorship).* Athens: Epikairotita.

Passas, I. 1980. *Εγκυκλοπαίδεια 'Ήλιος' (Encyclopaedia 'Helios').* Athens: n.p.

Pesmazoglou, I. 1972. 'The Greek economy since 1967', in R. Clogg and G. Giannopoulos (eds), *Greece Under Military Rule*. London: Secker and Warburg.

Pesmazoglou, V. 1999. 'Ελληνική δικτατορία (1967-1974) και ΕΟΚ: οικονομία, πολιτική, ιδεολογία' ('The Greek dictatorship (1967-1974) and the EEC: Economy, Politics, Ideology'), in G. Athanasatou, A. Rigos and S. Seferiadis (eds), *Η Δικτατορια 1967-1974* (*The Dictatorship 1967-1974*). Athens: Kastaniotis.

Preston, P. 1986. *The Triumph of Democracy in Spain*. London: Methuen.

Pridham, G. 1984. 'Comparative perspectives on the new Mediterranean democracies: a model of regime transition?', in G. Pridham (ed.), *The New Mediterranean Democracies*, pp. 1-29. London: Frank Cass.

Pridham, G. 1991. 'International influences and democratic transitions: problems of theory and practice in linkage politics', in G. Pridham (ed.), *Encouraging Democracy*, 1-30. Leicester: Leicester University Press.

Pridham, G. 1991. 'The politics of the European Community', in G. Pridham (ed.), *Encouraging Democracy*, 212-45. Leicester: Leicester University Press.

Pridham, G. (ed.) 1984. *The New Mediterranean Democracies*. London: Frank Cass.

Pridham, G. (ed.) 1991. *Encouraging Democracy*. Leicester: Leicester University Press.

Przeworski, A. 1988. 'Democracy as a contingent outcome of conflicts', in J. Elster and P. Slagstad (eds), *Constitutionalism and Democracy*, pp. 59-80. Cambridge: Cambridge University Press.

Psalidopoulos, M. 2016. 'Διλήμματα και προτεραιότητες της οικονομικής πολιτικής: από τη δικτατορία στη μεταπολίτευση' ('Dilemmas and priorities of economic policies: from the dictatorship to the Metapolitefsi'), in Ίδρυμα της Βουλής των Ελλήνων για τον Κοινοβουλευτισμό και τη Δημοκρατία, *Η δικτατορία των συνταγματαρχών και η αποκατάσταση της δημοκρατίας: Πρακτικά συνεδρίου* (Hellenic Parliament Foundation for Parliamentarism and Democracy, *The Dictatorship of the Colonels and the Restoration of Democracy: Minutes of a Conference*), pp 572-602. Athens: Hellenic Parliament.

Psomiades, H. 1982. 'Greece: from the colonels' rule to democracy', in J. Herz (ed.), *From Dictatorship to Democracy: Coping with the Legacies of Authoritarianism and Totalitarianism*, pp. 251-73. London: Greenwood.

Rodakis, P. 1975. *Η δικτατορία των συνταγματαρχών* (*The Dictatorship of the Colonels*). Athens: Mycenae.

Rueschemeyer, D., Stephens, E. and Stephens, J. 1992. *Capitalist Development and Democracy*. Cambridge: Polity.

Schmitter, P. 1986. 'An introduction to Southern-European transitions from authoritarian rule: Italy, Greece, Portugal, Spain and Turkey', in G. O'Donnell, P. Schmitter and L. Whitehead (eds), *Transitions from Authoritarian Rule: Prospects for Democracy*, Vol. 2: Southern Europe, pp. 3-10. Baltimore, MD: Johns Hopkins University Press.

Schmitter, P. 1991. 'The influence of the international context upon the choice of national institutions and policies in neo-democracies', in Lawrence Whitehead (ed.), *The International Dimensions of Democratisation: Europe and the Americas*, pp. 26-54. Oxford: Oxford University Press.

Shain, Yossi. 1995. 'Democratisation and the international system: the foreign policy of interim governments', in Yoshi Shain and Juan Linz (eds), *Between States*, pp. 255-304. Cambridge: Cambridge University Press.

Share, D. 1986. *The Making of Spanish Democracy*. London: Praeger.

Sorensen, G. 1993. *Democracy and Democratisation*. Oxford: Westview Press.

Sotiropoulos, D. 1999. 'Η κοινωνικη πολιτικη της δικτατοριας' ('The social policy of the dictatorship'), in G. Athanasatou, A. Rigos and S. Seferiadis (eds), *Η Δικτατορια 1967-1974 (The Dictatorship 1967-1974)*, pp. 115-31. Athens: Kastaniotis.

Stavrou, N. 1976. *Allied Politics and Military Interventions*. Athens: Papazissis.

Stern, L. 1978. *The Wrong Horse: The Politics of Intervention and the Failure of American Diplomacy*. New York: Times Books.

Syrigos, A. 2016. 'Ελληνο-τουρκικές σχέσεις 1967-1974: από τη συνάντηση στον Έβρο στην εισβολή στην Κύπρο' ('Greek-Turkish relations 1967-1974: from the meeting of Evros to the invasion in Cyprus'), in Ίδρυμα της Βουλής των Ελλήνων για τον Κοινοβουλευτισμό και τη Δημοκρατία, *Η δικτατορία των συνταγματαρχών και η αποκατάσταση της δημοκρατίας. Πρακτικά συνεδρίου* (Hellenic Parliament Foundation for Parliamentarism and Democracy, *The Dictatorship of the Colonels and the Restoration of Democracy: Minutes of a Conference*), pp. 313-36. Athens: Hellenic Parliament.

Theodorakopoulos, T. 1976. *The Greek Upheaval: Kings, Demagogues and Bayonets*. London: Stacey International.

Tomai, F. 2009. 'Ο ρόλος των ΗΠΑ στην κρίσιμη διετία 1965-1967 μέσα από τα επίσημα έγγραφα του State Department' ('The role of the US in the critical biennial 1965–1967 through the official documents of the State Department'), in Manolis Vasilakis (ed.), *Από τον ανένδοτο στη δικτατορία* (*From the Unrelenting Struggle to the Dictatorship*), pp. 71–90. Constantine Mitsotakis Foundation. Athens: Papazissis.

Tovias, A. 1991. 'US policy towards democratic transition in Southern Europe', in G. Pridham (ed.), *Encouraging Democracy*, pp. 175–93. Leicester: Leicester University Press.

Treholt, A. 1976. 'Europe and the dictatorship in Greece', in R. Clogg and G. Yannopoulos (eds), *Greece Under Military Rule*, pp. 320–44. London: Secker and Warburg.

Tsingos, B. 2001. 'Underwriting democracy: the European Community and Greece', in L. Whitehead (ed.), *The International Dimensions of Democratization*, pp. 315–55. Oxford: Oxford University Press, 2001.

Vanhanen, T. 1992. *Strategies of Democratisation*. London: Taylor and Francis.

Veremis, T. 1987. 'The military', in K. Featherstone and D. Katsoudas (eds), *Political Change in Greece: Before and after the Colonels*, pp. 214–29. London: Croom Helm.

Veremis, T. 1997. *The Military in Greek Politics: From Independence to Democracy*. London: Hurst Publishers.

Verney, S. and Couloumbis, T. 1991. 'State-international systems interaction and the Greek transition to democracy in the mid-1970's, in Geoffrey Pridham (ed.), *Encouraging Democracy: The International Context of Regime Transition in Southern Europe*, pp. 103–23. Leicester: Leicester University Press.

Voulgaris, Y. 2001. *Η Ελλάδα της Μεταπολίτευσης, 1974–1990* (*Greece in the Metapolitefsi, 1974–1990*). Athens: Themelio.

Weiner, T. 2007. *Legacy of Ashes: The History of the Central Intelligence Agency*. New York: Doubleday.

Whitehead, L. 2002. *Democratisation: Theory and Experience*. Oxford: Oxford University Press.

Woodhouse, C. 1982. *Karamanlis, The Restorer of Greek Democracy*. Oxford: Clarendon Press.

Woodhouse, C. 1985. *The Rise and Fall of the Greek Colonels*. New York: Franklin Watts.

Xydis, S. 1972. 'The foreign policy of the military regime', in R. Clogg and G. Giannopoulos (eds), *Greece Under Military Rule*. London: Secker and Warburg.

Yannopoulos, G. 1972. 'The state of the opposition forces since the military coup', in *Greece under military rule*. Eds Clogg, R. and Giannopoulos, G. London: Secker and Warburg.

Zacharopoulos, G. 1972. 'Politics and the army in post-war Greece', in R. Clogg and G. Giannopoulos (eds), *Greece Under Military Rule*. London: Secker and Warburg.

Zournatzis, S. and Mihalopoulos, G. 1990. *21η Απριλίου 1967: Μύθοι και Αλήθεια (21st of April 1967: Myths and Truth)*. Athens: n.p.

Journal articles

Abadi, J. 2000. 'Constraints and Adjustments in Greece's Policy on Israel', *Mediterranean Quarterly* 11, no. 4: 40–70.

Cizre, Ü. 1997. 'The anatomy of the Turkish military's political autonomy', *Comparative Politics* 29, no. 2: 151–66.

Danopoulos, C. 1984. 'From military to civilian rule in contemporary Greece', *Armed Forces and Society* 10, no. 2: 229–50.

Danopoulos, C. 1991. 'Democratising the military: lessons from Southern Europe', *West European Politics* 14, no. 4: 25–41.

Duman, Ö. and Tsarouhas, D. 2006. '"Civilianization" in Greece versus "Demilitarization" in Turkey: a comparative study of civil–military relations and the impact of the European Union', *Armed Forces and Society* 32, no. 3: 405–23.

Eisenstadt, T. 2000. 'Eddies in the third wave: protracted transitions and theories of democratisation', *Democratisation* 7, no. 3: 3–24.

Huntington, S. 1984. 'Will more countries become democratic?' *Political Science Quarterly* 99, no. 2: 193–218.

Kallivretakis, L. 2014. 'Greek–American relations in the Yom Kippur War concurrence', *Historical Review* 11: 105–25.

Karakatsanis, N. 1998. 'Do attitudes matter? The military and democratic consolidation in Greece', *Armed Forces and Society* 24, no. 2: 289–313.

Karl, T. L. and Schmitter, P. 1991. 'Modes of Transition in Latin America, Southern and Eastern Europe', *International Social Science Journal* 128, 269–84.

Klarevas, L. 2006. 'Were the eagle and the phoenix birds of a feather? The United States and the Greek coup of 1967', *Diplomatic History* 30, no. 3: 471–508.

Maragkou, K. 2014. 'The relevance of détente to American foreign policy: the case of Greece, 1967-1979', *Diplomacy and Statecraft* 25, no. 4: 646-68.

Pedaliu, E. 2011. 'A discordant note: NATO and the Greek junta, 1967-1974', *Diplomacy and Statecraft* 22, no. 1: 101-20.

Rustow, D. 1970. 'Transitions to democracy: towards a dynamic model', *Comparative Politics* 2, no. 3: 337-63.

Sakkas, J. 2004. 'The Greek dictatorship, the USA and the Arabs, 1967-1974', *Journal of Southern Europe and the Balkans* 6, no. 3: 245-57.

Schedler, A. 2001. 'Taking uncertainty seriously: the blurred boundaries of democratic transition and Consolidation', *Democratisation* 8, no. 4: 1-22.

Schmitter, P. and Karl, T.-L. 1991. 'Modes of transition in Latin America, Southern and Eastern Europe', *International Social Science Journal* 43: 269-84.

Tzortzis, I. 2012. 'Fake or failed? A Greek would-be *reforma pactada*', *Southeast European and Black Sea Studies* 12, no. 2: 315-33.

Tzortzis, I. 2017. 'Blame it on Kissinger? The international factor and the failure of the "Markezinis Experiment"', *Mediterranean Historical Review* 32, no. 1: 65-82.

Verney, S. and Tsakaloyannis, P. 1986. 'Linkage politics: the role of the European Community in Greek politics in 1973', *Byzantine and Modern Greek Studies* 10: 179-94.

Online sources

Demetrios Tsevas, Public Attorney. 1974. *Report to the Chief Public Prosecutor of Athens on the preliminary investigation concerning the Athens Polytechnic Events of November 1973*, 14 October 1974, http://www.tovima.gr/files/1/2012/11/14/porismatseva14.pdf

Index

activism (*see also* Polytechnic demonstrations; resistance)
anti-American 171
anti-bailout deal demonstrations 1
demonstrations by workers 57, 127
demonstrations of 1965 21
demonstrations of 1968/1971 49
student movements 56, 135, 138, 188, 206n.11
student unrest of 1973. *See* Polytechnic demonstrations
Adenauer, Konrad 157
agents provocateurs 128, 222n.43
Agnew, Spiro 150, 151
agricultural sector 17
aid 17
Alivizatos, N. 19, 23, 65
AMAG (American Mission for Aid to Greece) 17
amnesty, for political prisoners 66
Andrews, K. 127, 128
Androutsopoulos, Adamantios 104, 105–6, 108, 135, 140–1, 186, 216n.113
Anghelis, Odysseas 62, 70, 97, 99, 130
Apogevmatini 90
Apostates (Renegades) 21
Arab–Israeli conflict. *See* Yom Kippur War
Arapakis, N. 84, 85, 163, 166, 186
arms embargo 149
arms trade 230n.38
Asia Minor, withdrawal from 7
Aslanidis, George 34, 38
ASPIDA 27, 195n.21
Athens University faculties, decision to occupy the campus 123–5 (*see also* Polytechnic demonstrations)
austerity, memorandums of 1

authoritarianism
authoritarian regimes 9
of Ioannidis 136
transition from 143, 174–5, 185–6
the United States and 146
Averoff, Evangelos 41–2, 51, 61, 62, 87–8, 106, 138, 142, 152, 189
Axis occupation (1941) 8

Barkman, Karl 43, 65, 66, 69, 83, 89–90, 95, 97, 113, 127, 158, 161, 191
Battle, George 147
Bonanos, Grigorios 70–1, 79, 81, 100, 102, 106–7, 111, 112
Brandt, Willy 159
Brillakis, Antonis 92

castrated parliament 82–94
Ceausescu, Nicolae 159
censorship 66, 118, 119, 133, 174
Central Intelligence Agency (KYP) (Greek) 100–1, 126, 128, 198n.57
Chief of the Armed Forces 70
Christian Greeks. *See* chapter 2
Christianiki 67
Christoloukas, Chief Constable 125, 134
CIA
Communist Party of Greece (KKE) and 165
Generals' coup (1967 coup) 146–7, 227n.3, 228n.7
Ioannidis and 166–7, 233n.93
myth of the omnipotent CIA 167
November 25 coup and 144
Polytechnic demonstrations and 144
civil service 19

civil society
  awakening of 4
  democratic transition and 6, 10, 137
  lack of support for Markezinis 2
  Markezinis experiment and 117–21, 136, 138
  Papadopoulos regime and 47–54
  passivity of the people 47, 50, 52, 192
  Polytechnic demonstrations and 57
civil war (1944–1949) 8, 14
class
  emergent middle class 17–18
  political class 4
  working classes 18
clientelism
  the Generals' coup and 52
  the military and 18, 23
  politics and 18, 23
Cold War 15, 146, 157, 162
communism
  anti-communism 25, 26, 52
  fear of 23, 24, 137, 138–9
Communist Party of Greece (KKE) 15, 16, 46, 85, 91–2, 95, 119, 138, 165, 167
conspiracies
  conspiracy theories 5, 136–7, 141–2, 144, 145, 170, 192
  Ioannidis and 38, 216n.111
  the military and 25–7
  by naval officers 61–2
Constantine II of Greece 21–2, 35, 61, 63, 148
Constitutional Court 19, 74, 92
constitutions
  constitution (1952) 16, 19, 23, 108
  constitution (1968) 41, 43, 45, 63, 64
  constitution (1973) 64, 73, 98, 108
construction 18
Consultative Committee 52–3, 177

corruption
  bribary and 195n.22
  elections and 17, 26, 27, 157, 194n.10, 197n.43
  the Generals' coup and 51
  in the military 70–1, 209n.61
Couloumbis, Theodore 42–3, 53, 85, 90, 95
Council of Europe 45, 152
Council of Ministers 71
Council of the Nation 64
coups
  1909 coup (Goudi coup) 7
  1922 11 September coup 7
  1951 coup 25
  1967 Greek counter-coup attempt (royal coup) 4, 35, 41, 60
  1973 25 November coup led by Ioannidis 100–3, 104–5, 108, 139, 140–1, 142, 143, 144, 175, 187, 233n.93
  coup attempt in Spain February 1981 184
  Generals' coup (1967 coup). See Generals' coup (1967 coup)
  naval conspiracy 61–2, 87, 207n.32
Crete 164
crisis of 1965–7 20–2, 27, 30
culture, politics and 16
Cyprus
  1967 crisis between Greece and Turkey 35
  1974 Cyprus crisis 2, 6, 107–8, 110, 111, 136, 146, 167, 168, 169, 185
  Greek–Cypriot relations 160
  Ioannidis and 169
  Markezinis government and 160
  Papadopoulos regime and 153–5
  the United States and 148, 154, 168
Czechoslovakia, Soviet invasion of 46

Danopoulos, C. 77
Daskalopoulos, Head of Greek police 125

debt, of Greece 50, 119 (*see also* economy)
Demirel, Suleyman 182
democracy
   1949–1961 14–19
   breakdown of in 1965–7 20–2
   conditions needed for democratization 83, 186
   democratic transition and civil society 6, 10, 137
   democratic transition by regime self-transformation 8–10
   democratization and Papadopoulos 181–2
   democratization and Markezinis 68–9, 133–4
   democratization studies 8–10
   elections and 94
   the international factor 10
   Ioannidis and 34, 42
   Karamanlis' request for restoration of 40
   limited 'democratization' 68–9
   the military and 78
   pressures for democratisation 18–19
   Spain and democratization 8, 179–80
   third wave of democratization 6
   transition to 4, 6
Democratic Defence 48
deportation camps 105
détente, between the Western and Eastern blocs 159
Diamantouros, P.-N. 31, 185
dictatorship(s)
   of the colonels (1967) 1, 8, 29–30, 110 (*see also* chapter 2)
   dictadura (new dictatorship) 99–109
   ending of 4, 8
   Metaxas dictatorship 33
   moving from a 'hard' to a 'soft' form of 63
   transition to democracy and 10

diplomacy
   of the Netherlands 43
   of the United States 42–3, 147, 150
   dissidence, suppression of 136

EAM–ELAS–Polytechnic 138
Ecevit, Bulent 182
economy
   deficit of Greece 50, 119
   economic development 17–18
   economic growth 18, 33, 50, 93, 152
   Generals' coup (1967 coup) and 49–50, 54, 56
   international economic recession 162
   Papadopoulos regime and 151–2
EDA (United Democratic Left) 14–15, 17, 19, 21, 29, 53
EENA (Union of Greek Young Officers) 26
Egypt
   Nasserite dictatorship 24, 33
   remnants of the army escaping to 8, 25
   Yom Kippur War 162
EK (Centre Union)
   Andreas Papandreou/radicalization and 20–2
   constitutional amendment and 19
   creation of the 15
   elections of 28 May 1967 and 21–2
   electoral fraud and 17
   the ERE and 19
   factionalism/fatal crisis in the 20–1, 27
   Generals' coup (1967 coup) and 28, 43–4, 45, 146
   the Markezinis experiment and 84, 89–90, 96
elections
   1958 elections 24
   1961 elections 17, 21, 26, 27, 197n.43

1963 elections 20, 26
1964 elections 20
1967 elections (proposed) 21, 22
1974 elections 142, 157
corruption and 17, 26, 27, 157, 194n.10, 197n.43
democracy and 94
Generals' coup (1967 coup) and 41, 43, 45
the Karamanlis government and 109, 194n.10
reform and 10, 95, 96, 194n.7, 194n.10
requirements for free and fair elections 156
in universities 57, 58, 122
Eleftheros Kosmos 60, 97
elites
  anti-elitism 26, 33
  dictatorial 10
  economic 93-4
  elites/counter-elites and the Markezinis experiment 95-9, 113, 114
  Generals' coup (1967 coup) and 39-47
  the military as 24
  opposition elites and the Markezinis experiment 10, 82-94, 112
  outgoing dictatorial 9
  political 2, 3, 4, 5, 6, 39-47, 108, 186
employment 17, 18
energy provision 17
Enosis 154
EPEN (National Political Union) 190
Epikaira 138
EPOK (National Cultural Movement) 58-9, 72, 177, 206n.18
ERE (National Radical Union)
  dominate position of 14
  the EK and 19
  electoral fraud and 17, 194n.10

Generals' coup (1967 coup) and 27-8, 29, 40, 41, 43-4
Kanellopoulos and 14, 21, 194n.10
Karamanlis and 14, 21
the Markezinis experiment and 84, 89, 96
the military and 26
ES (Greek Rally) 14, 44
ESA (Greek Military Police) 2, 36-7, 62, 81, 82, 100, 105, 128, 134, 136, 185
Etzioni-Halevy, E. 10
European Economic Community (EEC)
  Greece and 11, 56, 151-2, 153
  Greece becoming a republic and 156
  Markezinis experiment and 146, 160-1, 206n.7
  trade and 151
Evelpides cadets 36, 44
Evren, Kenan 182
exiles 45, 118
extremists 34, 184

factionalism
  the EK (Centre Union) and 20-1, 27
  Generals' coup (1967 coup) and 32-3, 34-9
  in the military 25-7
Farakos, Grigoris 12, 46, 110
foreign factor 47-8, 136, 144, 170 (*see also* international factor)
foreign influence, in politics 11, 146
foreign investment 17
foreign policy
  Markezinis and 159-60
  Papadopoulos regime and 150-1, 229n.26
foreign press, giving a positive impression to 95, 119
France, trade with Greece 152
Free Greeks 48
free market 50

Index

Garoufalias, Petros 21, 27, 61, 62
Generals' coup (1967 coup) (*see also* chapter 1)
   Andreas Papandreou and 28, 29
   CIA and 146–7, 227n.3, 228n.7
   clientelism and 52
   corruption and the 51
   developments/faction struggles within the regime (1967–72) 34–5
   economy and the 49–50, 54, 56
   EK (Centre Union) and 28, 43–4, 45, 146
   elites and 39–47
   ERE (National Radical Union) and 27–8, 29, 40, 41, 43–4
   factionalism and 32–3, 34–9
   factors leading to 26
   Kanellopoulos and 29, 41, 42–3, 44, 88, 197n.47
   Karamanlis and 39–40, 41, 42, 43, 44
   Makarezos and 34, 38, 45, 56
   Markezinis and 44, 59
   the military and 22–5, 35
   monarchy and 34–5, 198n.48
   officer corps and 33
   Papadopoulos and 31, 33–4, 36, 37–9, 40–1, 43–5, 198n.52
   Pattakos and 34, 38, 147
   politics and 41
   power and 34–5, 37–8
   Prometheus Plan and 198n.53
   punishment of the 1967 coup instigators 185
   resistance and 48–9
   returning to some kind of 'political normality' 40–4, 197n.47
   rights and 41
   security regime of 48
   timing of the coup 198n.52
   United States and 146–8, 228n.7, 228n.14
   'wrong coup' of 21 April 1967 22–5, 27–9
Genevoix, Maurice 17
Georgalas, George 93, 114, 151
Ghizikis, Phaedon 100, 101, 104, 106, 109, 140, 143
Gill, G. 134–5
Gillespie, C. 186
Glezos, Manolis 92–3
government, parliament and 22
Great Britain
   archives of 11
   British Foreign Office 11
   concerns for the future of Greece 168–9
   election fraud and 157
   Greece becoming a republic and 156
   the Greek army and 8
   Markezinis experiment and 158–9
   views on the opposition parties 162
Greece
   anti-Americanism 170–1, 192, 228n.14
   becoming a Republic 7, 63, 65, 66, 156, 231n.49
   debt of 50, 119
   European Economic Community (EEC) and 11, 56, 151–2, 153
   Greek–Cypriot relations 160
   Greek–Turkish conflict (1897) 7
   Greek–Turkish relations 148, 168
   public archives 11
Greek Federation of Industrialists (SEB) 68
Greek Industrialists' Association 93
Greek Rally (ES) 14, 44
Grigoriadis, P. 36, 100, 122–3, 144, 160
Grivas, Georgios 154

Haralambis, D. 18, 52, 69, 104, 155
Heath, Edward 159
Hooper, Robin 100, 101, 112–13, 159, 160
human rights abuses 152, 185 (*see also* rights)
Huntington, S. 9, 63, 82, 113, 143

IDEA (Sacred Link of Greek Officers) 25-6
identity, political 18
ideology, the military and 23-4
Iliou, Ilias 43, 53, 91-2, 187
import substitution 50
industrialization 50
inflation 119
infrastructure, restoration/modernization of 18
institutional engineering 16-17
institutionalization, of a dictatorship 10
institutions, politics and 14-19, 16
international community, giving a positive impression to 95-6
international factor (*see also* foreign factor)
  democracy and the 10
  the Markezinis experiment and 145-6, 156-62, 170
  Papadopoulos regime and the 148-53
investment, foreign 17
Ioannidis, Dimitrios
  authoritarianism of 136
  conspiracies and 38, 216n.111
  coup of 100-3, 104-5, 108, 139, 140-1, 142, 143, 144, 175, 187, 233n.93
  Cyprus and 169
  democracy and 34, 42
  liberalization and 2, 6
  Markezinis experiment and 3, 4, 5, 77
  the military and 106
  the monarchy and 60
  the officer corps and 78-9
  overthrowing of 111
  Papadopoulos and 103, 110-11, 132-3, 140-1, 176, 216n.107, 216n.108
  plan to overthrow Papadopoulos and Markezinis 80-2
  Polytechnic demonstrations and 82, 138-9, 143
  power of 36-8, 71, 207n.32, 210n.4
  reign of terror of 105-7
  surveillance activities of 210n.4
  torture and 185
  the United States and 166-7, 168, 233n.93
Iordanoglou, Chrissafis 122, 124
Israel, Yom Kippur War 162

Johnson, Lyndon B. 148, 228n.16
Juan Carlos I of Spain 179, 180

Kanellopoulos, Panayotis
  1973 25 November coup led by Ioannidis and 104-5, 108
  Constantine II of Greece and 21-2
  declaration of the 'Republic' and 65
  election fraud and 194n.10
  ERE (National Radical Union) and 14, 21, 194n.10
  Generals' coup (1967 coup) and 29, 41, 42-3, 44, 197n.47
  under house arrest 132
  liberalization and 66, 67
  the Markezinis experiment and 84, 85, 88-9, 90
  student demonstrations and 57, 125-6, 128, 129, 134, 137, 141
Karakatsanis, Neovi 46
Karamanlis, Constantine
  attempts at democratic consolidation (1963-5) 19-20
  election fraud and 194n.10
  ERE (National Radical Union) and 14, 21
  Generals' coup (1967 coup) and 39-40, 41, 42, 43, 44
  Markezinis and 142
  the Markezinis experiment and 84, 85-6, 96-7, 187

the military and 109
monarchy's support of 14, 19–20,
   194n.4
the naval conspiracy and 61
the officer class and 197n.44
Papadopoulos and 64, 84
Polytechnic demonstrations and
   142
popularity of 93, 108, 212n.36
Rallis and 87
request to return to Greece 21, 68
resignation of 20
restoration of democracy and
   59–60, 108–9, 189–90
United States opinion of 158
Karter, Georgios 39, 44, 93, 103
Keeley, Robert 29
Kissinger, Henry 145, 158, 163, 164,
   165, 166, 168
Kollias, Constantine 34, 35, 40
Konofagos, K. 47, 125, 126, 129, 132,
   136
Konstantopoulos, Savvas 97, 142
Kornetis, Kostis 129, 136, 143–4
Kyrkos, Leonidas 92, 138

Ladas, Ioannis 34, 38, 62, 80
law(s)
   Law 509 92
   the state of emergency and 16
Legg, K. 18, 31, 50
legitimacy, the Papadopoulos regime
   and 149
Lehman, Dick 147
Leontaritis, G. 62
liberalization
   controlled 39
   democratic transition and 9
   early liberalization January–
      September 1973. *See* chapter 3
   Ioannidis and 2, 6
   Kanellopoulos and 66, 67
   Markezinis experiment and 2, 5, 6
   opposition elites and 83–94, 120

Papadopoulos and 39, 118
the student movement and 122,
   138
Linz, Juan 10, 66, 94, 113
loans, foreign 50

Makarezos, Nikolaos
   1973 25 November coup led by
      Ioannidis and 100, 102
   Generals' coup (1967 coup) and
      34, 38, 45, 56
   Karamanlis/Markezinis and 85
   the Markezinis experiment and
      96–7
   transition to democracy and
      200n.12
Makarios, Archbishop 154, 155, 160,
   168
Makedonia 85, 90
Manesis, A. 47
Mantoglou, A. 124
Markezinis experiment (*see also*
   reforma (1973))
   civil society and 117–21, 136, 138
   the end of 101–2, 167, 176
   ERE (National Radical Union)
      and 84, 89, 96
   European Economic Community
      (EEC) and 146, 160–1, 206n.7
   failure of 77–8
   Great Britain and 158–9
   the international factor and
      145–6, 156–62, 170
   Ioannidis and 3, 4, 5, 77
   Kanellopoulos and 84, 85, 88–9, 90
   Karamanlis and 84, 85–6, 96–7,
      187
   legacy of 186–92
   liberalization and 2, 5, 6
   the military and 78–82, 96
   opportunity missed or a ruse that
      failed? 109–15, 183
   opposition elites and 10, 82–94,
      112

Papadopoulos and 3, 4–5, 31
Papandreou (Andreas) and 90–1
as a point of historical and
    political reference 3–12
Polytechnic demonstrations and
    2, 3, 117–18, 167
the right wing and 83–9
summary of 2
tactics of the elites/counter-elites
    and 95–9, 113, 114
United States and 158–9, 164–6,
    167
what if it had succeeded? 179–86
what was it and why did it fail?
    173–9
Yom Kippur War and 162–5
Markezinis, Spyros
1973 25 November coup led by
    Ioannidis and 101
Cyprus and 168
democratization and 133–4
economic elites and 93–4
economy and 119
failure to gain support of
    opposition elites 82–3
fall of 111–12, 196n.37
foreign policy and 159–60
Generals' coup (1967 coup) and
    44, 59
as his own worst enemy 190–1
international image of 157–9
Karamanlis and 142
limited 'democratization' and 68–9
Markezinis cabinet 4, 5
martial law and 133
the military and 82, 96, 98–9
Papadopoulos and 3, 71–5, 80,
    95–6, 97–8, 134
Polytechnic demonstrations and
    98, 99, 117–18, 123, 125,
    129–30, 133–4, 139, 143, 190,
    219n.12, 219n.14
as Prime Minister 83, 95, 98–9
Progressive Party of 21, 44, 190,
    236n.21

reasons for his failure 4–5
resignation of 80, 102
retrospective recognition of
    186–7, 191–2
the United States and 5, 164–7,
    170
Marshall Plan 17
martial law
    constitution (1973) and 64
    following the Polytechnic
        demonstrations 98, 103, 132,
        133, 139–40, 143
    Ioannidis and the failure to lift
        105
    lifting of 4, 38, 43, 45, 66, 118,
        174
    Markezinis and 133
    Mitsotakis and 43
    Papadopoulos and 99, 139–40,
        143
Mavros, George
    asked to form a coalition
        government 108
    Cyprus and 168
    EK (Centre Union) and 43, 45
    European Economic Community
        (EEC) and 161
    under house arrest 132
    the July plebiscite and 65
    the Markezinis experiment and
        89–90
    Papadopoulos and 43, 44
    Polytechnic demonstrations and
        57, 129, 137, 141
McCloskey, Robert 164–5
media
    anti-Americanism and 171
    giving a positive impression to
        foreign press 95, 119
    Markezinis and 157–8
    propaganda and 51, 67, 69
    public mood and 119
memory, collective 1
Metaxas, Ioannis 8, 33
Meynaud, Jean 37

Index

military
  clientelism and 18, 23
  conspiracies and 25–7
  corruption and 70–1, 209n.61
  democracy and 78
  ERE (National Radical Union)
    and 26
  factionalism in the 25–7
  Generals' coup (1967 coup)
    and 35
  ideology and 23–4
  Ioannidis and 106
  Karamanlis and 109
  loss of civilian control of the 26
  Markezinis and 82, 96, 98–9
  the Markezinis experiment and
    78–82, 96
  military-as-institution 2, 183,
    184
  military police 105 (*see also* ESA
    (Greek Military Police))
  military service 56, 57, 122
  the monarchy and 22, 23, 25, 26–8,
    197n.45, 198.n.49
  nationalism and the 23–4, 33
  officer corps. *See* officer corps
  Papadopoulos and the 78
  politics and the 7–8, 22, 23–4, 26,
    73, 184, 196n.35, 197n.44
  the Polytechnic demonstrations
    and 131–2, 137, 138
  power of 13, 41, 47, 64, 111
  professionalism and 22–3
  public opinion of 196n.39
  radicalization of the 24
  social status and prestige of 24–5,
    26
military coups. *See* coups
Military House of the President of
  the Republic 81
Miller, James 159
Millet 155
Minister of Defence 4
Mitsos, Achilleas 12, 53, 67, 119, 120,
  127, 128–9, 135, 144, 178

Mitsotakis, Constantine
  (Konstantinos) 20, 43, 85, 90,
  189, 191
modernization 20, 33, 50, 72
Modiano, Mario 133
Momferratos, Nikolaos 85, 236n.26
monarchy (*see also* names of
  individual monarchs)
  abolition of 7, 62, 207n.34,
    231n.49
  crisis of 1965–7 and 30
  fleeing to Rome 35
  Generals' coup (1967 coup) and
    34–5, 198n.48
  as guarantors and personification
    of the state 194n.4
  Ioannidis and 60
  the military and 22, 23, 25, 26–8,
    197n.45, 198n.49
  politics and 15–16, 19–20, 21–2, 29
  restoration of 15–16, 38
  support of Karamanlis 14, 19–20,
    194n.4
Le Monde 40, 95, 169, 187
Moskos, Charles 24
Motherland Party, Turkey 182
Murtagh, P. 49, 166, 167
myth (*see also* conspiracies)
  constitutive 188
  of the omnipotent CIA 167
  Polytechnic myth 192

Nafpliotis, Alexandros 160
Nasser Hussein, Gamal Abdel 24, 33
'Nasserites', in the officer corp
  196n.37
National Assembly 7
National Cultural Movement
  (Ethnikon Politistikon Kinima
  – EPOK) 58–9, 72, 177,
  206n.18
National Liberation Front 138
National People's Liberation Army 138
National Resistance Council 49
National Schism (1910s) 25

nationalism, the military and 23–4, 33
nationalist discourse 51
NATO 11, 147, 148, 152, 157, 166
naval conspiracy 61–2, 87, 207n.32
Netherlands, diplomacy of 43
networks, political clientelist 18
New Democracy Party 189
New York Times 133, 159
Nixon, Richard 149, 157, 158, 165
Notaras, G. 47, 48
Novas, George 90

O'Donnell, G. 9, 175
officer corps
  anti-communist and corporatist-oriented 8
  extremism of 184
  Generals' coup (1967 coup) and 33
  ideology and 23–4
  Ioannidis and 78–9
  Karamanlis and 197n.44
  'Nasserites' 196n.37
  perceived predominance of 30
  professionalism and 22–3, 77–8
  social status and prestige and 24–5, 26
oil shock 162
Olson, Mancur 52
Ozal, Turgut 182, 183

Palamas, Christos 85, 162, 163, 165, 167, 187
Panagoulis, Alexandros 49, 118
Panhellenic Liberation Movement (PAK) 45–6, 48, 49
Panspoudastiki 128
Papadopoulos, Georgios
  1973 25 November coup led by Ioannidis and 100, 102
  assassination attempt 49
  conspiracy theories 144
  corruption and 197n.43
  criticisms of 93
  Cyprus and 154–5, 168
  democratization and 181–2

EENA (Union of Greek Young Officers) and 26
fall of 2, 102–3, 110–11, 196n.37
foreign policy of 150–1, 229n.26
Generals' coup (1967 coup) and 31, 33–4, 36, 37–9, 40–1, 43–5, 198n.52
Ioannidis and 103, 110–11, 132–3, 140–1, 176, 216n.107, 216n.108
Karamanlis and 64, 84
liberalization and 39, 118
loss of support for 74–5, 78, 79
Markezinis and 3, 71–5, 80, 95–6, 97–8, 134
Markezinis experiment and 3, 4–5, 31
martial law and 99, 139–40, 143
the military and 78
nepotism and favouritism of 51
Polytechnic demonstrations and 117–18, 124, 126, 130, 131, 132, 136, 139–40, 143, 216n.106, 225n.93
power and 41, 59, 64, 79
as President of the Republic 63, 70
presidential powers of 64–5
public opinion of 118–19
reforma (1973) and 55, 77–8, 93
student demonstrations and 57, 58
the transition process and 63–4
the United States and 5, 164, 165, 166–7, 170
weakness of 178
Papadopoulos regime
  civil society and 47–54
  the international factor 148–53
Papagos, Alexandros 14, 25, 44
Papandreou, Andreas
  the ASPIDA group and 27, 195n.21
  demonstrations at his memorial service 120, 123
  Generals' coup (1967 coup) and 28, 29

Index

the Markezinis experiment and 90-1
the monarchy and 21
the Panhellenic Liberation Movement (PAK) and 45-6, 48
the Polytechnic demonstrations and 139-40, 167, 188
radicalization of the EK (Centre Union) and 20-2
undermining other anti-junta groups 45-6, 49
Papandreou, George 15, 19-20, 21, 27, 49, 195n.24
parliament
  castrated 82-94
  government and 22
Parliamentary Committee for the Restoration of Democratic Legality 65
PASOK 188, 189
Passas, Ioannis 72, 73, 114, 198n.57
passivity, of the people 47, 50, 52, 192
Patriotic Front (PAM) 48
patronage 18
Pattakos, Stylianos 34, 38, 75, 100, 102, 105, 147
Paul of Greece 14, 21
Pedaliu, Effie 34
people's movement 91
Pesmazoglou, John 94, 112, 153
Pipinellis Memorandum 45
Pipinellis, Panayotis 45, 150
plebiscite 63, 65-6, 67, 69-70, 208n.56
police (*see also* ESA (Greek Military Police))
  police state 8
  the Polytechnic demonstrations and 125-6, 128, 130-2, 219n.12, 221n.33, 221n.40, 223n.57, 224n.84
  the relaxation of policing 119
political prisoners 4, 43, 45, 47, 66, 67, 87, 105, 118, 174

politics
  the centre: the EK and the centre-left 89-91
  clientelism and 18, 23
  conspiracy theories and 137, 141-2
  the credibility and passivity of the left 46
  culture and 16
  exclusivist political system 17
  foreign influence in 11, 146
  Generals' coup (1967 coup) and 41
  institutions and 14-19
  the left wing: the KKE and EDA 91-4
  the military and 7-8, 22, 23-4, 26, 73, 184, 196n.35, 197n.44
  military police 105
  the monarchy and 15-16, 19-20, 21-2, 29
  parliament/government and 22
  patronage/corruption and 30
  political elites 2, 3, 4, 5, 6, 39-47, 108, 186
  political identity 18
  political participation 18
  post civil war 14-15
  the right wing 83-9
Polytechnic demonstrations
  1973 25 November coup led by Ioannidis and 100
  casualties of 134, 223n.71
  conspiracy theories about 144, 192
  decision to occupy the campus 123-5
  the demonstrations and their aftermath 56-9
  the downfall of Papadopoulos and Markezinis and 117-18
  ESA (Greek Military Police) and 82
  the Greek people and 221n.38
  Ioannidis and 82, 138-9, 143

the liberalization experiment and 188
Markezinis and 98, 99, 117–18, 123, 125, 129–30, 133–4, 139, 143, 190, 219n.12, 219n.14
Markezinis experiment and 2, 3, 117–18, 167
the military and 131–2, 137, 138
Papadopoulos and 117–18, 124, 126, 130, 131, 132, 136, 139–40, 143, 216n.106, 225n.93
Papandreou (Andreas) and 139–40, 167, 188
the police and 125–6, 128, 130–2, 219n.12, 221n.33, 221n.40, 223n.57, 224n.84
police firing on demonstrators 131, 219n.12, 223n.57
political implications of the events 136–44
the students and the people 121–36
violence and the 131–2, 139, 141
Polytechnic trials 125, 128, 134, 140, 143, 222n.43, 224n.71
Portugal 40
Potts, James 166
power
balance of 94
Generals' coup (1967 coup) and 34–5, 37–8
of Ioannidis 36–8, 71, 207n.32, 210n.4
the military and 13, 41, 47, 64, 111
Papadopoulos and 41, 59, 64, 79
state 19
primary sector 50
Progressive Party 21, 44, 190, 236n.21
Prometheus Plan 32, 198n.53
propaganda 51, 67, 69
Przeworski, Adam 9
Psaroudakis, Grigoris 67
public administration 17
public mood 118–19
public works 18, 50, 51

radicalism, social 33
radicalization, of the military 24
Rallis, Georgios 12, 65, 67–8, 86–7
rapprochement 39
reform, elections and 10, 95, 96, 194n.7, 194n.10
reforma (1973) 33, 55, 71, 74, 77–82, 88, 92, 93 (*see also* Markezinis experiment)
reforma pactada 8
refugees, Greek from Asia Minor 7
religion 51–2
repression
ESA (Greek Military Police) and 36
the Polytechnic demonstrations and 121
Republic, establishment of 7, 63, 65, 66, 156, 231n.49
resistance
the Generals' coup (1967 coup) and 48–9
lack of 47 (*see also* passivity)
Polytechnic demonstrations and 144
student movements 56, 135, 138, 188, 206n.11
Revolutionary Committee 37, 38, 101–2
Rigas Ferraios 12, 122
rights
economic and social 19
Generals' coup (1967 coup) and 41
human rights abuses 152, 185
political, civil and individual 16, 134
right to strike 19
Roberts, J. 18, 50
Rodakis, P. 167
Roufogalis, Dimitrios 126
'royal coup' (1967) 4, 35, 60
Rueschemeyer, D. 18
rural out migration 18
Rustow, D. 10

Salazar, António de Oliveira 40
Schmitter, P. 9, 175
School of Military Cadets (*Evelpides*) 36, 44
secondary sector 17, 50
secret services 128
security regime, of the Generals' coup (1967 coup) 48
Seferis, George 49
self-interest 177
self-transformation attempt 2–3, 5, 8
Shain, Yossi 66, 113
Sifnaios, Panayotis 122, 124, 125, 130, 136
Simitis, Costas 48
Six-Day War 147
sleaze 79
social autism 177
social mobility 23, 24
social progress 33
social radicalism 33
social resentment, of the military 25
social status and prestige, the officer corps and 24–5, 26
Sorensen, G. 11
Soviet Union
  Communist Party of Greece (KKE) and 15, 91
  invasion of Czechoslovakia 46
  Markezinis experiment and 159
Spain
  coup attempt February 1981 184
  democratization and 8, 179–80
Der Spiegel 95
standard of living 18, 52
state
  the deep state 19–20
  intervention in everyday life 16
state of emergency 16
state of siege 28, 64
Stavrou, Nikolaos 149
Stepan, A. 10, 94
Stephanopoulos, Stephanos 90
Stevens, E. 18
Stevens, J. 18

student movements 56, 135, 138, 188, 206n.11 (*see also* activism; Polytechnic demonstrations)
Suarez, Adolfo 179–80, 235n.4
Sunalp, Turgut 182
Symvouleutiki Epitropi (Consultative Committee). *See* Consultative Committee
Syria, Yom Kippur War 162

Talbot, William Philips 146, 147, 149
Tasca, Henry 100, 149, 158, 159, 166, 167, 170, 187, 236n.16
taxation 50
terror campaign 67
tertiary sector 17
Theodorakis, Mikis 48, 93, 190
Theodorakopoulos, T. 28, 50, 53, 105, 109–10, 114–15, 141, 192
The Times 95
To Vima 97
torture 37, 105, 152, 185
tourism 18
Tovias, Alfred 165
Treaty of Association 161
Treholt, A. 152–3
Truman Doctrine 17
Tsatsos, Constantine 84
Turkey
  1967 crisis between Greece and Turkey 35
  1974 Cyprus crisis 2, 6, 107–8, 110, 111, 136, 146, 167, 168, 169, 185
  democratization and 182–3
  Greek–Turkish conflict (1897) 7
  Greek–Turkish relations 148, 168
  presidential powers in 65

unions 19
United Nations 162
United States
  1973 coup and 187
  American factor/Yom Kippur War 5, 145

anti-Americanism of Greece
    170–1, 192, 228n.14
archives of 11
arms embargo 149
attitudes of the Greeks people
    towards 148
CIA. *See* CIA
concerns for the future of Greece
    169, 170
Cyprus and the 148, 154, 168
diplomacy of 42–3, 147, 150
free and fair elections and 156
Generals' coup (1967 coup) and
    146–8, 228n.7, 228n.14
Greece and NATO and 157
Greek politics and 11
Ioannidis and 166–7, 168, 233n.93
Karamanlis and 158
Markezinis and 5, 164–7, 170
Markezinis experiment and
    158–9, 164–6, 167
military interests in the region
    148, 151, 162–5, 168, 170
Papadopoulos and 5, 164, 165,
    166–7, 170
Papadopoulos regime and 145
Polytechnic demonstrations and
    144
Truman Doctrine/Marshall Plan 17
views on the opposition parties 162
Yom Kippur War and 162–5
urbanization 18

values
    middle class 17
    of the military 24
Vanhanen, T. 186
Varvitsiotis, Ioannis 85, 88
Velos 62
Venizelos, Eleftherios 7
Veremis, T. 17, 32
victimhood 26
violence, the Polytechnic
    demonstrations and 131–2,
    139, 141 (*see also* torture)
Voice of Truth 167, 219n.16
Voulgaris, Yannis 30
Vradyni 59, 86, 105

Weiner, Tim 146–7
Western Europe, relations with
    Greece 152–3
Whitehead, L. 55, 161
Woodhouse, Ch. 33, 36, 74, 84, 139,
    147, 151, 152, 156, 167, 168
workers, demonstrations by 57, 127

Yannopoulos, G. 48, 50
Yom Kippur War 5, 147, 162–5

Zacharopoulos, George 23
Zagoriannakos, Dimitrios 70, 81, 98
Zoitakis, Georgios 36
Zournatzis, S. 56, 72, 101, 130, 132
Zumwalt, Elmo 150, 163

www.ingramcontent.com/pod-product-compliance
Lightning Source LLC
Chambersburg PA
CBHW051544020526
44117CB00047B/1693